Po Tsangpo

Camp 22
Tsachu   Take-Out
Cable Crossing (Camp 21)
Abu Lashu

Tsangpo

Camp 20
Payi
Azadem
Tso Dem
Senchen La
Waterfall Camp (Camp 19)
Go La
Camp 18

Tsangpo

Hidden Falls   Rainbow Falls

Luku

Northeast
Straits
Tso
amemba
Kintup Falls
Camp 13
Gully Camp (Camp 15)
Gogden (Camp 17)
Camp 10
Beach Camp
Pine Camp (Camp 12)
Snow Camp (Camp 14)
Luku La
Cave Camp (Camp 16)
Camp 9
Kondrasong La
Clear Creek
Pemakochung (Camp 8)
Churung Chu

Yangden Tsangpo

Sanglung Glacier

4800

Namcha Barwa
25,446 ft

6000

2400

Tsangpo Expedition

	River paddled
	Ground route
	Grand portage
	Hidden Falls party
	Trek out
●	Camp
■	Settlement
4800	Contour (meters)

0   2   4 mi

HELL

OR

HIGH

WATER

HELL

OR

HIGH

WATER

SURVIVING TIBET'S
TSANGPO RIVER

PETER HELLER

RODALE

Printed in the United States of America
Rodale Inc. makes every effort to use acid-free ∞, recycled paper ♻.

Book design by Joanna Williams

Library of Congress Cataloging-in-Publication Data

Heller, Peter, date.
    Hell or high water : surviving Tibet's Tsangpo River / Peter Heller.
       p.   cm.
    ISBN 1–57954–872–5 hardcover
    1. Kayaking—China—Tibet.   2. Kayaking—Brahmaputra River.   3. Tibet (China)—Description and travel.   4. Brahmaputra River—Description and travel.   I. Title.
GV776.7.T55H45   2004
797.122'4'09515—dc22   2004014410

Distributed to the trade by Holtzbrinck Publishers

2 4 6 8 10 9 7 5 3 1 hardcover

RODALE
WE **INSPIRE** AND **ENABLE** PEOPLE TO IMPROVE
THEIR LIVES AND THE WORLD AROUND THEM

FOR MORE OF OUR PRODUCTS
WWW.RODALESTORE.COM
(800) 848-4735

to MY PARENTS

John and Caro

And to MY GRANDMOTHER

Barbara Cheney Watkins

who loved a river story

CONTENTS

ACKNOWLEDGMENTS

Thanks to Gerta Bella, whose encouragement meant so much, and who didn't live to see the completion of this project. And to Kim Yan, who was my rock.

Thanks to Space Imaging and the people there—Bob Leitel, Mike Martinez, and especially John McKune Jr.—for their emphatic interest and indispensable satellite shots and for many hours spent acquiring images, piecing them together, and laying over them a true lat-long grid. Thanks to Linda Lidov for being the first to bring space imagery to the expedition.

Thanks to Dale Vrabec, scientist and Himalayan historian, who patiently and enthusiastically shared years of unsurpassed research. And to Robbie Barnett at Columbia University and Ganden Thurman at Tibet House. Thanks to Shane Sigle and T. Andrew Earles at Wright Water Engineering.

To my agent, Kathy Robbins, and to Jeremy Katz at Rodale, thanks for being fired up and full of encouragement and insight.

Thanks to Don and Jon at Confluence Kayaks. And to Leslie, Landis, Callie, Sascha, and Lisa for their suggestions and for being great friends and listeners throughout.

Thanks to the folks at Poggio's.

Thanks to my magnificent editor, Jay Heinrichs.

And to Hal Espen, who dropped me in and backed me up and whose vision and support never faltered.

May it become the sound of the dharma, the six syllables;

When I am chased by snow, rain, wind and darkness,

May I receive the clear, divine eye of wisdom.

—TIBETAN BOOK OF THE DEAD

Did she put on his knowledge with his power

Before the indifferent beak could let her drop?

—WILLIAM BUTLER YEATS, "LEDA AND THE SWAN"

The austere serenity of Shangri-La.

Its forsaken courts and pale pavilions shimmered in repose

from which all of the fret of existence had ebbed away,

leaving a hush as if moments hardly dared to pass.

—JAMES HILTON, *LOST HORIZON*

PUT-IN

The only sound was wind, rippling and snapping the prayer flags that ran down the riverbank and freezing the paddlers' hands as they zipped into drysuits. It came from upstream, from flat across the Tibetan Plateau, and it drove dry snowflakes onto the beach and darkened the jade-green water with patterns like woven fabric.

The kayakers moved quickly, pulling on life vests and helmets, and didn't speak. It was already afternoon. After 10 years of planning, there wasn't much to say. They were seven of the best expeditionary paddlers in the world, from four countries, led by Scott Lindgren of Auburn, California. They had come to Tibet to paddle the Tsangpo Gorge, arguably the last great adventure prize left on Earth. It is a Himalayan chasm so shrouded in mystery and danger that a legendary waterfall in its depths, sought by explorers for more than a century, had never been photographed until late in the 20th century. And it is a place, like Everest, that shimmers with myth and menacing superlatives.

The Yarlung Tsangpo, "the Purifier," is one of four major rivers that flow off the slopes of Mount Kailash in western Tibet, a mountain that is holy to Buddhists and Hindus. The river runs at great volume due east for almost a thousand miles, paralleling the Himalayas and draining the runoff from their entire north slope, and then abruptly bends south, plunging through the barrier of mountains to emerge, flat and stately, in the jungles of Assam, India. In its hidden course through the mountains, the river and its tributaries carve the Tsangpo Gorge. Just before the main

1

current sweeps around the Great Bend, it is joined by the Po Tsangpo flowing in from the north. From there, the Yarlung Tsangpo crashes through its Lower Gorge, which also has never been run, on its way to the Indian border, about 80 miles away.

For centuries, the Gorge has lived in legend as the site of fabled waterfalls and magic portals to other worlds. It was the inspiration for Shangri-La in James Hilton's novel *Lost Horizon*, and in Tibetan Buddhist mythology, it cradles the most sacred landscape—Pemako, a *beyul*, or Hidden Land, a place of transformative power and refuge. A ruined monastery called Pemakochung is one of the holiest pilgrimage sites for Tibetan Buddhists seeking enlightenment. An ancient Buddhist text unearthed by a lama in the 17th century declares, "Just taking seven steps toward Pemako with pure intention, one will certainly be reborn here. A single drop of water from this sacred place—whoever tastes it—will be freed from rebirth in the lower realms of existence." Tibetan Buddhists believe that the Gorge is the home of the goddess Dorje Pagmo, "the Diamond Sow," Buddha's consort and a symbol of enlightenment. The Gorge is her body, the highest peaks her breasts, and the river her spine. Two tribes live there, the only Buddhist hunting cultures on Earth. They have little conception of a greater Tibet.

The Tsangpo cuts beneath the perpetual snows of 25,000-foot peaks, running so far below them that much of the canyon is subtropical. Snow leopards and rare mountain tigers hunt the higher slopes, which are covered in bamboo and flowering rhododendron, while farther down the canyon, the forest turns to jungle and reverberates with the cries of tropical birds. Bengal tigers, some of the largest ever seen, haunt the Lower Gorge.

Measuring from the tops of the peaks that define it, the Tsangpo is the deepest river gorge in the world, three times deeper and eight times steeper than the Grand Canyon. (In places, the river falls even faster: Imagine taking the Grand Canyon stretch of the Colorado River, with its two-story waves and churning currents, and tilting it to more than 15 times its actual steepness.) Along its course, the Tsangpo cascades over the famed Rainbow Falls, the Lost Falls of the Brahmaputra, and the Hidden Falls of Dorje Pagmo. (Hidden Falls wasn't documented until 1998, in a controversial race of discovery—claimed by both Himalayan explorer Ian Baker and a team of Chinese scientists.) One stretch of river called the Lost Five Miles is said to thunder through 60 to 70 cataracts, each 10 feet high, in rapid succession.

In an age diminished by the belief that there is no magnificent adventure left undone, the Tsangpo Gorge remained a fearsome anomaly. Nobody had ever successfully paddled the 44-mile stretch of the Upper Gorge from the town of Pe to Clear Creek, beyond which high waterfalls make the Gorge impassable. No human being had ever traversed the length of it at river level. A section of the Gorge, despite numerous assaults, had never even been seen by a Westerner.

Now, on this wide beach just below the town of Pe, Lindgren and his paddlers set their boats on the water's edge. Their apprehension was palpable. There was no guarantee that any of them would come back alive. The last team to make a serious attempt on the Tsangpo—an American group led by Wickliffe Walker in 1998—made only 27 miles before seasoned kayaker Doug Gordon drowned.

If anyone could get it done, though, it would be these seven. Most of them had been kayaking since they were children, and in recent years each had paddled close to 300 days a year. Lindgren, 30, is the alpha dog of expedition kayaking, an Emmy Award–winning adventure filmmaker who has spent the last decade pulling off audacious first descents of some of the Himalayas' most daunting rivers. He specializes in river runs that combine maximum remoteness and extreme audacity—and he's done much of his paddling while hauling a 22-pound Bolex movie camera. He has an improbably perfect record for avoiding disaster and bringing everyone home intact.

For the Tsangpo team, he picked his closest kayaking friends, all veterans of previous Lindgren epics. South African Steve Fisher, 25, is known for his prowess in big, violent water. Mike Abbott, 29, from New Zealand, and his paddling partner, Englishman Allan Ellard, 26, are famed for wild descents, many in the Himalayas. Dustin Knapp, 24, of Jacksonville, Oregon, is the star of many of Lindgren's extreme paddling films; he has launched off so many hair-raising waterfalls and giant drops that he's stopped counting. Twin brothers Johnnie and Willie Kern, 29, from Stowe, Vermont, have a reputation for fearlessness—for years in the States, a truism went: "If the Kern brothers won't run it, nobody will."

The kayakers snugged into the tightly padded cockpits and sealed the openings with neoprene sprayskirts. One by one, they picked up their paddles, shoved off the sand, and glided onto the freezing waters of the Tsangpo. Looking at the flat green water meandering beneath black-timbered ridges at close to 10,000 feet, you wouldn't guess that just downriver, it shears through the wall of the Himalayas and all hell breaks loose.

Three women from Pe stood beside me. They wore belted ponchos of yak skin and watched with the solemnity of guests at a funeral. Maybe they saw it that way.

CHAPTER ONE

THE ASSIGNMENT

On a late August afternoon in 2001, in the Trinity Alps of northern California, I carried my kayak up the bank of the sky-clear Cal Salmon River and stashed it with a pile of others against the wall of an equipment shed at a small lodge. It had been a fun day. I was on a weeklong retreat with a group of editors from *Outside* magazine, and I had been doing what I love to do as much as anything in the world: paddle with good people on a whitewater river in wild country.

I began kayaking in college and had paddled with passion ever since. I had worked as a river guide, paddle maker, and kayak instructor, and in my late twenties, I began to write about rivers. On assignment for magazines, I traveled the world with a kayak, taking part in expeditions of varying degrees of seriousness. When I was 30, a young New Zealander named Roy Bailey and I were the first to kayak the Muk Su, a river in the old Soviet Union that flowed between the republic's highest peaks, in the Pamirs of Uzbekistan and Tajikistan. We paddled big, violent, freezing Class V water without mishap for 17 days in a remote canyon. We ran out of coffee.

On that warm evening in northern California, with fat bees buzzing through the beds of asters and fireweed at the edges of the lawns, the charm of the day was that this was emphatically *not* expedition paddling. It was as far from it as one could get without spinning around in a paddle boat at Club Med. After we stripped off our life jackets and helmets and hung them on a line behind a hammock, we ate pesto and artichokes and

5

watched the last sunlight fire the fir trees on the highest ridge, then jumped into a wood-fired hot tub. After a while, everybody left but me and Hal Espen, *Outside*'s editor. I liked Hal. He was a bearish man, packing some extra weight, but strong. One eye went in a different direction than the other. He had sandy, tousled hair and a soft-spoken affability. I was so relaxed in the bubbling water that I almost fell asleep. Then Hal said, "We're thinking of sending you someplace, ah, thrilling."

I sat up. "Oh, yeah?"

"Have you heard of the Tsangpo Gorge?"

It may have been the breath of the down-valley night wind, but I don't think so: A wave of goose bumps spread over my shoulders. "Yes," I said.

Three years before, I had attended a memorial service for 42-year-old Doug Gordon. Doug was a world-class paddler, a top slalom racer who had been very kind to me when I was a beginning boater. In 1998, on a *National Geographic*–sponsored expedition attempt on the Tsangpo, only 27 miles into the Gorge, Doug died paddling. He was well-loved, and on that overcast November day, the Quaker meetinghouse in rural Connecticut was filled to the galleries. One of my old friends, Landis Arnold, a kayak importer, stood up and talked about Doug. His voice cracked, and tears streamed down his face. "Going to the Tsangpo," he said, "is like going to the moon."

For a kayaker, and for a century's worth of overland explorers who had repeatedly tried to penetrate it, the Tsangpo Gorge was as alien and forbidding a place as our planet could offer. To commit to go there was to be willing to die.

"Oh, and they won't let you paddle it," Hal said.

Relieved but still confused, I mumbled, "Paddle? Who?"

"Scott Lindgren, the expedition kayaker from California. He's hand-picked six of the best kayakers from around the world. *Outside* is a sponsor."

"Well," I thought, "all right." Now I was really *very* relieved. I had read the accounts of Gordon's expedition. The whitewater was so fierce, the main current down the middle so cataclysmic, that even ferrying—paddling from bank to bank—was death defying. I had never covered a river story where I wasn't in a boat. But I was a recreational paddler now; I had no business going anywhere near the Tsangpo in a kayak.

"What am I supposed to do?"

"Trek through the Gorge with the ground support team," Hal said.

"When are they leaving?"

"There's some uncertainty about the permits, but they're shooting for mid-January."

"That's the . . . that's the middle of winter."

My mind was racing. The only way out of the Gorge was to claw 5,000 feet over a Himalayan pass. Nobody had even seen the pass in mid-winter. Nobody—not local hunters, not explorers—would go near those passes after November or early December. They were buried in snow. And there was another problem: I couldn't walk. Not really.

What neither Hal nor any of the other editors at *Outside* knew was that I couldn't amble three miles around the lake in front of my house in Denver without limping in pain. I'd eaten ibuprofen like popcorn and hidden the fact that I had wrecked my left hip; after years of jumping off high rocks and carrying too much weight, the joint had lost its cartilage and was bone on bone. Even here, on this retreat, I had deliberately chosen a bike-riding option over a hike on our afternoon off. A trek through the Tsangpo Gorge would be something like 200 miles of some of the most brutal terrain anywhere.

"It's their only window," Hal said.

"Window?" I wiped the drops of steam out of my eyelashes.

"The middle of winter. They want to hit the river at its rock-bottom lowest level to give themselves the best chance. After the monsoon and before spring runoff. My sources tell me it'll still be monstrous water."

"Oh. Sure."

"Think about it. We'll talk more."

I thought about it as I walked over the grass barefoot, back to my room under the first soft stars. Seven men were going to squeeze into tiny plastic boats and ride the Everest of rivers down into the deepest gorge on Earth while the Himalayan winter raged over their heads. It was beyond audacious.

That night, Hal gave me a large folio-size book called *The Riddle of the Tsangpo Gorges*, a republication of the journal of botanist Francis Kingdon Ward's 1924 expedition. He was the first person ever to make it through most of the Gorge on foot. The book was full of stunning photos, including a few that Ward had taken and some dramatic color pictures shot by modern explorers. I took the book to bed with me that night and flipped through the pictures again and again. Here was 108-foot Hidden Falls, a Holy Grail for Asian explorers for more than a century. Here was the sacred "keyhole" in the rock below the falls, reputed to be a magic gateway to Edenic realms. I put the book down. This was the assignment of a lifetime.

. . . .

Two months later, in late October, Scott Lindgren shouldered his way into the Friday-night Power-Flamenco crowd at the upscale, low-ceilinged club El Farol in Santa Fe, the town where *Outside* is based. The meeting was a kind of test set up by the editors—Expedition Leader meets Sponsor's Writer, sort of a see-if-the-two-chemicals-in-combination-will-explode kind of thing. The week before, on the phone, I'd told him about my injury, and he hadn't seemed too concerned. Tough guys deal with their own tweaks. That wasn't where his issues lay.

Lindgren came through the pack of ostrich-booted, conch-belted dinner club cowboys with the disdainful heedlessness of a wolf trotting through a herd of sheep. He was 30 years old, of medium height, with unkempt straight brown hair that fell almost to his shoulders. Surprisingly thin, he wore an orange-hooded fleece sweatshirt, loose khaki shorts, and flip-flop sandals. He had high cheeks; a round, boyish face; full lips compressed into an angry scowl; and blue-gray eyes that looked out from under a strong brow with no love lost for a world full of dumbasses and halfwits. I'd already gathered from our phone conversation that he wasn't exactly pleased about the night's meeting. This was *his* trip.

In May of 1998, he'd come *this* close—about 30,000 cubic feet per second close—to tiptoeing into the Tsangpo Gorge with his old paddling friend Charlie Munsey and poaching the river. No permits, no years of trying to obtain official government sanction, just two buddies, two of the finest extreme paddlers around, in kayaks stuffed with beans and *tsampa* (roasted barley flour, a Tibetan staple). Fast and light. Under the radar. Pure. This was how Lindgren had always done things—a few friends, kayaks loaded with food and cameras. He would talk repeatedly about the "purity" of his river exploits.

It wasn't about money; he never cared about that. He and his younger brother, Dustin, had grown up poor, and he was proud of it, proud that he'd been able to do everything he'd done—the world travel, the expeditions, the ski trips, the films—all on a shoestring and a prayer. He drove a dilapidated '87 Subaru wagon that he'd picked up for $1,500 and put 50,000 kayak road trip miles on it in less than a year. He lived and worked in a bungalow of offices by the interstate in Auburn, California, with an industrial carpet like Astroturf and a hot plate.

It wasn't about fame, either. Other river teams were clawing to be the first down the mythic Tsangpo. A trophy like that would barely fit on the wall of the Explorers Club, but he'd already backed off once when other teams were clamoring at the gates.

In the spring of 1998, when he and Munsey were there the first time, a race was on. An old Special Forces Vietnam vet and expeditioner, Wickliffe Walker, and Tom McEwan were putting together a team of former whitewater racers and Olympians—including the ill-fated Doug Gordon—for a run in the fall. An international team, led by rocklike

German paddler Lucas Blücher, was casing the river. Several other Americans and Brits, including remnants of the old *Men's Journal* Adventure Team, were hustling for sponsors. The winter of '98 had been a record snow year in Tibet, one of the worst. Yaks had floundered and died by the thousands. People had frozen to death. With all that snow, the spring runoff was abnormally turgid.

Lindgren and Munsey got to the Yarlung Tsangpo at the head of the Gorge at the town of Pe, took one look at the swollen, freight-training current, and turned around. They then planned to paddle from the town of Pelung 18 miles down the Po Tsangpo to the confluence with the Yarlung Tsangpo, and if things looked good, the hell with the fall trip; they might just continue right into the big river and go on to India. The border was only 80 miles downstream.

Again they got skunked. The Po Tsangpo was raging with runoff. It was brown and ferocious. It cut down into its own incised, walled-in canyon. They kayaked about three miles and were buried in house-size waves and swept by a racing current, on the edge of control. They tried to hug the shore and paddle along the seething edge but were forced out into the middle by ledges and giant boulders. Ferrying across the torrent was toying with death. They pulled out. They hiked down to the sacred confluence, still hopeful. But if the main river, the Yarlung Tsangpo, was out of control at the start of the Gorge at Pe, here, after joining forces with the Po Tsangpo, it was simply monolithic. Lindgren and Munsey were deeply impressed by the scale and beauty of the walls and snow mountains that climbed around them—and by a local Buddhist Monpa hunter who casually fished by throwing dynamite into the river—and they turned around again and hiked out.

Lindgren didn't even consider going back that fall. According to Munsey, the Walker-McEwan expedition had originally planned a November attempt, but when they heard that Lindgren and Munsey were also shooting for November, they moved their trip up a month. Had they waited the extra month and let the river subside from the rains, the outcome might have been different. Lindgren wanted no part of a rush for the starting line. He said later, "There was a 50-year monsoon that summer. Because of the monsoon and the race with other teams, I decided to pull the plug."

Purity. Lindgren didn't want to do Tibet's sacred river that way, in the kind of race that killed Robert F. Scott near the South Pole. He wouldn't be forced to make bad mistakes in judgment. "People have been calling my death for years," he said to me that night in Santa Fe, "but I keep coming back alive. Nobody has ever died on my watch."

He had been paddling wild rivers in the Himalayas since he was 20. "I grew up there," he said. "I've got enough experience on the water by now. I can pretty much pick out a disaster." The fame of a big First was less important than doing it right, on the river's terms. This humility was paradoxical for the aggressive and fiercely independent young explorer. "The river decides," he would say again and again.

In early October 1998, the four Americans sponsored by *National Geographic* launched their boats into the Tsangpo below Pe. The three kayaks and one decked canoe were big and loaded with 15 days' supply of food. They weighed 100 pounds. The river runners were all fine technical paddlers, bred on the rocky, low-volume rivers of the East, and they mostly came from racing backgrounds, where the challenge was not surviving the raw violence of the river or its remoteness but fine-tuned boat control.

When they got to the river, they saw it in flood. Lucas Blücher, who was riding along the roaded section near Pe on a pink mountain bike and scouting for his own trip, tried to warn them off. They embarked nonetheless. They sneaked wherever they could down threads of current along the edges, grunted their packed boats over house-size boulders, and portaged for miles. They were brave and dogged, and they were making their way slowly downriver as the walls of the greatest gorge closed in.

On Day 12, 27 river miles from the put-in, Doug Gordon ran an eight-foot waterfall off a ledge, got caught, upended in the violent hydraulic beneath it (picture the turbulent whitewater beneath a dam), missed the Eskimo roll he needed to right himself, got swept into the main current, and was never seen again.

Tom McEwan, one of the expedition members, had shot video where he could, and *National Geographic* made a movie out of it. Lindgren could not contain his disgust at a venerable institution of exploration that now pandered like daytime TV. "There was very little consideration for preparation, commitment, or risk," he said of the movie on our second day in New Mexico. "It was all about 'Four Go In, Three Come Out.' They were more interested in getting an underwater reenactment of Doug Gordon drowning than in his character. They focused on his underwater struggle. It was a completely selfish, self-serving point of view that glamorized Doug's death. I feel sorry for Mrs. Gordon."

. . . .

When we met at the fancy restaurant in Santa Fe, Lindgren was accompanied by Les Guthman, who was the head of Outside Television. After they were seated, Lindgren stared at the linen tablecloth, his face half hidden by the fall of long hair. He could barely make civil conversation. I'd ask him a question like "How did you pick the six paddlers?" He'd shake himself out of a sullen reverie. "I'm not making any compromises on this trip. They all paddle 200 to 300 days a year. There isn't a more qualified team on the planet." He'd say it aggressively, as if I had just asked him why he was wearing white socks.

I could understand the surliness. Scott Lindgren had always had almost complete control of his story. Now he was being asked to relinquish some of that—on this, his most ambitious and dangerous trip. In exchange for sponsorship and pulling together more than half a million dol-

lars in a deal with General Motors, *Outside* insisted that their writer—
me—would write the article and the first book. Lindgren didn't trust
journalists. He was ambivalent about the whole setup. He was being
forced to swallow something distasteful, and he had never been forced to
do anything since he'd first learned to throw a hard punch. On the other
hand, he was getting the resources he needed, and complete command of
all decisions on the ground. Should the stakes prove too high, it would be
his decision to pull out.

Les thought a hike might loosen things up, so the next morning we
drove together to Bandelier National Monument and strolled through
Anasazi ruins along a creek blazing with orange cottonwoods. Les's attempt
at bonding wasn't a big success. At one point, when we were alone, Lindgren said, "People have one chance with me. They fuck up, I cut them off."

The next day at the magazine offices, where Lindgren gave a pre-
sentation of his assault plan to the editors, I told Hal and Les that I had a
slight problem with one part of the *Outside* Tsangpo expedition.

"What part?" Hal said.

"The part where we walk and climb along the side of the river."

I broke the news about my hip.

Hal pulled me into an empty office and closed the door. He was
flushed and breathless. He pulled out a chair, flipped it around, and motioned me into another.

"I just spoke to my doctor," I said, talking quickly. "She said I can't
hurt it any more than it already is."

"That doesn't sound exactly reassuring."

"She said she can inject me with some stuff, and then it's just a
matter of how much pain I can take."

Hal's roving eye went to the ceiling and then settled on my left
shoulder. He took a deep breath and let it out in a soft whistle. "We're
about to pull the trigger. I need to know right now if this is an issue. Is
this an issue?"

Sometimes life crystallizes hard and sharp. Zero ambiguity. This was a big story, and I imagined turning it down because of joint pain. I suddenly pictured myself driving back to Denver in the airless relief of having chosen the comfortable option. The injury and what it had forced me to turn away from would then become the central fact of my life. I looked at Hal and answered, "No, it's not an issue. I can deal with discomfort. I'll get the story."

"Listen, I don't want you to get caught up in some kind of wishful thinking because you want to go," Hal said.

"It's not an issue."

Hal then did something that surprised me. He looked at me and said simply, "Okay."

I had just committed to going into the Tsangpo Gorge. For up to 50 days. I wasn't sure of anything—of myself or Lindgren—but I knew this: Once you commit to something risky and bold, life unfolds with increasing richness and wonder.

. . . .

I arrived at Scott Lindgren Productions in Auburn, California, on January 8, 2002, 10 days before our planned departure for Hong Kong and Lhasa. Scott had just flown to Beijing to negotiate last-minute details of our permit, but I was told the rest of the paddling crew would be at the headquarters: 331 Rio Vista Drive. It turned out to be an optimistic address. There is no Drive. There's a cut, not even an alley, between the Travelodge and the sprawling Lou LaBonte's Restaurant, which hails the traffic on I-80 with a giant pink-and-blue neon sign. Behind that is a desolate parking lot. There is no Rio, and no Vista, except the Dumpsters behind the motel, a low-income apartment complex, and one brave pine tree growing out of the tarmac where heroin addicts congregate. At the top of the parking lot is a low, drab cream-colored office complex almost wholly taken up by Scott Lindgren Productions.

If the early-1990s Subaru wagons with kayak racks and the score of kayaks stacked on the patio didn't give the place away, you would know what it was as soon as you opened the glass door. The low, dim room betrayed itself as a kayaker's hive by the strong must, the smell of fleece and neoprene and nylon gear that has never quite dried out. There was also sweat, which had to do with the filmmaking side of the operation—the rankness of too many guys in close quarters laboring at desks and monitors for days on end with no open windows.

This is the nerve center of one of the top extreme kayak video production companies. It's also Scott Lindgren's apartment and a crash pad for his brother, Dustin, and a handful of buddies who star in the films and work on their production. For the past two weeks, Scott, Dustin, Willie and Johnnie Kern, and Dustin Knapp had been working 22 hours a day editing footage of their latest video, *Liquid Lifestyles 4: Aerated*, which had premiered at Disneyland the previous Sunday. The team finished the movie at 5 P.M. Saturday and drove straight to Anaheim for the showing. The film is a montage of footage from nearly vertical rock flumes in Mexico, 40-foot waterfalls in British Columbia, huge ocean surf in Sumatra, big-water gorge paddling on the Grand Canyon of the Stikine in British Columbia, and an insane, bobsled-style waterfall slide down a granite slab in Yosemite. Dustin Lindgren calls it "kayak porn."

The first person I met was Willie Kern. He was tall, broad-shouldered, and bulky, with a goatee and wide-set, intelligent eyes, and he had shades propped on the brim of a baseball cap. Willie was never in a hurry. He was deliberate, respectful, serious, and competent. He had a generous laugh and smoldering humor that broke out in dry asides. He smoked cigarettes outside. Willie was a seriously radical paddler. If he weren't so good at running waterfalls and tight, cascading creeks, he'd be crazy.

I pointed to a Liquid Lifestyles poster of a kayak midway down monstrous 80-foot falls and asked if the paddler was Willie. "That's Johnnie, dang him," he said. "My stunt double. I'll be using him a lot on the Tsangpo."

Johnnie was Willie's fraternal twin and looked like him, with a long, trimmed moustache and soul patch, but while Willie was everywhere, setting up and seam-sealing tents, experimenting with freeze-dried food recipes on the MSR stove on the patio, fielding phone calls, and endlessly going over the satellite images of the Gorge with the other paddlers, Johnnie never left the desk at one end of the main room. From 7 A.M., when Scott called on the sat phone from Beijing, until midnight, Johnnie was at the computer—barefoot, chewing tobacco. He e-mailed sponsors, arranged plane tickets, and organized, organized, organized. He, too, was deliberate, unruffled, and methodical, a radical paddler and respected boat designer. He was smaller than Willie, a little shorter, broad-shouldered but slender. They both slept in their clothes, on the floor, in whatever corner of the room wasn't occupied, and heedlessly ate whatever Burger King meal someone brought in.

Both brothers knew exactly what they were getting into. They were, in a sense, kayak orphans: After their father died when they were 13, their older brother, Chuck, became their role model, mentor, and friend. Two and a half years older, he was fast becoming the best all-around paddler in the world. By all accounts, he was beautiful on the water—smooth and controlled in violent rapids, with never a wasted stroke. But in 1997, Chuck's life was cut short by whitewater. Four years later, one of their closest friends, Brennan Guth, drowned on a river in Chile.

Steve Fisher shambled out of a video editing room. Steve—25, South African—was known for his skill in big, dangerous water and for his off-river bravado. He'd placed third in an extremely competitive World Freestyle Championships, and in 1998, he'd pushed the kayaking limits by running the Zambezi at 750,000 cubic feet per second (cfs), the second highest level ever recorded. In 2000, he had aced the televised Camel Challenge extreme whitewater race in Chile after drinking all comers under the table the night before and then refusing to use a vital piece of the sponsor's kayak gear because, as he told them to their faces, it was "a piece of shit." He had put down first descents all over the world, won every kind of extreme paddling competition, and invented many of the balletic and aerial "rodeo" moves that have become the basic repertoire of play kayaking. He created the Freewheel, for example, a kayak cartwheel in the middle of a high waterfall. He cut his teeth as a teenager on the Zambezi, and he has the blond, clean-cut, sleepy-green-eyed good looks and easy confidence of a South African movie star.

There was something about Steve, for all his superhero exploits, that was profoundly quirky. At one point he announced, out of the blue, "I've eaten monkey—terrible. Worst meat you can imagine."

Charlie Munsey, just arrived from Idaho, cocked his head. "That's damn near cannibalism," he said.

. . . .

One of the first things Willie Kern said to me, after "Make yourself right the fuck at home" with a wry look around this crowded dump of an HQ, was "Check this out." He took me to a computer monitor. A thin green ribbon, blurred to white, snaked through a field of black splashed with ragged stars and reefs of colder whiteness: The Tsangpo, uncurling and stretching, snapped in candid nakedness by a satellite 423 miles in space. "It doesn't have a lot of sediment in it—it's pretty green," he said. "Anyhow, it's cool—you can see bridges on this. It's pretty hilarious. We've started to correlate some of the old photographs with the sat images. It's fuckin' amazing."

The most compelling difference between a river expedition like the Tsangpo and a great mountaineering exploit is that on the river, the objective is hidden. A mountain stands up to be scrutinized. Climbers scope it for the best routes and draw dotted lines on photographs. The most dangerous sections reveal themselves as avalanche chutes and cornices and rockfall. But in the bottom of the Tsangpo Gorge ran a river of great power, and few people on Earth could say with any certainty what it looked like. One reason is that a river is alive. It falls and jumps and leaps, never the same for a single instant. It sings in summer and roars in the spring. Huge waves and calamitous ledges at medium flow may get filled in and smoothed over—"washed out"—at high water levels. Or the reverse— a flat section at low flow may boil with crashing swells at flood.

Only a few expeditions in history had ever gone through the Upper Gorge, between Pe and Rainbow Falls, and only one was a river expedition whose members had an eye for river features, for what was within the realm of possibility for a person in a kayak. The Walker-McEwan team had gone only 35 miles, much of it on foot. That left 10 unscouted miles to Rainbow Falls and all of the Lower Gorge.

Francis Kingdon Ward had taken a few photographs of the river on his arduous 1924 trek, as had a couple of scientists named Ludlow and Sherriff during a 1947 hike partway into the Upper Gorge, and these grainy black-and-white reproductions took on iconic importance for Scott Lindgren's kayakers. So did the series of satellite images shot over the Great Bend and donated by a company called Space Imaging, of Thornton, Colorado.

Another difference between mountains and rivers: You can never "conquer" a river. For a river, the lowest place around is not enough. A river must go lower. Put onto a stream in a kayak, and you're likely to drop from sight—away from the road, between two mountains. A river can't get away fast enough. It falls toward the coast in a headlong rush to empty itself in the salt. Tibetan Buddhism emphasizes the inherent emptiness of all things; a river seeks to prove the point. Every wave and crease and current dissolves and is re-formed moment to moment, in a journey toward complete undifferentiation. A river's last act is to empty itself of its self. How can you conquer something that only seeks to disappear?

. . . .

That night, the door of 331 Rio Vista cracked open and Allan Ellard stuck his head in. Shoulder-length blond dreadlocks swayed around his sun-reddened face. "Knock, knock," he said, and smiled shyly. Allan is English. Tall, maybe 6'2". Behind him, a bit shorter, a bit more slender, dark-complexioned, and with shave-cut black hair, came his paddling partner and best friend, the Kiwi Mike Abbott.

They were a couple of the most experienced Himalayan river runners alive. For most of the past decade, they had spent a long season in Nepal, guiding rafts and exploring the remotest streams in kayaks. They had put down dozens of first descents on several continents and were known for doing hellacious expeditions on a budget of $5. "Wait," Mike had said once. "Is this an expedition? It doesn't cost near enough." They'd buy a sack of rice and one of beans and throw their kayaks onto the roof racks of the jammed public buses. Then they'd climb into the kayaks. Better view from up there. They'd get stoned and duck under low-hanging power lines. "One chap riding on the rear ladder didn't duck fast enough," Mike said. "The wire caught him under the chin, and off he went." They'd play a game, letting their boats shoot to the front of the roof at sudden stops. Once, Mike toppled, boat and all, over the rail and hung on by one arm as the bus accelerated. Allan hauled him back up. After their recreational bus ride, they'd get serious and hike into some terrifying gushing mountain cataract and kayak it with the optimistic "No worries," twinkle-in-the-eye excitement of two friends on a complete lark. This was the same style and resilience I'd seen time and again on my own trips with New Zealanders and Aussies and Brits—a bred-in-the-bone toughness and humor still found among members of the old British Empire.

Mike and Allan were also super athletes. In the last kayak freestyle world championships, a competition of wild tricks and rodeo moves in the thumping white crash of a big hydraulic, Allan came in 12th, and Mike was 13th. Mike dependably placed first in big-cash-prize, international all-around kayak competitions. He'd share the winnings with his mates. He was always flat broke. After winning the Asahan Whitewater Festival in Sumatra, he immediately spent most of his take on a ticket to Peru to paddle and visit a girlfriend. The rest got stolen, and he laughed about it. Easy come. Scott told me that on any given day, he thought Mike was the best paddler in the world. (On the other day, it would be Steve Fisher.) The first night Mike pulled his drysuit out of his duffel, everybody gathered around, amazed—it was ripped and patched, in tatters. No worries: It was only cold water. . . .

Those were the paddlers. Willie and Johnnie, Allan and Mike, Steve. Plus Scott, who was away in China, and Dustin Knapp, arriving soon, who at 24 was the youngest member of the expedition.

Allan was the group's computer wiz. Within minutes of his arrival, he was snugged into the tiny bedroom that Scott shares with his longtime girlfriend, Jenning Steger. While other paddlers sat on the rumpled bed, Allan commandeered the computer set up in the corner, reloaded the satellite disks, and began to configure them in contiguous zoomed-in sections. The kayakers began to take a mile-by-mile tour of the Tsangpo.

From then on, for the next three days, Allan rarely moved from the keyboard. His raw-knuckled, scarred right hand rolled the pointer onto stretches of river, then clicked for a zoom, bigger, bigger, until the boys were actually scouting a rapid—"Looks like some rocks here, the river rising up and piling into this wall. Here, there's a big diagonal feature, and that looks like a hole, right across. A bit beefy. You'd want to stay left here. No bank, that must be cliff. . . . "

At one point, Allan murmured gleefully, "You know you're fucked when you're scouting from space."

The stretches of river were being identified spontaneously, without deliberation, by a kind of unspoken collective acknowledgment, with names such as the Northeast Straits, a long straightaway, and the Crease, a choked maelstrom of white at the crux of an acutely angled bend. Many sections of the unfurling virtual river were "blown out": So much glare reflected off the whitewater that the ribbon blurred to an undifferentiated photo-paper white. All heads came closer to the screen as the paddlers strained to make out the components of the cataract. But of course, they couldn't. It was as if the sheer ferocity of the water stunned the digital code into a string of smitten zeroes. The satellite, from its safe distance of more than 400 miles in space, could snap a picture of the proud river goddess Dorje Pagmo, but it could not look into her heart or trace the entire length of her spine. The force and beauty of her uncurling majesty rendered entire sections incognito.

There was another white nexus on the map that became a fixture for discussion, only this time it was the white of snow: the Senchen La, the 12,000-foot pass we'd need to climb in the most audacious portage in history. Even in the May flyover pictures, it was blanketed with snow, and what wasn't snowbound looked like impossibly steep ravine, couloir, cliff face, and ridge. I spent a long time looking at the Senchen La.

. . . .

Scott realized after his aborted attempt with Charlie in '98, when the sheer power of the Po Tsangpo caught them by surprise, that he'd have to alter his entire strategy. He would need to launch the kind of grand, 19th-century-style expedition that had become obsolete a long time ago.

First, he'd need light boats, and that meant a substantial support team to carry food—a small army of porters and expedition personnel numbering nearly 100 men. Second, the expedition needed the resources to operate carefully, methodically, and independently for up to 50 days.

Third was the midwinter timing. If they could paddle the Tsangpo when it was flowing at its rock-bottom low, he might have a chance.

It would be expensive. Lindgren, a maverick by temperament, knew he would have to court major corporate sponsorship. With the help of *Outside*, he got GM to commit to the money and to ship three army-green Chevy Avalanches to Beijing to be driven on to Lhasa. The company would outfit the vehicles with extra-beefy wheels and two spare tires apiece. Part of Charlie's job would be to photograph the hybrid

SUV/pickup trucks loaded with kayaks in flattering Tibetan ruggedness.

The size of the group and the duration of the trip, Scott realized, would turn the job of securing visas and permits from Beijing into a complicated and protracted diplomatic struggle. But the greatest challenge his expedition faced was physical: how to get the kayaks up and over the Senchen La in order to avoid Rainbow Falls and Hidden Falls. The answer came to him in a dream.

He would take two sets of boats. The kayakers would paddle the Upper Gorge in the first set. He would send the second set down the trail along the Po Tsangpo into the Lower Gorge with Rob Hind, a 32-year-old Englishman with 10 years of Himalayan outfitting experience. Once the paddlers got blocked by the falls, they'd sink their boats, climb unencumbered over the pass into the Lower Gorge, and pick up the new kayaks. But Scott would come to find that a dream can make poor prophecy.

. . . .

Ten days before launch, the "to do" list, written on an 8 × 5-foot marker board in the Auburn HQ, was not getting any shorter; in fact, it had swelled to more than 100 items. The long columns read like a poem, a distilled catalogue of expedients and dangers. Items such as "jerky" and "coffee" might have been found on any cattle drive. "Small GPS's," "ham radios," and "sat phones" were expected—it was the third millennium. But other sections spoke to the demands of a very different kind of river trip.

GROUP GEAR
Shovel/probe—RACK
Snowshoes 2; ice axe/cramp 2
2 60m spectras ropes, 7–10mm
Pitons/hammer
Saw/axe
Fishing pole

Extra sleeping bag
Avalanche transceivers x2

The shovel was for digging out victims of avalanche. The probe was for finding them. "RACK" was technical climbing hardware, ice screws and nuts. "Cramp" was crampons. An avalanche transceiver sent and received a locator beacon between victim and searcher after a slide. I wondered how just two would help, with so many on the climb.

Below that was "disposable blondes." For reviving the victim, presumably.

The only item with three stars was "tar tape." This is a kayak repair shop in a roll. Warm it up and slap it on, and it will fix any gouge. The stars were eloquent. Highlighting the most essential item, they meant that as far as the paddlers were concerned, the Tsangpo still came down to an individual in a little boat that had better not leak.

Steve Fisher was talking about monkeys when Charlie Munsey walked in. Up until a month before, Charlie had been part of the paddling team, but in December, Scott had said simply, "Charlie's not paddling. He'll be ground support."

Charlie had been eyeing this river for a decade, talking to other people who had been there, collecting maps and history and weather data. Thirty-four years old, part Indian, with the neat, handsome, dark features of a '50s teen idol, Charlie was enigmatic. He wore his thick black hair short in a bebop cut, and he spoke articulately in a soft, insistent tenor punctuated by ironic laughter. He seemed sensitive, almost thin-skinned, as well as game. He had the grace and toughness of a natural athlete, which, by all accounts, he was. He had been a competitive bump skier in Sun Valley, Idaho. He'd been on the *Men's Journal* Adventure Team, which sent world-class outdoorsmen on dramatic exploits and produced weird advertorials for Johnnie Walker whiskey. By the time he was 30, he had completed the North American "Triple Crown"—kayak descents of the Alsek, the Stikine, and the Susitna rivers. To this day, only six men have done it.

For the past few years, Charlie had been laying off extreme boating and concentrating on photography. *Outside* had assigned him as the Tsangpo expedition's main photographer. The previous October, we had met in Santa Fe. "I think this will be my last big one," he said then over a beer. "The more friends I lose, the older I get."

Extreme kayaking is a very costly sport. In the past three years, five men I had paddled with perished on rivers. Over the same period, Scott lost 13. No activity in the world, except perhaps mountaineering, saw such attrition among its best practitioners.

Why do people do it? Because there is no other activity that throws one, with such intimacy, into the embrace of so much changeable living force. Rivers pulse, throb, swirl, and rush. Standing waves rear up, crash, and subside. Whirlpools open and deepen, cyclone down an eddy line, and vanish. Eddies boil up. Tongues of current surge, cover the side of a boulder, and fall back. The power of a river can send a kayaker shooting across from one bank to another with the speed of a diving swift—as if on a zip line, straight across, without losing a single foot to the downward-tearing current. It can toss a kayak vertically on end, even airborne. The river is so powerful. It lifts you, crashes on you, launches you. Lean your boat a fraction of a degree the wrong way, and you flip so fast you don't remember going over. Angle your body in opposition in the wrong place, and you tear all the muscles in your arm or torso. But learn to move with it, harness just a little bit of its force in the direction of your intention, and you become another animal altogether, a mer-human. You move with a grace you never imagined owning, vouchsafed to you in some prehuman contract when your animal spirit could fly, and at the bottom of the rapid, you know you have never experienced anything so close to the divine.

That's why we paddle. Despite the grievous losses of friends and brothers. Despite the cold and the danger.

. . . .

The team doctor Scott had recruited waffled, couldn't come, then decided yes, he would, but in the meantime, Scott, in Beijing, took him off the permit and replaced him with Ken Storm Jr., the explorer who had "discovered" Hidden Falls with Ian Baker in 1998. Ken, 49, had trekked through the Upper Gorge in '93. He lived with his sister in Minneapolis, where he worked in the family book and game distribution business and collected rare books. Charlie had been talking to Ken on the phone and abruptly said, "Hell, Ken, you should just come with us," and Ken immediately accepted. So we traded the doctor for a guide; probably, in the boys' estimation, it was a good swap in the equation of overall safety, though Willie ominously referred several times to Wick Walker's memoir, *Courting the Diamond Sow.* "In Wick's book," Willie said, "the doctor was crucial in diplomacy with the Monpa villages and porters." I'd remember that line.

Two days after I got back to Denver to pack up my own gear, I got a call from Johnnie Kern. "Go down to REI and buy an avalanche transceiver. We decided we all better have one." That made sense to me. He told me which one to get.

The next day, he called again.

"Did you buy the transceiver?"

"Yup."

"Better go down and trade it in for a GPS. Sorry to run you around."

"Why?" I said.

Johnnie told me they were looking hard on the sat maps at the approach to the Senchen La. They decided that if an avalanche did cut loose, it would be of such magnitude that it would take out the entire expedition. There'd be no one left to search. A GPS was therefore more cost-effective. I thanked him. I went back to REI. Then I went up the street to a lawyer I knew and made out my first formal will.

CHAPTER TWO

LHASA TO PE

Half of the Tsangpo expedition's core team of Westerners crossed the Pacific on January 18, 2002. We were the kayakers Willie and Johnnie Kern and Mike Abbott; photographer Charlie Munsey; Andrew Sheppard, the climbing coordinator from Banff, Alberta; and myself. We had seven of the kayaks. The rest of the team would fly the next day with seven more boats. In Lhasa, we would meet up with ground support team leader Dave Allardice, a New Zealander who was coming up from Nepal with five climbing Sherpas, men with experience on Everest and Amadablam, as well as Rob Hind, who was flying from Austria and would lead the relief party trekking into the Lower Gorge with the second set of kayaks.

Nobody slept much. I asked Willie if he'd had to say goodbye to a girlfriend in the past few days, and he said he'd just ended a relationship. He described a graceful rock climber and competitive kite surfer. "She's great," he said wistfully. "But—ultimately the kayak won." He laughed. His brother, he said, was also flying solo. He said the hardest thing was saying goodbye to their mom. A former New Englander, Julie Kern worked at a guest ranch in Arizona. She lived alone, and they thought about her all the time. "We love our mom," Willie said.

Andrew listened to techno on his mini-disk player. He was a surprise. I'd heard from all the Americans that he was a mountain icon. His unearthly aerobic fitness had earned him a nickname: the Third Lung. Scott had talked of his strength: "He'll pick up a Sherpa, bro, and carry him over the pass." Willie told me that Andrew was consistently ranked among the top 50 skiers in the world by *Powder* magazine. He'd grown up on skis in Banff and starred in a bunch of extreme skiing films. He worked on a highway stabilization crew in Alberta and British Columbia, rappelling off cliffs and setting dynamite charges, blowing off loose rock and avalanches. He was a respected ice climber and mountaineer and had been a junior national champion in cross-country skiing, which in Canada is as close as you can come to sitting near the hockey players on Mount Olympus. He was 30 years old, about 5'11", in a loose fleece jacket and wide gangster pants that bunched up around his feet and dragged, fraying on the ground. His cornsilk-blond hair hung down the middle of his back, and he had a strong nose, almost a beak, and dark-blue eyes. He shuffled along with his hands in his pockets and a cap pulled low over his brow. He looked like the kid in the back of history class happily chewing spitballs. He did not look like a jock.

I asked him what the last fun thing had been. He thought for a second and said, "Just did a Toyota commercial. That was the last fun thing. Four of us jumped out of a helicopter on skis. Sixty feet. If the light had been good, we would have jumped into this horn. It would've been sick."

Two rows up, Johnnie and Mike bent over Charlie's seat and pored over the topo maps of the Gorge sent by Lucas Blücher, the German. Johnnie's head was shaved to near stubble and gleamed roughly in the cabin light. He had cut it himself with an electric razor. I could see a couple of bald patches on top where the blade had slipped. His long, drooping moustache was gone. He said that with his facial hair, he was getting a lot of comments about how he was looking like Willie, so he'd gotten rid of it.

Being mistaken for each other hadn't been a problem for Johnnie and Willie as kids. They grew up in Massachusetts, in a white clapboard Cape in a semirural town on the North Shore of Boston, where their father, a heavy-truck salesman, stacked cordwood under the pines in the backyard. He was a big, beefy, clean-cut man who wore button-down shirts, and when he wasn't working long hours, he was launching his sons into the local swimming hole or coaching them to climb trees. He encouraged them to take risks, to push themselves. Chuck, two and a half years older than his brothers, excelled in school and at sports, was a popular student, and became an Eagle Scout. The twins looked up to him with the kind of solid admiration only younger brothers can have. Willie was a lot bigger than Johnnie. He was the one who would get stuck too high in a tree and start yelling. Johnnie was quieter, and slender like his mother. He wore big glasses and was teased at school for being a four-eyes.

When the twins were 12, their mother left the marriage. That was the first sorrow. She had been living in quiet desperation for years. Eleven months after the separation, their father died of a heart attack. He was 61 years old.

. . . .

In the midnight dimness of the 747, everybody crowded the aisle to look at maps covered with circles and arrows and route lines. Lucas Blücher had marked portages in red—Critical. Green sections meant Boat. Black was Walk. He had straight pin lines pointing to and underscoring elevations. A very methodical German. "Option One" and "Option Two" were scrawled over his possible routes. Problem areas on the river were marked by bold circles.

Willie went back to his seat and pulled some pages out of a small yellow drybag he'd use in his boat. They were temperature graphs of Lhasa and flow-level graphs of the Lhasa River just downstream. The river is a large tributary of the Tsangpo and could give a good indication of what levels to expect down on the main river. So much of this attempt would depend on the river level. Scott had said he hoped for volume of

2,000 to 8,000 cfs. The boys looked at the graphs. The temp and water flow over the months corresponded almost exactly—very flat from January through May, then spiking very high and staying high until they plunged again in October and November.

Charlie said, "I think that six-week shot, first of February through middle of March, is gold." He mentioned that according to a reputed gauge where the Lhasa River hits the Tsangpo, the lowest it's ever been is 6,000 cfs—not promising for Scott's target. "But now you've got two years almost of drought," he added.

Nine hours later, we landed in Hong Kong. Red dawn on the dark water. Morning had caught up with us. In the glitzy airport, the polished floors reflected the illuminated signs of the duty-free shops that spilled over with watches, liquor, and electronics. A robot female voice announced the flights and gates. Some of the boys bought mini-recorders. They slept in the cushioned chairs of the coffee bar. Then we boarded a flight for Chengdu, the last city in western China before the mountains rise into the Land of Snows.

We were in Chengdu for two nights while the second group of paddlers, including Scott, caught up with us. The team had been split and its entrance into China staggered so as not to overwhelm and alarm Chinese Customs with 14 kayaks. The delicacy of the negotiated permission to enter the Tsangpo Gorge with boats was becoming more apparent every day. Scott was worried that despite the $130,000 spent on our permit, until we were actually in the Gorge and on the water, the Chinese could change their minds and pull the plug at any moment.

The Chinese were skittish about another river expedition into the Gorge. For one thing, every other serious attempt had ended in death. In September 1993, Yoshitaka Takei of Japan put in with another kayaker near the confluence with the Po Tsangpo. He flipped within the first mile and drowned. Then there was Walker-McEwan and Doug Gordon in 1998. The Chinese reaction was to close the Gorge to all river runners.

Then there was the bad PR. The Chinese have ambitious plans for the development of the Tsangpo Gorge as a tourist attraction—the Grand Canyon of China—and internationally publicized deaths in the Gorge only worsen its aura as a forbidding and frightening place.

To add insult to fatality, in January 1999, a few months after news of Gordon's drowning got wide press, *National Geographic* reported that Ian Baker and Ken Storm Jr. had at last discovered Hidden Falls, a great historical geographic prize that the National Geographic Society claimed had eluded all previous explorers. "If there is a Shangri-La, this is it," Rebecca Martin, director of the society's Expeditions Board, announced blithely. "This is a pretty startling discovery—especially in a time when many people are saying, 'What's left to discover?'"

Preposterous, the Chinese shot back. Yang Yichou, a geologist with the Chinese Academy of Sciences, had known about the falls for years, they said, and had documented it during a 1998 survey of the Gorge. What's more, Che Fu, a Chinese army photographer, had photographed the falls way back in 1986, and just to prove it, they produced the picture. For *National Geographic* to claim discovery was the height of arrogance. It would be like Lewis and Clark telling the Blackfoot Indians that they had discovered the Great Falls of the Missouri. And in all of the historical bickering, nobody seems to remember the Monpa people, who have inhabited the Gorge for two centuries and for whom Hidden Falls holds great mystical significance as a portal to paradise. It was a Monpa hunter who led Storm and his companions, Gil and Troy Gillenwater, straight to the ledge overlooking Hidden Falls in 1997.

Then there was Scott himself. He was about to make an attempt on one of the great adventure prizes left in the world—in Chinese territory. If the government understood the significance of the expedition and the prestige of a possible triumph, would they grant permission? Would the United States have wanted the first ascent of Mount McKinley or the first river descent of the Grand Canyon to have been made by Chinese? This is why, the first night the expedition was all together in Lhasa, Scott explained that we were on a "scientific expedition" into the Gorge and that we would all have two roles—our actual roles on the river trip and the ones assigned to us on a roster of fictitious scientists submitted to the Chinese. I would be a zoologist, Johnnie a geologist, and Steve a botanist—pretty good for a guy who didn't know a primula from a pansy.

. . . .

The first batch of us landed in Chengdu on January 20, with Barry Manilow singing over the plane's speakers. I had been here once before, on another river expedition in 1989. That time the music was "Home on the Range." I had vivid memories of the 40-minute ride from the airport into the city center: flat fields, low rust-brick buildings roofed with heavy tile, hedgerows of spindly trees, a stream of bicycles on the potholed road, a pair of oxen pulling a cart.

This time, we boarded a little charter bus and ramped onto an elevated highway. Heavy traffic, all motorized. And the highway shot through miles of commercial buildings, factories, and warehouses, past tall apartment complexes, over an art deco suspension bridge spraying red cables. The city now extended past the airport, and it felt awash in a tsunami of growth. The air was a uniform gray. As we jammed into the streets of downtown, where I had been so impressed by the throngs of bell-jangling bicyclists—office workers, bureaucrats, laborers, and schoolchildren, all peddling en masse toward, it seemed, an ever-present statue of Mao—it was now nothing but Hondas and VWs and Toyotas. Mao was nowhere in sight. Communism had been exported to places like Nepal, where at this moment, in a fit of anachronism, actual Maoist guerrillas were mounting an uprising.

We traveled down Safe Street, block after block of showroom stores featuring safes and vaults, and turned into Tire Street, with stacks of car and bike and motorcycle tires in all the store windows. We jostled in traffic with fashionable Audi-driving yuppies talking on cell phones and families in Lexuses and fancy Land Cruisers. We passed a line of "barber shop" brothels with striped barber poles and purple-tinted opaque glass and young women in tight clothes standing in curtained doorways, and one of the boys yelled, "Hey, it's tug shops on Tug Street!" Then we arrived at the Hotel Miushu, which had a bronze plaque and a marble lobby and rose over the rank Jin Jiang River.

The next morning, as a bunch of us walked through the crowded market alleys, Johnnie talked about extreme paddling. "The teachings always say, 'Look away from the misery, look away from the fear.' In kayaking, you look back, it turns the head, turns the torso, turns the boat—self-fulfilling prophecy." He said that he and Willie had a shared image, a dream-picture they cherished like an heirloom: It was a paddler approaching a cliffed-out corner in a deep, unknown canyon and paddling around it.

. . . .

Scott, Steve, Allan, Dustin Knapp, Dustin Lindgren, and Ken Storm Jr., the explorer from Minneapolis, arrived that evening. Scott had shaved his long hair down to a monk's stubble. With long sideburns, a soul patch, and wraparound shades, he looked like a barroom badass from Aryan Nation. The mood was celebratory.

Ken Storm Jr. was a surprise. He was round-faced and pale, with fine, thinning hair; big steel-rimmed glasses; and a mild, Mr. Rogers Midwestern accent. He was the most unlikely-looking explorer. He wore a crushable bush hat with one side of the brim rolled up and snapped, making him look like a retiring antiquarian book collector playing adventurer. He *was* an antiquarian book collector. He owned first editions of *Walden* and F. M.

Bailey's *No Passport to Tibet*, along with handwritten letters that Kingdon Ward wrote to Bailey from the Gorge. But he was also a Tibetan explorer with impressive bona fides. This was his *sixth* trip into the Gorge. Most of the earlier ones were in the more easily accessible Lower Gorge, but in 1993, he became one of the few Westerners in history to trek from Pe down into the Upper Gorge and, when blocked by Rainbow Falls, to climb out over a pass just south of the Senchen La and into the subtropical Lower Gorge. He knew the route out of the Upper Gorge at Clear Creek, up onto the Senchen La, which was crucial to our plan and possibly to our survival.

Ken had been skewered in Michael McRae's book, *The Siege of Shangri-La*. He felt he had been wronged in the eyes of history, although history, if it reads *National Geographic*, will always know Ken Storm Jr. and Ian Baker as the "discoverers" of Hidden Falls in 1998. Never mind the Gillenwaters, two brothers from Arizona who first spotted the falls with Storm from a distant ledge in 1997, and whom *National Geographic* neglected to mention. Or David Brashears, who took a picture of the falls from the very same ledge in '93 and who couldn't get the society to publish his articles when he returned.

I asked Ken about all this right away in Chengdu, to clear the air. Of his '97 expedition with Baker, he said, "Ian held back." He had broken away from the other three when Storm and the Gillenwaters stumbled onto the falls. Looking down from high up on the river wall, they saw the Tsangpo drop over a river-wide ledge. It was clearly big—obviously a massive falls and probably the fabled Hidden Falls explorers had been searching for since Victorian times. When they reported their discovery to Baker, the four made a pact to keep the find quiet until the following year, when they would attempt to climb down right to the lip and photograph and measure the falls before announcing the discovery to the world. That's exactly what they did—but without the Gillenwaters. Ken said the brothers had decided not to go on that return trip: "They had no interest in the story. It was only after the fact."

That seems reasonable. What isn't so clean is that the earlier trip and the brothers were never even mentioned in the National Geographic Society's announcement, magazine article, and TV documentary. It wasn't as if they didn't know the history: Ken told me that before the society's big announcement, he sent them a chronology and a film of his trips in the Gorge, with a scene in which he and the Gillenwaters gazed down at the falls.

. . . .

One of the peculiarities of the People's Republic, one that seems to reflect the perversity of rigid central state control, is that all across the land, regardless of when the sun rises and sets, the local time is Beijing Time. There is no Mountain Time or any other time zone. In western Sichuan and Tibet, far to the west, that makes everything late. Even in midwinter, the sun doesn't set until 7 or 8 P.M., and dawn doesn't break in Chengdu until after 8 in the morning. Seven A.M. is still night.

With the diesel throb of our airport bus idling in the hotel's drive, and all the gear loaded, Scott made a head count and came up three short. He swore. He reentered the hotel and five minutes later was followed out by his brother, Dustin; Andrew Sheppard; and Steve Fisher, all looking the worse for wear. They had been carousing in nightclubs with locals until, 15 minutes before departure, they had passed out on their beds in their clothes. Scott was yelling at his brother, "You are not gonna be the trip drunk!" He told Dustin in front of all of us that if he didn't get his shit together, he was going home, no questions asked. And then as Scott passed me and a couple of the paddlers on the way to the bus, he said with a smirk, "I hit him like a bolt of lightning."

Dustin took it. It seemed to run off him. A bartender at the Sugar Bowl ski resort near Lake Tahoe, a talented videographer for his brother's movies, and an extreme skier who starred in radical ski films, Dustin ran at the same high rpm as his older brother. Where Scott contained and stored his power, though, Dustin spent his energy more freely. He was generous with everything—laughter, stories, money, gear, his time—and was always cheerful and rowdy. "I'm different than him," Dustin said later. "I'm a professional goer-outer. That's what I do."

We flew west over the eastern edge of the Tibetan Plateau that morning with the sun rising behind us and lighting the first peaks. The winter mountains rose as suddenly as a line of storm surf breaking on a long beach. There was one thin road leading into them and then it was an ocean of pitched white—ribbed glaciers pouring out of the valleys, the ranks of sharp-ridged buttresses blazing on their east faces and throwing their outlines into the steep ravines. This wasn't a long, parallel scarp like the Appalachians or the Rockies. This was geologic chaos buried in ice and snow. What a time to go paddling.

After two hours, we saw dry lower ridges, dun-colored—the Tibetan Plateau—and then a bright bend of pale-blue river, broad beside the houses of a village. It was our first glimpse of the Tsangpo. It was not frozen in the flat parts as Scott had hoped, and it was huge. A hush fell over the kayakers. What we were looking at was no map; it was a living river, with all the gathered power of its trans-Tibetan journey.

Then we dropped through the clouds, and the country was sere desert—yak-colored mountains with dunes that drifted into the lee of the ridges. The blue Tsangpo braided into its baked sand bed, two large channels carving tapered islands. "I was hoping that this would be a trickle," Scott said.

The jet dropped right over the river and landed in a broad floodplain.

． ． ． ． ． ． ．

Lhasa is at 12,000 feet. At night in January, it freezes hard, and the air is so thin and sheer that the early sun cuts straight to your skin and burns it red, and it warms the streets and packed earth of the courtyards. A few blocks from our hotel, the magnificently tiered Potala Palace presided on a hill over the city. It looked like a fanciful wedding cake. In the center of town, nested on three sides in a warren of old, narrow streets and facing its wide plaza, the Jokhang temple still sheltered the most sacred image in the land, a large, 1,400-year-old golden statue of Sakyamuni Buddha. Incense from *chortens* on the court outside the temple wafted a fragrant haze over the rooftops.

Now, in the time of Monlam, the Tibetan New Year celebration in which the gods and goddesses are said to gather in Lhasa, the streets were jammed with pilgrims in the dress of every province. Adorned in turquoise, jade, coral, and silver—with the women's long hair braided in countless patterns or loose and held in silver combs, and the long hair of the handsome, fierce Khampa men from the east braided and looped through yak-bone rings—thousands of ruddy-cheeked country people with knives at their waists and children in tow flocked to worship. En masse, like a slow current, spinning prayer wheels and chanting, they shuffled and prostrated in a clockwise circuit around the temple. They took time out to shop and barter at the hundreds of stands that lined their route and offered religious artifacts, knives, clothes, and horse tack. In front of the Jokhang, there was a continual rhythmic whisper from the pieces of cardboard or wood strapped to the palms of 100 hands that slid forward on the polished cobbles as the worshippers knelt and prostrated and stood again.

But there were also battered pool tables everywhere outside in the narrow streets. Solar reflectors heated teakettles in the yards. Cars and buses and bicycle rickshaws jostled at the crowded intersections, where Chinese pedestrians wore medical face masks against the smog. Whole blocks of back streets were devoted to selling sheet-metal woodstoves or bicycle tires or wooden chests. An entire neighborhood was lined with butcher shops strung up with the bloody sides of yak and dzo, the yak-cow cross. This was the Muslim quarter—Buddhists will not kill animals, but they will eat meat. And the Potala Palace, seat of the Dalai Lamas for seven centuries, was now a husk, empty of its leader and of all but a handful of monks. More than 5,000 of the Gelukpa order had been exiled or killed.

Outside the Jokhang, Chinese officers in handsome long uniform coats clasped their hands behind their backs and walked among the prostrating pilgrims, making no effort to avoid stepping on their hands. Security cameras mounted on roofs over the square monitored their movements. Since the 1950 occupation, tens of thousands of Tibetans have been killed (some authors put the figure at over a million) and many more tortured, imprisoned, and exiled. The lucky ones fled. Beginning in an especially cruel period of collectivization in 1955, again during the uprisings of 1959, and during the Cultural Revolution in the late 1960s, Red Army soldiers emptied monasteries and nunneries of adepts, monks, and nuns who had taken vows of chastity and tortured them in public, sometimes forcing them to copulate with each other before killing them, according to the International Campaign for Tibet and *Introduction to Tibetan Buddhism* by John Powers.

But in the mid-1990s, the Chinese proudly announced that they had just spent more than $6 million to renovate the Potala. It attracted foreign money. The Chinese turned Tibetan Buddhism into a tourist attraction. Besides, Beijing now had an elegant solution to dealing with any stirrings of Tibetan separatism without incurring international charges of human rights violations: They were simply using market incentives to overrun the country with hundreds of thousands of Chinese immigrants. The International Campaign for Tibet reports that ethnic Chinese settlers now outnumber Tibetans in central Tibet. Native Tibetans are becoming an increasingly marginalized minority in their own country.

At the Himalaya Hotel, a glassed-in temporary storage area off the pillared lobby that was meant for a few guest suitcases was stacked wall to wall with red and yellow kayaks and gear. It looked like an aquarium for big plastic fish.

When we arrived at the hotel, Dave Allardice, the New Zealander and leader of the ground team, met us with five Nepali Sherpas. He swept into the lobby on a tide of good cheer.

"It's nice and low, eh? I've never seen it that low," he sang out as he shook hands all around. Tall and craggy, with an aquiline nose, sharp blue eyes, and tousled blond hair, Dave knew almost all of us well. At 44, he had been running rivers in the Himalayas most of his life. He created what became one of the largest river outfitting companies in the world, Dave Allardice's Ultimate Descents in Nepal, which takes paying clients in rafts down some big hairball rivers like the Bhote Kosi and the Marshyangdi. Half of the kayakers—Scott, Mike, and Allan—had worked for him as guides and gotten their start in the Himalayas. The first time I asked Mike if he'd worked with Dave, he raised his eyebrows. "Worked *for* him, you mean? A bit too much. Bloody exploited, I'd say!"

When Dave saw me, he grabbed my hand and gave me a hug. I had taken an EMT class with him years ago, and we had both been on a hair-raising expedition to the Pamirs. "I heard you were on this. I was glad when I heard it, too!" He patted my stomach. "Got a bit of an insurance policy, I see." Dave is a storm of energy. His nickname is the Gasman, for his ability to make things go. He is the granddaddy of Himalayan River running; he wrote the book on it, *White Water Nepal*. He's a notorious hardman, a sort of New Zealand/Himalayan version of Crocodile Dundee.

Once, in the Tien Shan mountains, on a warm-up before the Pamirs, Dave and I were humping over a low snow pass. We carried heavy burlap sacks of Russian-packed provisions on our shoulders. We climbed over the saddle and were making our way down a snow field. After several hours of lugging the sacks, Dave turned to me and said, "What do you reckon's in these?"

"Dunno," I said. "Heavy, though. Coconuts?"

We dropped the sacks in the snow and I untied the twine. They were filled with watermelons. Dave looked at me. He looked in the bag.

"Watermelons," he said. It was too astounding for comment. We glanced at each other and without a word dumped the melons in the snow. We opened up our river knives and sliced into them. The rest of the expedition caught up with us, and we broke open and devoured every last one. It looked like a massacre. The slope was littered with busted rinds and the snow was stained red.

Now, in the lobby, Dave introduced the Sherpas, who stayed in a tight clutch. Each put his hands together and bowed to each Westerner as he was introduced. There was Passang Sherpa, 35; Kusang Sherpa, 34; Passang Ringi Sherpa, 25; Jangbu Sherpa, 34; and Kannuri Sherpa, 39. Jangbu, the cook, would be the chief. He was the smallest man, with the biggest smile. He had been high up on Everest several times and had summited Amadablam. Kannuri was his brother. He was a bona fide Buddhist lama and a mountaineer, having trained for much of his life in a mountain monastery. That made three sets of brothers on this expedition—the Kerns, the Lindgrens, and the Sherpas.

Mr. Liang arrived. An official from the geology department of the Chinese Academy of Sciences, he was the one who finally got Scott his permit. Mr. Liang and his crew had driven with the three brand-new Chevy Avalanches all the way from Beijing. He was a tall, beefy man with a big smile and white teeth, and he was a fixer. "This dude, Mr. Liang, pulled off in 11 days what nobody else could do in three years," Scott said. Who was the affable Mr. L.? He scowled when he wasn't smiling, grunted his orders, and was obeyed like a general. His card read, with a Chinese flair for the poetry of bureaucracy:

LIANG LIMIN

President

Division of International Scientific Expedition

Institute of Geology & Geophysics

Chinese Academy of Sciences

Beijing Volunteer International Scientific

Expedition Service Centre

On our second night in Lhasa, we all went out to a celebratory dinner at the White Pagoda Restaurant, right at the base of the Potala Palace. There was very loud and sad "Tibetan Opera," belted out by alcohol-sullied, silk-clad Tibetan "tribesmen," and big plates of fried lung and bottles of beer. I began to ask Mr. L. about the geology of the Gorge. He nodded and smiled and knocked my glass, getting more and more confused, until Peter, his hip young aide and interpreter, interrupted. "He doesn't know about geology. He's a driver."

I met our interpreter, Tsawong Gurmey from the Windhorse Adventure travel agency, a tall, slender, smooth-faced man with almond eyes and shoulder-length black hair. He wore a thin black leather jacket. He was half-Chinese and half-Tibetan and spoke English with a rising lilt at the end of his sentences, as if he were constantly surprised that the right words were issuing from his mouth. He took me to the crowded central market across from the Potala to buy fishing gear and extra notebooks. When I commented on the handsome Khampa, who I thought looked like Plains Indian warriors, he said, "Actually, Khampa people are very strange. Black in hair are more strong. Red in hair are weak. Yes!" He told me he had been in the Gorge in 1998 with the Chinese. He said it was a very wild place, with tigers, and that in the Gorge there was a people called the Poisoners of Kongbo who still practiced ritualistic murder. He said they take a special egg and bury it in the ground for weeks. When they dig it up, it is mortally toxic. They scrape some of the egg under a fingernail, and when they make you tea, they dip that finger in it. When you're dead, they raise a white flag over the house, bragging to the neighbors. "They get your luxury, your luck," Tsawong said. "Yes!" Rich out-of-towners like us, and lamas with lots of accumulated merit, are especially targeted. The thought made Tsawong suddenly glum. "Even we dead," he said; then, as if trying to console himself, "Also we use our body to the vulture to make food."

Back at the hotel, he whispered to me that his uncle was a lama and a *tulku*—a living incarnation of the Buddha. This uncle went to Dharamsala, India, and visited the Dalai Lama—Tsawong says "D.L." in case he's overheard by the Chinese. He gave me a simple red string holding a loop of braided and knotted thread. "The D.L. give him this. For protection." It fit perfectly over my head.

On the roof, the gear and food were sorted into piles. Dave looked at the 2,000 vacuum-packed meals and 80 pounds of chocolate, and winced. "Let's go, boys," he said to the Sherpas, and they took off. A few hours later, they came back with 200 pounds of potatoes, sacks of onions, dried yak, and beans. Dave had been in the Himalayas in winter and knew the value of good fuel.

On the fourth day, we all visited the Tsang Kung Buddhist nunnery for a *puja*, a prayer ceremony and blessing. Off a narrow alley not far from the Jokhang, a small door opened into a spacious courtyard surrounded by second-story galleries and potted flowers. We were ushered up a flight of steep outdoor steps and into a dim, fragrant temple festooned with silk banners and lit by butter candles. All along the walls were elaborate statues of Bodhisattvas and Buddhas, and in the middle, kneeling in rows, purple-robed nuns sat cross-legged, chanting, their shaved heads gleaming in the uncertain light. The chant was punctuated by the ringing of a handbell. Scott gave them a wad of cash, enough to ensure their prayers for us every day we were in the Gorge. "Damn good insurance," Dave said.

. . . .

Ken Storm Jr. brought a deep wealth of knowledge about the Tsangpo—geographical, ecological, and historical. Also, along with his profound distrust of journalists, he brought the news that his former co-explorer, Ian Baker, had just gotten a $500,000 advance for a book about the Gorge. This news went through the expedition like the rumor of gold in *Treasure of the Sierra Madre*.

On the third day in Lhasa, while eating lunch with Ken and Steve Fisher in the hotel's gallery dining room, I said something that would hound me the rest of the trip. We were at a white-linen-covered table and served by lovely Tibetan girls who, with their sunburned high cheeks, looked out of place in long silk Chinese kimonos. Ken was talking about the barriers the Gorge throws at people, how many times in history hopeful explorers have been turned back at the gates. He said something about having clean intentions going in, how they can't be self-serving. "I have some personal business to transact on this trip," he said seriously.

In the spirit of this thought, I said that I would also have to be careful to keep my intentions pure. I said the Tsangpo story could be my *Into Thin Air*, referring to Jon Krakauer's bestseller about Everest. I said I didn't simply want to use the Tsangpo as a means to write a book—just as the kayakers didn't seem to want it to be all about being the First Down. Whoops. Ken immediately reported to Scott that I was looking to write a sensational bestseller. They were both convinced I would get rich off the trip, *their* trip. Scott had been planning it for 10 years, and Ken had devoted a decade of his life to the Gorge. They had a huge amount personally invested. Now I would sweep in and make a killing, some journalist who couldn't spell Tsangpo until six months ago.

Next morning after breakfast, Charlie told me that Scott wanted to talk to me. Good. I walked into his room. He was sitting up in his bed. Ken and Charlie sat on the other bed. Scott said, "I've been working on this trip for 10 years. Peter, some things have been said that fucking disturb me." I looked at Ken, who had a pained and kind of pious expression. Scott said that he hadn't been keen on taking a writer, or big sponsorship, period. He said when he'd met me in Santa Fe, he'd gotten a good vibe; otherwise, I wouldn't be here right now.

He said, "Everyone on this expedition is here for a reason. All of the kayakers have devoted their lives to paddling. All of them have been paddling since they were little kids. I probably started the oldest—I started when I was 17. I've led this double life—my paddling in the Himalayas and paddling at home. It's all I know how to do. It hasn't been about conquering a river or making films—it's been about a passion for a sport. I never had anything. Until the last few years, I put together all the trips on my own. I stayed true. It's hard. That's the thing about the sport. Four years ago, my best friend drowned."

I watched Scott. What he was saying wasn't a plea for sympathy. It was something else he was trying to express, something about the root of who he was.

"Was that Chuck?" I said.

"Yeah. Willie and Johnnie watched their brother disappear. They called me, and I drove out to Colorado and helped retrieve the body. We keep paddling. It's been laser focus. It's the same for all these guys."

I waited. Scott stared at me. His mouth was compressed. "I am frankly fucking concerned that you come in here looking for controversy. I don't want you writing about controversy, Tibetan separatism. I have a lot riding on this. I wanna come back and do more rivers. You could ruin my future relations with Mr. Liang and my future business in China."

Nobody had ever told me what to write or not write when I was doing an expedition story. I suddenly felt the increased tenuousness of my position. My assignment was to write about the first descent of the Tsangpo, and I would not be on the water myself. There was a lot I wouldn't see from shore. I needed Scott and the paddlers to tell me what went on every day on the water. I needed cooperation and trust.

"I am going to write a story that is true," I said. "I am not a yellow journalist. I'm not here to sensationalize anything. I cannot *not* write about what the Chinese have done in Tibet. I will do it in proportion, with tact. It's not the focus of the book. You have to trust me on that." Tact. I heard the word come out and shuddered. I thought, "Fuck, don't lose your integrity here." Next to *Chinese* and *Tibet*, *tact* was a yuppie in a killing field.

Scott was shaking his head. "You've got the power!" he said. It was more of a cry than a statement.

Then Scott told me that he was going to make another film on the trip, separate from the *Outside* river-running movie, a parallel documentary about the spiritual aspects and sacred places within the Gorge, with a lot of narration by Ken. He told me that when he was off interviewing Ken about these things, he didn't want me around taking notes. "To protect our investment," he said. Ken nodded. I got it. Scott was carving up the turf. If there was money to be made, stories to be controlled and sold, he was laying down the boundaries. It was Yalta.

"Fine," I said. "What you all do off the river is none of my business. I don't want to steal Ken's story. I'm on kind of a spiritual journey of my own, and whatever I discover under my own steam, that's what I'll write about."

Scott and Ken looked at each other. They seemed unsure.

"Fair enough," Ken said. Scott nodded. Charlie stared at the rug. I walked out.

. . . .

We drove east out of Lhasa across dry plateau, over a high pass, and down a frozen creek with hamlets on the bank and dried hay flung in the trees. In the evening, in the middle of nowhere, we entered a city. Bayi stands on the banks of the Gyamada River some 20 miles from its confluence with the Tsangpo—the last major tributary before Pe and the Great Bend. In thickly falling snow, a yellow taxi led our convoy down a wide boulevard—four lanes of clean-swept concrete divided by a neat median of newly planted pines. On either side, low, white-tiled shop fronts with green glass windows gave the whole street the feel of a lavatory. Beyond, new office buildings rose into the twilight, seven and eight stories, some all blue glass, faceted like gems, and others in mock pagoda style, half-built and caged by scaffolding. The city was empty. We turned onto another four-lane avenue, where we were the only cars.

Scott sang over the Talkabout walkie-talkie: "Holy fuck, bro. Four years ago this was a dirt road. None of this shit was here." We passed a landscaped park with a little lake and pagoda gazebo, petrol stations with new pumps, a school compound with a cannon-size yellow pencil on a pedestal at the deserted gates, and rows of new condos with faux tile roofs sweeping up at the corners—all of it like an architect's model blown up to living scale. It was a city in waiting, planned and stocked and completed like a new exhibit at the zoo or a colony on Mars. We pulled up to a freshly minted six-story hotel and piled out. Three police vehicles pulled in behind us. We were told later that we were the first foreign group here in a year and a half and that this was a tightly restricted area.

Later that night, I stepped outside to smoke my pipe. The snow had stopped, the temperature had dropped into the single digits, and the moon lit a bank of cloud and diffused a soft radiance over the silent city. I noticed new banners hanging from the poles of the street lights, so I broke my curfew and walked down to have a look. The flags were cheerful artists' renditions of the Great Bend of the Tsangpo curving between two mountains. They had already begun the advertising campaign.

. . . .

The estimable Mr. Liang evidently carried some weight in these parts because the next morning, after hard-boiled eggs and gruel in what looked like a storeroom at the hotel, we were on the road again, past yaks rooted among the orange-stemmed willows and Chinese soldiers tending rows of plastic-sheeted greenhouses. In less than an hour, we turned into the big river and found ourselves on the left bank of the Tsangpo.

The first thing you noticed was the size. The riverbed might have been a mile across. The trucks braked in a cloud of dust, and the kayakers tumbled out and jogged to the edge. The river itself flowed low in a blue channel; someone yelled "Twelve hundred!"—the volume of the water flow looked to be 1,200 cfs—and someone else pointed out another bigger braid, and then another. Al said softly, "Pretty deep and wide there, isn't it?" Then your eyes traveled along the barricade of steep mountains that backed and hemmed the far shore: Tibet's Great Wall, the Himalayas, which had protected and hidden this country for centuries. They were snowy and rugged, probably all 20,000-footers, and on the other side of them was India. When you looked downstream, there was a spire of rock and snow that dwarfed the rest, a massif with a horned summit and a single cloud plume sailing off its crest like a streamer: Namcha Barwa, 25,446 feet.

We crossed a bridge of stone arches guarded by a red-and-white bar gate and a Chinese soldier in a long coat standing stiffly on a box. He looked as if he'd rather be shooting hoops with the rest of his squad, who were playing a full-court game outside their barracks. Seeing us, they yelled, "Michael Jordan!" and "If I were Michael Jordan, I would not be here!" until an officer hustled out and shut them up. On the other side of the Tsangpo, we turned downstream beneath the mountains and followed a rutted, muddy road lined with brushwood fences and big logs that had been skidded out of the thick forests on the lower slopes. The sun dropped behind the peaks behind us, and it got cold fast. Just before dark, our convoy pulled out onto a gravel bar beside the river, and we made two big fires in the lee of a lumber shed. It was the last day of January.

The night came on clear, and we could hear the river ripping against the stone bank. A heavy moon loosed itself from a high, snowy ridge to the southeast and set off into a dense current of stars. Mr. L. sat cross-legged by the fire next to Scott, drinking a bottle of rice wine, and the discussion was getting heated. It was 15 degrees and the temperature was still dropping. A stiff wind batted the flames, and Mr. L. was sitting too close to the fire. He was well into his second bottle and lying with increasing gusto. When the bottle exploded between the fire and his crossed legs, he grunted at the interruption and shifted his weight back like a man clumsily dodging a punch. One of his drivers caught a shard just above an eye and cried out. Mr. L. swung his head and frowned, his glasses reflecting the firelight. He called for more wine, and then he slapped Scott's knee and showed his teeth. "The road to Pelung is not possible. Closed this morning. It is not possible. Don't worry," Mr. L. said through the interpreter Tsawong, who looked embarrassed.

The road to Pelung was only an essential part of Scott's assault plan: Pelung was a little frontier town and the trailhead for the Po Tsangpo, which burrowed into its own steep canyon and ran south before it joined the Tsangpo near the apex of the Great Bend. Scott's dream-inspired plan was to send Rob Hind, a Sherpa, and some porters down the Po Tsangpo with the seven extra boats and a pile of food for the second-half attempt on the Lower Gorge. Pelung was also our way out: After scouting and paddling the Lower Gorge, we planned to trek out along the Po Tsangpo to Pelung and the Chengdu-Lhasa Highway. Now Scott sat on the ground in a puffy silver expedition parka, the hood pulled over his closely shaved head, hugging his knees and glaring into the fire. He looked as if at any moment he might grab the new bottle of rice wine and break this one over Mr. L.'s head.

Scott's voice rose. "You say you saw about the road on the TV at the hotel this morning? Why weren't we told about the road this morning?"

Skinny Tsawong wet his lips and pushed his long, straight hair out of his face. "He say he had meetings in the morning," the interpreter said, "so he forget to tell you about the road." Tsawong held up his long, fine-boned hands and crossed them. "Road Bayi to Pome, closed. They repair. Tomorrow. Until July." Mr. L. patted Scott on the knee. Tsawong continued, "Mr. Liang say it may be possible because even you have special permit from Beijing, so we make a discussion with the official, maybe we can pass. He say, Don't worry. He want what you want."

Scott's eyes cut to his Chinese host. He was trying to keep a lid on his anger. Mr. Liang was changing the rules at the 11th hour, and we were at his mercy. Until we were on the river and beyond the reach of a road, cheerful Mr. L. could shut us down. A new and brutal possibility loomed: If the road to Pelung was truly impassable and we had to scrap the plan of bringing an extra set of boats into the Lower Gorge, then the kayakers would have to carry their original boats up and over the Senchen La.

The next morning, Mr. L. took off for Pe to talk to the local military. As the sun lit the far bank of the river, Scott looked up at Ken. "You've never actually climbed over the Senchen La?" he asked.

Ken shook his head. "I made the traverse in summer. We missed the trail and went straight over to Luku."

Scott looked around at his men. He said, "Ken was saying in one day, walking normally, without boats, you can get to the top of the Senchen La. In one day."

Dave said, "It's nothing going over with the Sherpas. If we can make it in a day, they can make it in a day with boats."

Andrew came out of a reverie. He said, "You're stronger in one single group."

How fluid and flexible the strategies and plan of attack had to be, even for an expedition this ambitious! As with whitewater paddling itself, the conditions kept changing, and Scott had to be nimble and keep his eye on the prize. The group consensus seemed to favor scrapping the Rob Hind Lower Gorge party and abandoning Scott's plan of bringing in an extra set of boats below Hidden Falls.

"Maybe we should air it out," Steve said. "Ask the Chinese what's really going on in their heads."

Scott winced. "If you do, bro, you might find things you don't want to know. I'm more on the surface here."

Steve said dryly, "Maybe that's why you've had a girlfriend longer than us."

Scott grinned. "There's a word for that. I'll teach it to you right now: compromise."

"And another," Dave said. "Retail therapy."

"No, Jenning's cheaper than me," Scott said.

The conversation shifted. They began to talk about how to include the Chinese in filming. "We could have Mr. Liang give a talk on the geology of the area," Steve said. "That would be interesting," I thought. Mr. L. could explain the difference between a rock and a hard place.

"This may be a blessing in disguise," Charlie said.

They decided to take a break. The sun had been working its way across the gravel bar and finally poured into camp. It was 10:10 A.M.—Beijing Time. The group scattered. Scott and Ken and Charlie stood talking, still in intense discussion. Suddenly Scott looked up and announced, "That's it! Rob, we're going from the top. All of us. We're gonna have 70 men!" he said. "Fucking 70 men can do a lot of shit."

Johnnie was beside me, drinking tea. I asked him if he ever waits and waits to put on the river. He smiled. "All good things take time," he said.

After noon, Tsawong and Mr. L. returned from Pe in his blue Toyota Land Cruiser. Tsawong announced that at first the military officer said we couldn't go. Then they gave him boxes of food and liquor, and he said okay. Tsawong said, "Many man from Pe went to help on the road to Pelung." We all looked at him, stony-faced. Nobody could believe they were keeping up the pretense of that lie. "But we said we need 50 porters, he said okay. So we move to Pe after lunch. Start trekking day after tomorrow! Yes."

Yes. Dave and Scott called all these shenanigans the Asia Factor. "Through the veil," Ken kept saying. I was beginning to catch his drift.

We broke camp and drove downriver through the town of Pe, a burgeoning village of stone and timber houses and muddy courtyards behind walls stacked with firewood—yaks and chickens and piles of hay sharing the yards with children. We passed an army base behind high green walls and came around a bend where the perspective opened so that we could see both giant peaks, Gyala Peri on the left, the north, and Namcha Barwa so close to it on the south, and I thought, "The Tsangpo flows between them. No way." There wasn't room. Where could the river go?

. . . .

The haggling with Mr. Liang had nearly become war. It was too cold to sit outside, so Scott and Mr. Liang, with Chinese Peter and Tsawong to interpret, all crammed into one of the Avalanches and idled the engine with the heat on. Charlie was there, too. The windows steamed. They wrangled and negotiated for something like six hours straight. Occasionally, I could hear cries from inside, "Eyes! Eyes! Look me in the eyes and say that!" That would be Scott, making a fork out of two fingers and jabbing them emphatically at his eyes. "You lied! I am a man of my word!" Scott again. Some baritone shouts from Mr. L. Once in a while, a door would fly open, and big Mr. L. would tumble out and stalk off a few feet and light a cigarette, his beefy face mottled with anger. Charlie would hustle after him, imploring, "Come back, come back! He didn't mean that. . . ." And Scott would fly off up the road, shaking his head and smoking.

Mr. Liang was doing his best to take the money and scuttle, or half scuttle, the trip. First it was the closed road to Pelung, which was a brash and admirably imaginative lie. Then it was that we could not kayak past Pemakochung, halfway into the Upper Gorge. It was too dangerous, and we didn't have permission from the military. Then the final blow: Porter rates had suddenly gone up significantly, like 250 percent, and each porter would now cost 250 yuan, or about $30 per day. This was a problem. We needed to allow 50 days and had brought enough cash to pay 50 porters about 100 yuan per day. At this new, outrageous rate, we could afford only 20 days in the Gorge.

Charlie told me that Mr. L. had told his assistant, Peter, that his entire sojourn away from Beijing, including the drive, would be a month. He had never planned on allowing us the full 50-day scope of a successful

Tsangpo expedition. He didn't want to sit in the Insta-City of the Living Dead, Bayi, for a month and a half. He was going to take the 130 grand and give us three weeks, or less.

At about three in the afternoon, the logjam broke. Everybody piled out of the truck. Mr. L. had relented and agreed to paying the porters 100 yuan per day.

Dave said, "Mr. Liang knew he had to give a little. All he's been hearing since Lhasa is that people die on the Tsangpo. If someone dies, it's big news back home—under the Institute of Geology of Mr. Liang."

The entire powwow moved in under the cook tarp for toasts. The police chief from Pe and the headman were there for the payoff. They were extremely happy: Scott had been forced to agree to give the Pe "school" $4,000 from our operating cash as a gesture of goodwill. Mr. L.'s hand was on Scott's shoulder, fatherly, holding a cigarette.

Dustin Lindgren said, "It's all okay now. He, Mr. L., just offered me a beer. Scott had a breakdown just now. He needs everybody to pick him up, give him a hug. He needs to get his head wet. He needs fluids. He hasn't been eating. Last night he went off. He got kind of irrational. Don't let him get in the position where he's trying to play catch-up with you guys."

Allan said gently, "No way that will happen on the river."

Dustin smiled. "Yeah," he said, "he'll probably get into full-on Scotty mode."

"When he gets on the river, he'll relax," Johnnie said. "That's how it is for all of us."

I smiled at the professionalism of the kayakers who would *relax* once they got on Tsangpo whitewater.

THE RIVER

The kayakers move fast. Their hands are freezing. It is already afternoon. They unstrap the boats from the roofs of the trucks. They zip into drysuits. They pull harnessed life vests over their heads. All the gear, unused for weeks or months, is stiff, contracted, difficult. The latex gaskets at the wrists and necks of the drysuits are almost too tight to work into. The vests snag. Willie backs up to his brother and without a word holds his arms out like a martyr, and Johnnie tugs the life vest down over his wide lats and pushes him away with a pat on the back, a gesture he's made 1,000 times since they were teens.

There's almost a race to the water. Spare paddles are shoved into sterns, behind the seat. Compact bags of 8-millimeter safety rope are strapped at the kayakers' waists. Carabiners and small aluminum Tibloc ascenders are clipped to life vests. The life vests—designed by Allan with a trip like this in mind—are sewn with integral webbing harnesses, as tough as any climbing harness, and the kayakers can use them for climbing if they need to. First-aid kits are stuffed into the boats. Thin helmet liners like swim caps are stretched over heads. Tight neoprene sprayskirts like odd tutus are worked up legs and over hips and adjusted flat against waists. The skirts will be stretched and snapped over the rims of the boats' cockpits to seal out all water.

Johnnie shrugs into the arms of his drysuit and squeezes his head into the black gasket. The crown of his head, then his ears, emerge from the taut latex ring like a newborn's. His face is beet red. The seal clamps on his throat. "I did not stretch this neck gasket enough," he croaks.

Willie looks up from where he's squatting next to his orange boat, cramming a small, cylindrical yellow drybag behind his seat. Each paddler has one. It holds extra neoprene gloves, a fleece hat, duct tape, a GPS, reduced satellite images, a radio, and a little food. "It's chilly, ay?" he says.

Then silence. Just the wind and the familiar put-in sounds: The bang of watertight, heavy plastic Pelican boxes that hold cameras and first-aid kits hitting the sides of the boats. The clink of carabiners, the rustle of nylon. Velcro being ripped apart and refastened.

Each man puts his own house in order. Kayak, paddle, life vest, helmet, sprayskirt: the five items you absolutely cannot paddle without. Plus paddling shoes with sticky rock-climbing soles. Gloves. Throw rope.

. . . .

Jorge Luis Borges wrote of a God who sees a whole horse race in a split second—the start, the first turn, the backstretch, the finish. All of it at once. It was how he reconciled God's omniscience with Free Will, how He can always know the outcome but allow each being its choices. Obliterate time. There are so many gods in the Tsangpo Gorge: the demons of the Bon religion that the Buddhist saint Padmasambhava was said to have battled in the Gorge. Dorje Pagmo, the diamond sow, Buddha's consort. Dorje Draksen, the merciless protector of the Gorge, who resides in the black sulfur mountain across the river from the ruined monastery of Pemakochung. Sakyamuni Buddha himself, who was an actual man who lived in history and is considered here to be a god. And the river gods, whom devoted paddlers know to exist.

I have the blunt thought, rare for me at a river put-in, that some of us may not make it to the end of this journey alive. There's a paddler's adage that all kayakers are between swims, meaning that sooner or later, every kayaker, regardless of skill, will be forced to pop his sprayskirt and eject from his boat in the middle of a river. I once went 10 years without a swim, paddling a fair amount of Class V water, and then swam and almost bought the farm. Here on the Tsangpo, a swim would almost certainly mean death. For the ground team, too, the trek has its dangers.

Some people are born with a system that hums at redline rpm, and they discover they have the ability to kick into smooth, powerful overdrive when their companions freeze or break or run. Maybe it's part of the constitution of an adventurer, the constant need to find a situation that can match that potential energy.

Steve straps on his helmet. He looks the way he always does: relaxed and fresh. "Today we make history," he pronounces. "Scott Lindgren, Johnnie Kern, Willie Kern, Allan Ellard, Mike Abbott, Dustin Knapp, and Steve Fisher are going to run the Yarlung Tsangpo River." It's an announcement, obvious, redundant, and so self-pleasing that I find myself laughing. His weird accent gives almost everything he says an authoritarian, well, authority. Or maybe it's not the accent at all; maybe it's the perfect teeth, the slow, level green eyes.

Dustin Knapp has his digital video camera out and is filming. Mike, the expedition co-leader, says to the lens, "Feeling a bit nervous, but everyone psyched to hit the water and get into river mode. It's as strong a team as you could have."

Dustin was raised in Oregon and the woods of northern California as a Seventh Day Adventist, homeschooled and strictly vegetarian. He is short, 5'6", and slight, and he looks about 15. He wears tinted wraparound athletic glasses, on the water and off. Quiet, mild-mannered, gentle. Self-contained. He smiles often, but the smile comes across his face slowly, as if he lets the humor of a thought fill him up, a deliberate private appreciation. On anybody else it would look like irony, but his demeanor belies a scary poise on dangerous whitewater. He is the Clark Kent of the Tsangpo. At the end of the day, he portages less and runs more rapids than anybody else.

Earlier, I asked Dustin why he seemed happy most of the time—content. "Does this have something to with your faith?"

He cocked his head a little and let the slow smile cross his face. "Well," he said, "it takes just as much energy to be miserable, so why not be happy?" I asked him again about his faith, and this time he didn't smile. "I'm lost," he said.

. . . .

Willie calls the group together: "Let's huddle up." As river safety coordinator, he quickly goes over the voice and paddle signals. "One whoop is good; two is stop. Three is a situation. Always point positive. Level paddle is stop." By pointing positive he means point to the way down, not at the obstacles, so that someone on the bank or ahead in a boat, giving directions on a route through a rapid, will always point at the good line. Pointing a paddle in any direction means go there.

Johnnie points with his right arm outstretched and crosses his left hand across it near the shoulder. "This is go right halfway," he says.

Willie says, "First aid, injury is . . ." He crosses his arms in an X. Then he looks around at the tight circle like a quarterback and says, "Shitfire, I think we all speak the same language. Waving an arm is radio. Both arms is attention. Feels good?"

"No," brother Johnnie says. "That's confusing." He points two hands at the sides of his helmet for radio. "Radio," he says. Everybody nods.

They all turn their Talkabouts to Channel 1—not likely to be much competition for the channels out here—and break for their boats. They drag them to the water's edge and lay the paddles beside them. We are on the right bank of the river, where the ground crew will stay for many days. The boaters slip into the tightly padded seats with a swift, practiced rocking motion—a hand propped on each side of the cockpit, wriggling one hip under a hooked hip pad, then the other. Their seats and thighs and knees are padded out with gray, closed-cell foam, like a ski boot, to transfer every microadjustment of their hips to the boats. Their feet press up against padded bulkheads; their knees are apart and up tight against the decks. Their lower backs are braced by wide, padded back belts, which they snug down tighter. They reach behind them and work their sprayskirts over the coamings, or rims, at the rear of the cockpits and stretch the tight, Kevlar-reinforced neoprene forward. They hook it to the front of the coamings and then snap the sides in place, tight as a drum.

They are completely sealed in their boats. Nobody is going to get torn out of their kayak by accident. The kayaks are part of them, an extension of their bodies. The way they are locked in, nobody is going to find it easy to eject and swim even if they want to.

Willie shoves off the beach, the first on the river. He sits tall in his boat, paddle resting across his sprayskirt. He drifts and spins in the wind, suddenly weightless. He grins. "Sitting in a boat feels so gooood!" he calls. Then he's over and up again, a fast roll for the Chinese and Tibetans watching on the beach. He shakes the water off his head like a dog. "Yow! Cold!"

One by one they launch. Scott, who's been filming, finally squeezes into his yellow Gus, the kayak Johnnie designed for this trip, and tucks the Pelican camera box between his legs. "I haven't even sat in this boat."

"How's it feel?" Mike says.

"Perfect."

Willie's resonant voice comes across 20 feet of water. "Right answer," he says. He makes a wide, smooth sweep with the right blade of his paddle and spins the boat and starts paddling downstream. Scott salutes the group of us huddled against the wind onshore, gives a thumbs-up, and lays into a steady stroke. It's close to 1 P.M. The river is flat as far as we can see, two miles or so to a right-turning bend where the wooded ridges on either side come together.

. . . .

The first thing the kayakers noticed about paddling on the Tsangpo was the temperature of the water. It could not have been much above freezing. Willie's roll had given him an ice cream headache. Even in neoprene gloves, their fingers stiffened. Mike said they were wearing so many clothes they felt like Michelin Men, and it was difficult to move.

The second thing was the altitude. The put-in was at 9,600 feet. Nobody had been training at any altitude or, for the past few months, training much at all. They set a steady pace downriver, working against the lateness, eight river miles to the first camp. The paddlers were short of breath, laboring much more than they should have been. Their muscles felt leaden. Shoulders burned. Backs were sore. It felt good to stretch and move, but they all knew they had lost their edge, and it was disconcerting.

They hit the first rapid at the end of the flat straightaway where the river constricted and turned to the right. A thousand feet above them, on a spine of ridge on the right bank, was a ruined monastery, all softly moldering stone in the long grass, with a line of tall white prayer flags whipping flat in the wind. Even upwind, they could hear the sound of the river's welcome. A river that puts its head down and plunges after a long flat stretch usually announces the leap with a rush or a roar. The Tsangpo sounded like jet engines. A big wave crashed at the rapid's entrance; Mike spun his boat upstream, caught the face of it with two quick strokes, and surfed, his boat bouncing down the steep swell and coming alive under him like an animal. He peeled off the wave and paddled for a wide tongue of water that fed between a hydraulic and a boulder.

Below were big rapids, wave trains—a line of rolling haystacks—and boulder gardens, a maze of truck-size rocks with fast chutes of whitewater between them. Ledges plunged six feet into foaming backwash. One rapid fed directly into the next. The waves broke over their heads, numbing their faces and freezing their teeth. They all quickly realized what would make this the most challenging paddle of their lives: The current out in the middle was a force that quickly overmatched them. Whatever the difficulty of the moves in the boulder-strewn channels and ledges along the sides, out in the middle, a solid, powerful Class V freight train threatened to sweep them out of control into the next drop.

"There was an approach rapid to it," Willie said, describing the last drop before the river barreled into a steep quarter-mile canyon with violent hydraulics. "You end up in the wrong place on that and you would hate your day."

So they planned their lines with minimum exposure to the main current. They might have to do a fast ferry across to the other side, or maybe a looping sally out from the edge around a boulder or big hole, and dash back. But even those moves were a challenge. The eddies that they planned to hit, their havens of safety behind rocks or along the bank, took all their concentration and strength to reach. "It was fucking ferocious," Willie said. "Getting into an eddy and *huh huh huh*—trying to catch your breath." They were in literally over their heads, and the immersion was shocking cold and powerful. And this was the moderate water. This was just the intro to Tsangpo.

But the greatest challenge wasn't whitewater or cold water; it was the difficulty of planning their moves. They knew the Tsangpo would be a great, interlocking puzzle. Where they came out at the bottom of one rapid was not necessarily where they wanted to start the next. There would be little or no time for recovery in between. The bank on one side of the river where they finished a difficult drop might be the wrong side for scouting the next. A sheer rock wall might prevent them from carrying up a bit to correct the mistake. They would have to move very, very slowly, taking the river one small piece at a time and planning ahead as best they could. An instant's inattention, placing them just past the last safe eddy on that piece of the puzzle, could easily mean entrapment or death.

They also knew that because of the steepness, horizon lines would continually block their line of sight. A horizon line is an edge of water from bank to bank or across a channel, like the lip of a ski jump. It means that on the other side, the river falls away. It might be an easy, sloping 10-foot slab, or it might be a 300-foot waterfall. If you're brave, and the water is slow enough, you can drift to the very lip, back-paddling so you won't go over. If the water is backed up, you hold steady and peer over the edge, ready to drop over or to sprint back upstream if it looks deadly. When the water is fast, you can often "boat scout" by hitting the very last safe eddy before the edge and trying to see what you can. It is an art, and all of the Tsangpo boaters were masters at it. But they would have less opportunity to boat scout here than on any other river they'd ever done.

They got out onto the bank and scouted half the rapids on foot that afternoon. Sometimes two would break to one bank and scout, giving directions for the others by signaling with their hands and paddles. Two fingers forked to the eyes meant "Better look for yourself." Skipping a flat hand over a closed fist meant "Boof," or jump the lip, to clear a bad hole beneath a ledge. This shore scouting takes time, and it was almost night-fall when the paddlers came to the Mini-Gorge, a broad left bend falling steeply through a series of big holes. It was the first serious drop.

Scott and Steve went first, charging the rapid and threading the first set of hydraulics and then catching an eddy on the left bank. They threw their paddles up on the rocks, shimmied out of their boats, and began filming right away. Mike, Allan, and Willie followed and hit the same eddy. Then Willie peeled out and sprinted for the gap in the middle of the river. The chaotic current pushed him too far to the right and flipped him; he rolled up too late to avoid washing down into one of the massive ledge holes. He disappeared. Directly below was an ugly shoal of big rocks and hydraulics. After what seemed like a dangerously long time, Willie burst out of the foam, shook his head clear, and then sprinted left and rode into green water. Dustin Knapp came around the corner and did the same thing—except when he dropped into the hole, the river shot him 40 feet to the right and ejected him upside down. He rolled and recovered quickly and used the chop of the waves to surf himself back to the center. He joined Willie in the flat water at the bottom. The two men sat their boats and caught their breath. Submersion in a Tsangpo hole was not play: Despite the warm gear, the helmet liners and gloves, it had shocked and numbed their heads and sapped their strength.

That was how it began, eight miles and the first demonstration of the Tsangpo's muscle. The Upper Gorge would present 44 miles of ever-steepening whitewater to Clear Creek. Just beyond it, the river squeezed between towering walls and poured over the two great cataracts, Rainbow and Hidden falls. From Clear Creek, the whole expedition planned to climb almost 5,000 feet straight up and traverse the Senchen La, a feat that had never been attempted in the dead of winter. They had no idea what the conditions would be—weather, snow, and avalanche danger were all unknowns. On the other side of the Senchen La was the subtropical Lower Gorge, where the kayakers would scout and paddle as much of the massive flow as they could—about 20 miles if they were lucky. In the gathering dusk, the rest of the paddlers caught up with Willie and Dustin, and they spun their boats and paddled the last mile of easy water to camp.

The whole project seemed as daunting now as it ever had. The river was low enough to expose its banks, allowing the kayakers to portage the unrunnable drops. That was key. If the banks held up and didn't peter out into sheer walls, they could make progress. But we weren't even in the Gorge proper, the Tsangpo was at the lowest level any local could remember, and it was kicking their butts.

. . . .

I stayed back on the dusty trail until the last porter had passed. It was an impressive procession, 64 porters, all wearing heavy Chinese army surplus camo pants and coats, belted long knives, and green army sneakers with heavy soles. Some were accompanied by their wives for these first few days. There were a dozen horses, in plumed and brightly decorated headgear, carrying loads. A few donkeys. The young policeman from Pe, who had black leather gloves strapped into the epaulette of his camo coat and an assistant to carry his gear. And Tsawong and his boss at Windhorse Adventure travel agency, a big fat man named Babu. Sixty-eight men plus 19 of us. Eighty-seven people plus camp followers were moving into the Gorge, including the wife of the headman from Pe, who wore a stylish sheepskin coat and heavy makeup, and their children. Mr. Liang and his entourage had left us at the trailhead and returned to Bayi to wait.

By the time I stood, the air had gone grainy with dusk. I turned away from the river and climbed a wide trail pungent with the tang of horse manure. The trail topped out on a broad bench that sloped gently down to fields hazed with the green of winter wheat. Where all day there had been low clouds clinging to the wooded slopes, there was now the apparition of Namcha Barwa, its summit floating above the layers of forest and cloud, radiant in the last sun. Swinging on my trekking poles to save my hip, I half trotted past a few tiny, walled houses—the village of Tripe—over a muttering creek and through a brush fence that led into a slope of descending terraced fields. The fields overlapped in scalloped arcs, stepping down the hill over fieldstone walls, and they were newly green. Grazing horses lifted their heads. At 9,500 feet in Tibet in early February, despite the freezing nights and the winter that raged on the peaks above, spring was already coming. This was not a good thing. The kayakers had Right Now to paddle the river. In a month or six weeks, the snows at 10,000 and 12,000 feet would begin to melt, and the Tsangpo would become monstrous.

Four men sat on a pile of thick logs, smoking in the twilight. I could see the scar on the hillside where they had skidded the logs off the ridge. Beside the men, a stack of hand-cut boards glowed honey yellow in the dusk, and the sharp raw scent of pine came off them. A partly sawn log lay propped across a pit. This was how they milled their wood: a two-handled ripsaw, a man on top and a man in the trench. I laid my cheek against one of the planks and sighted down 20 feet of face cut, and it eyed flat and true, minutely rippled by the strokes of the saw. It was the second display of world-class skill I had seen that day. I straightened and grinned and gave them a thumbs-up, and they smiled and offered me a smoke, which I declined. I walked down the trail toward the river, smelled a dinner fire, and soon saw its light through leafless oaks at the bottom of a pasture.

The temperature plummeted, freezing the drysuits into suits of armor. "I learned one lesson today," Dustin Knapp said, pulling his head through the latex neck gasket of his suit. "To scout for myself if I'm not sure."

Mike sipped tea, and his hoop earring glinted in the firelight. "The first day was a bit intimidating, feeling the power of the river."

Scott stared into the fire, brooding. Then he looked up. "I want everyone on edge," he said. "One fuckup out here—*one*—and the whole thing's over."

He didn't have to say it.

. . . .

"So far I haven't seen any big water—I see very technical, high-volume, very dangerous water," Steve said, sitting on a stump by the fire.

The Sherpas had strung two of the big tarps between trees and walled off one end of the kitchen hut with sacked porter loads of provisions. There were two fires, one for cooking next to their shelter and one for warmth. No fewer than four pots were under way, and the five men moved around them, adding shredded yak jerky and packets of dried soup mix, chopping onions on a small cutting board, molding dough into small pastries. Jangbu was in charge. He squatted by the fire, a black baseball cap shoved back on his head, and stirred the pot. The five barely talked. They worked intently but relaxed, and when they spoke, there was often laughter. I got the sense of a family, each long accustomed to his role and easy in his work, though I'm not sure who, aside from the brothers Kannuri and Jangbu, had ever worked together. A two-gallon aluminum kettle of sweet cream tea warmed at the edge of the second blaze. The lama, Kannuri, poured an enamel mug full and handed me the cup.

I sat on a log and talked to Steve about the conditions on the river. Like most paddlers, he spoke in Roman numerals:

Class I is moving flat water with a few riffles.

Class II is small rapids; waves to three feet; and wide, clear channels.

Class III is rapids with high, irregular waves and narrow passages. It often requires complex maneuvering and may require scouting from shore.

Class IV is difficult rapids with restricted passages, often requiring precise maneuvering in very turbulent water. Scouting from shore is often necessary, and conditions may make rescue difficult.

Class V is extremely difficult, long, and violent rapids with highly congested routes. Scouting is mandatory—everywhere but the Tsangpo, at least. Rescue conditions are difficult, and there's significant hazard to life in the event of a mishap.

Class VI is unrunnable. Or it used to be. Now it's defined in the official handbooks as nearly impossible, very dangerous, for teams of experts only at favorable water levels and with all precautions.

"This cold water adds a whole new dimension," Steve said. "If you've got a Class III rapid with a sticky hole halfway down, you're probably looking at a Class IV rapid. First, your functionality is reduced. Second, if you swim . . ." He took a sip of his tea, leaving the results of that disaster self-evident.

Willie was listening in. He drew on a cigarette. "This is fucking incredible," he said. "This is perhaps the largest undertaking in kayaking history. And it's Day 1." He laughed and took a deep drag. "You know what else is really important? I think there's such a great cohesiveness among the group. I think it's because we're totin' around a good supply of humility. Nobody's walking around like they own the place."

No shit. "The Place" was asserting itself.

Scott started talking about the Walker-McEwan expedition. "I can't believe guys with so much experience were that stupid—they all had Tornadoes. Ninety gallons. Hard to move around." He stabbed at the embers with a stick. Doug Gordon and his mates had used big cruiser kayaks. The boats our guys were paddling were all about 74 gallons in volume, significantly smaller. They were, on average, 8½ feet long, as opposed to the 11½-foot Tornadoes. Three of our kayakers—Scott, Johnnie, and Willie—were each paddling a boat called the Gus, which Johnnie, under contract with a company called LiquidLogic, had designed specifically for the trip. But Doug Gordon and his friends were from a different, older school of paddling, where big water meant bigger boats. The old philosophy was that the faster hull speed of a big boat, and its sheer mass, would give a paddler an advantage in punching through the sticky hydraulics that tried to grab and trap the boat in their crashing backwash. If Scott's group hadn't had gear to worry about, they would have gone smaller still. It was a completely different style of paddling, bred on the trick-rider, freestyle kayak rodeo circuit, where agility and freedom to move around in a crashing hydraulic—not the combined barreling inertia of boat and paddler—were everything.

"The four clowns had 60,000 at least," Scott added, referring to the river's volume in cubic feet per second. He shook his head at their dumbassedness. Jesus. "Clowns" was harsh. Gordon, Roger Zbel, and the McEwan brothers were all undeniably brave, and one had died. This display of arrogance didn't square with Scott's professed humility before the river. Or maybe it did. He *was* respectful of the Tsangpo. For someone as driven and cocksure as Scott, maybe one of the wildest forces in nature was the only thing that could get his respect. Maybe that's why he needed to run rivers: to stay merely mortal.

. . . .

Steve and Willie crawled into their bivy sacks—tubes of Gore-Tex, each just big enough for a sleeping bag, with a small tent-pole hoop at the head.

I went to my single-person tent, an odd, tension-supported structure. It required about 60 percent less open ground than a two-person tent. I had done my homework: Among the big boulders along the constricted sides of the river, sleeping space would be at a premium. I took a Celebrex pill, a mega once-a-day anti-inflammatory. It was my fourth today.

I woke to slapping on my tent door. I unzipped it. It was still dark and well below freezing. "Coffee or tea?"

Ringi Sherpa, the skinny, youngest one, held a tray. The beam of his headlamp played over blue enamel mugs, tinned instant coffee, powdered milk, sugar. Tall Kusang Sherpa stood behind him with the steaming kettle.

"Coffee," I said. "Thank you."

"Sweet or no sweet?"

"Sweet, please."

Kusang poured the water and stirred the cup and handed it to me. What a way to wake up. A moment later, I heard chanting from over by the cook tent, a low, resonant, rhythmic drone, the same I'd heard from the monks at the Jokhang. I put on my boots and down coat and took up the scalding mug. Kannuri was sitting, praying. I hoped he was praying for us.

Dustin Lindgren was already up. He was so excited he could barely contain it. He'd just called his pal Eddy in California on the sat phone to ask for the Super Bowl score. "He's in a strip bar in Roseville—7 to 3, *Pats*," Dustin said. "They just intercepted and ran it back for a TD—that'll be the biggest upset in Super Bowl history. That's what I *love* about Parcells—he doesn't like a winning team. . . ." Dustin was beside himself. He and Scott had a high school friend in the game, playing linebacker for the Patriots. I laughed. The stars were lining up. We were at the mouth of the deepest gorge in the world. Kannuri the lama was praying. The Patriots were winning.

TRIPE TO SELUNG CREEK

It took two hours to break camp and distribute loads. For the kayakers, there was no hurry; the next few days on the river would be relatively short, so they might just as well wait for the sun to break into the canyon and warm things up. But the ground team would have rugged treks just about every day, and we needed to get moving. The Gorge would quickly become deeply incised and layered: There was the great chasm of the Tsangpo, and then there were the drainages and deep ravines that cut down from either side. Between them were high spurs, ridges that on river-right flowed down off the Namcha Barwa massif and dropped straight to the river; there were high spines, forested and slabbed with rock, with sides that strained toward the vertical. While the kayakers faced their own challenges in snaking around these buttresses, the ground team would run out of riverbank and hit a rock wall. Then we would be climbing up and over, sometimes humping thousands of feet above the river, searching for a climbable notch or pass, and then back down to the Tsangpo to reach the paddlers' camp. Ken estimated that the total altitude gain for the whole journey on the ground, counting all these spurs, was 30,000 feet. That's 30,000 up and 30,000 down. Like climbing Everest from sea level. When he said that, I popped a Celebrex for good luck.

Dave had halved the porter load from the usual Himalayan 40 kilos. That is, 20 kilos of our stuff along with their own blankets and enough food for about 30 days. There were villages in the Lower Gorge where they could resupply. Dave estimated that these personal provisions would easily make up the 20-kilo abatement, bringing the average porter total back to the traditional 40 kilos—just short of 90 pounds.

Dave swung sacks of food out of the kitchen tent, hefted them for weight ("Yep, that'll do"), and reshuffled men and loads ("You look like a strong bugger, the tent bag for you. . . . What's your name? Tashi? You reckon you can carry the spare kayak to Clear Creek? You *want* the kayak? Mate, you're a brave soul. . . .")

Tsawong stood by with a notebook and checked men's names off the roster, occasionally getting into a loud argument with one man or another, pointing angrily with his pen at a burlap bag of rice, sucking his teeth in disapproval, pushing his long hair back behind his ear. He was very emotional for a Buddhist.

Ken Storm Jr. was ecstatic. When we were still roadside, the headman from Pe had insisted we take all Peians; in the crowd, Ken recognized several men who had portered his previous trip through the Upper Gorge in '93. They were expedition-tested and they knew the way. He'd made a special request and was allowed to take four of them along with us. One was named Sherab, a quiet, handsome 40-year-old who'd been their guide before. Sherab rarely spoke. His hair was a soft black brush of mane, his expression serious. He almost always held his prayer beads, wrapping them around his wrist when he needed both hands to climb or cut through brush, and he could be heard all day long humming a prayer between breaths. Ken immediately asked Sherab to carry his camera gear in his large bamboo pack basket. Ken used trekking poles as I did, so Sherab also proudly carried his ice axe. Ken and Sherab would lead the ground team's long train for most of the trip.

Another porter Ken remembered was Tashi, a youth with wide-set eyes and a sweet demeanor, who now wished to carry the extra Gus kayak. He must have been just a kid in 1993.

The porters from Pe didn't make a living hauling loads like the cadres of professionals in Nepal. They were farmers mostly, and they were hunters before the Chinese banned it in the Upper Gorge in 1998. They were Kongbos, of mostly ancient Tibetan lineage. Some showed up with bamboo-strip baskets and some with pack frames made of bent wood, but most arrived for duty with a blanket, a plastic-burlap sack of food, and a length of rope. One in every few men carried a sheet of plastic to use as a tarp. They wore light sweaters and thin socks, canvas sneakers, one set of camo pants, and a jacket. Some of the porters couldn't have been older than 17. Each grabbed a load and tied it up with shoulder straps and a tumpline for his forehead, and I considered them as courageous as any of the kayakers—or so tough they didn't give it a thought, or desperate for cash. Probably all three. They knew where we were going as well as anyone. With all my top-of-the-line gear from North Face and Arcteryx, with soft, warm wool socks and a down jacket—and one of them to carry most of it—I felt pampered, almost effete. But I reminded myself that even Colonel F. M. Bailey had porters. He had brandy and English biscuits. And Kingdon Ward had a tent he could stand up in, Yorkshire relish, and pâté de foie gras.

That morning, as we our hoisted our packs and the kayakers held their frozen drysuits by the fire, a tough-looking, sun-darkened older porter came over and picked up my green rubberized drybag. He wore high-top sneakers and had cloth wrapped snugly around his calves, like puttees from World War I. His hair was chopped straight across in short bangs. He had blunt features and cauliflower ears and looked like a boxer. He said his name was Tuli. At 42, he was my age. He nodded with approval at the padded shoulder straps of my bag and began tying his bundle to the top and fixing a tumpline for his head. I noticed that he had a tin locket box shaped like a house around his neck and that inside was a photograph of the D.L. I looked around at the other porters and saw more of the lockets. Now that we were out of Pe and away from the Chinese, the Dalai Lama was being given some fresh air.

The whole procession, more than 100 people plus pack animals, moved onto the trail that climbed off the fields of the bench and onto the steep side of the canyon. The track contoured a few hundred feet off the river, in dry oak brush and small pines. It could have been Colorado. Less than a mile below Tripe, we all stopped for the show. At 10:30, the sun was clear of the ridges, and it poured onto the dry slope, releasing a warm, faded pungency like thyme. Here the river made a U-bend to the left. Just at the apex, and above and below it, were big, continuous rapids. We were in the nosebleed seats and excited to see how the kayakers would deal.

. . . .

A river is often faster where it makes a tight bend because it is usually more constricted. Some feature of the topography has forced it into the turn, pressing it against whatever elevation on the other side bends it back. Between the rock and the hard place, the river narrows and finds its way. The Tsangpo reminded me of the surface of a calm sea suddenly churned up in a fracas of feeding dorado. The river barreled over boulder ledges, hit a jumble of even bigger boulders at the crux of the turn—some were gouging out deep holes—and finished in a run-out of waves 10 feet high. The left bank opposite us was almost all rock wall until the apex, where it crumbled and fanned into a rock beach.

Charlie set up his Nikon, and Dustin Lindgren found a vantage on a dicey ledge with a video camera. The headman and his fancy wife and six kids perched in the bushes. All up the trail, the porters dropped loads and tethered their horses. It was like a carnival.

When biologists take pictures of specimens, they often put a pencil in the foreground for scale. The 8½-foot kayaks served the same purpose for calibrating the size of a drop. This rapid looked like any other Class IV to V until Johnnie, in his orange Gus, stroked around the corner, hugged the right bank, and flew over a little ledge waterfall slotted between two boulders. He was tiny. I blinked. The waterfall I'd thought was four feet high was more than double that. The river telescoped into proper scale with a jarring Alice-in-Wonderland adjustment.

Johnnie dropped into the hole made by the curtain of falling water and paddled out of it left, toward river-center, without missing a beat in the rhythm of his flashing paddle blades. He spun his boat up into the eddy behind a boulder on the left, and just as he stopped, Dustin Knapp angled over the ledge, got half buried in the hole, and with a similar, continuous tempo buoyed out of the foam and swung up next to Johnnie in the green eddy. I saw their heads turn toward each other, a brief exchange, and then with a double stroke, Dustin accelerated upstream out of the pool toward the middle of the river and caught a jet of current; then his boat defined a smooth arc, leaning toward the inside of the turn like an F-16 peeling out of formation. He dropped through a tight sluice between boulders, about a six-foot spill, and powered out into the main current and around the maw of a giant hydraulic; he tucked back in behind it, just catching its crashing left edge as Johnnie peeled out behind him.

Like music: rhythm, tension, release. Lilting pauses, partial resolutions, crescendo—and the heady suspension just afterward as the airborne kayak plunged into the swoon of a short coda. There were repetition and variation as the two boats, like two instruments, followed the score. Twinnings, separations, reining in, and abandon. Allan and Willie came around the corner and took the left side against the wall, another series of ledge falls and sluices, catching a two-beat rest in a shadowed, circling eddy in the hollow of the cliff, and it was the same. And then Mike in his red boat passed them both and moved left to center, speared over a 10-foot ledge, angled hard right, and almost scraped the boulder on his left shoulder as he launched completely clear of the death hole below the fall. He landed in a flat boof. He idled in the eddy, a red boat on green water, to spot for the guys above as they pieced together the end of the first rapid and hit the rocky beach at the corner. The finale: an orange paddle thrown onto the stones by Allan, who got out to scout the next stretch.

The music analogy went only so far. It was clear, even in these relatively benign riffs on the second day, that if someone messed up, he wouldn't get a frown or raised eyebrow from the maestro. He'd probably die.

What was remarkable about the second segment—the colossal boulders and holes at the crux of the turn—is that a few of the kayakers decided to sally out into the meat of the main current and test the feel of it for the first time rather than hug the left-side "sneak" route. The sneak was a demanding enough technical maze through steep rocks, but with much less water volume. Scott was on the radio: "River crew to trail crew. Steve and Mikey are getting ready to go. I think they're gonna run left of center. Some of the boys want to go out in the middle a little bit and see how it feels."

Andrew: "Are their balls gonna fit in the boat?"

Steve, Mike, and Allan. Two went left and one went right of the gnashing holes at the top. Allan looked like he would be swept straight into the guts—he raised a gasp from the onlookers in the bush bleachers—but he made two powerful strokes left and barely cleared the holes. It was a confidence booster. They had met the push of most of the Tsangpo's volume, and they'd been able to move their boats.

When the last man cleared the second rapid, the ground crew hit the trail. Everybody was in a good mood. The sun burned into the cold air with the giddy reprieve of Indian summer. The trail dropped to the river and cut along the flats beside it through wheat-colored grass, willow trees, and tall brown ferns that grew to my shoulders. The river ran on our left, green and open, just big waves and easy boulder gardens, and upstream, Namcha Barwa bristled and gleamed. On the walls of the cliffs across the river ran a band of chalky rock above the water like a bathtub ring—30 feet high. That was the high-water scour. I closed my eyes for a second and imagined the flood that would tear that high along the wall.

We passed an abandoned wood hut in the ferns, climbed into a dim forest of mossy rocks and tall rhododendron trees in full leaf, dropped down through groves of pines, and emerged onto a beach of fine sand and smooth, cobbled stones. A clear stream ran down out of a cleft in the woods and crossed the beach. A log footbridge spanned it, and some of us stopped and drank and washed our socks and undershirts.

A perfect time of year. No Westerners had ever come here in February. I thought how, in any other season, we might be walking in sheeting rain. The ferns would be so alive with leeches, their leaves would seem to writhe. As the Gorge closed in around us and the river bored into it, the scale of the place was becoming more evident. It wasn't just the man-high ferns and the rhododendrons as tall as gambrel oaks. Nor was it just the vast wall of the canyon, so high and sheer that you had to tilt your head way back to see the top. Those phenomena were all connected.

The Tibetan Plateau was desert, shielded by the Himalayas from the wet monsoon weather that surged up from the Bay of Bengal and the Indian Ocean. But the Tsangpo Gorge was a breach in the wall, and the monsoon swept into it, funneled up the canyons, and dropped prodigious amounts of rain. This, and the abrupt elevation gradient between subtropical and arctic ecosystems, made it one of the most biodiverse places in the world.

The river was disconcerting. I'd paddled on whitewater around the world, some of it high volume. When a flow got big enough, when waves got to a certain height and power and holes could swallow an 18-wheeler, the rocks in the riverbed tended to disappear, and a kayaker was faced with a different kind of challenge. Instead of maneuvering through rocks and over ledges, he had to deal more with the water itself, with powerful features formed by water colliding with water and the bank. Giant haystacks—steep rollers like storm swells—huge holes, and dangerous breaking diagonal waves that fed like funnels from the sides to the middle of the river. The rocks would be well-submerged and no longer an issue. Here on the Tsangpo, though, the whitewater was bigger than anything I'd ever seen, and there were still rocks in the riverbed, and ledges. This meant that everything—the rocks themselves and the gradient—was just plain bigger, steeper.

· · · · · · ·

We walked to a creek that flowed out of the mountains and out along the edge of a small, stony beach scattered with oak trees. At the bottom end of the beach, the stream ran along a low cliff and emptied into the river. This was Selung Creek, a sacred spot for pilgrims and the gateway to the Gorge. The Tsangpo stretched in a flat pan downstream, silvered in the lowering sun and serene, spent of its fury. Most of the kayakers were sitting on their boats on the beach, the sun on their faces and their backs to the cold downstream wind. They wore their down parkas and smoked.

Scott sat on a rock in a blue ski hat, barefoot, and motioned with a piece of bamboo. "That was really low stress for the most part," he said with a trace of excitement. "Be awesome if we could go right to the fucking brink of it, to Rainbow. I'm floored. When those guys were here at high water, it was a completely different monster. I feel so at home right here, it's insane. So much like California. The trees, the oak, the granite, identical—no different."

Willie said to me, "Below the big rapids, it was just these beautiful boulder gardens. A lot of room to move around."

A boulder garden is what it sounds like: a rapid with large rocks scattered through the riverbed. It's a lot of fun. When the current hits a boulder, it compresses and often rides up on the rock in a "pillow" that can be a smooth hump of green water or a folding, foaming pile. The current also flows to either side of the rock, and because it's been compressed, it jets past the main stream. Behind the boulder is an eddy, a pocket circling back upstream, where a paddler can rest and take stock.

You aim for a boulder downstream and paddle for it. You can pull a big airplane turn, riding up on the pillow and sluicing around it in a fluid falling motion. If you do, you'll pick up speed and ride the jet and cross it at the same time, literally dropping into the eddy pocket—sploosh! The water there will grab the bow of your boat and hook it swiftly upstream, and you'll come to rest tucked neatly behind the boulder and facing up-river. Or you might aim a little lower and just miss the rock altogether. You angle across the fast jet of eddy fence and splash into the pocket from the side. Again, the eddy current whips your boat around to face up-stream. A look over your shoulder to the next boulder below—take aim—a hard stroke or two, and you're out of the pocket, turning downstream in an accelerating, canting arc as the main current catches your bow and swings you downriver. You power for the edge of the next big rock and—*whip!*—hook in behind that one; a beat or two and you're gone.

It's called eddy hopping, and it's a flying dance, rock to rock. You read the river from your boat and use the boulders to break long rapids into manageable sections. It all has a swooping, waltzlike rhythm. There's nothing funner.

Steve stacked a tower of flat pebbles between his feet. "At high water, yah?— lot of this would be cliffed out."

I thought of the high-water mark along the rock walls, 30 feet up. When the four were here in '98, it couldn't have been *that* high. You might as well close your eyes and step in front of a train.

Scott said, "I always said if we could make it to Pemakochung, that would be awesome. That's gonna be the telltale for us. Seeing the rapid and looking at the satellite."

The ruined monastery of Pemakochung sat at about Mile 30 on the river. We were now at 15. The pictures provided by Space Imaging didn't include these first miles of the river. The images comprised all of the Great Bend, but they started just upstream of Pemakochung, so the kayakers were now relying on topographic maps and their own scouting, and they had no idea how the sat photos correlated with the facts on the ground. Would the glare-obscured, "blown-out" sections be impassable?

Would the cliffs allow for any scrambling along the edge of the river? They wouldn't know until they got close to the monastery.

Young Dustin Knapp sat alone on a granite slab above camp. I wondered if he was praying. He seemed pleased. "That was *quality* whitewater," he said simply. Dustin was such an odd duck. He was an ultimate team player, quietly shouldering his load. On the river, he was happy to paddle ahead and film, then catch up; he scouted for the others. Off the river, he spent hours quietly editing film footage for Scott. But he didn't feel the need for the camaraderie of camp, the swapping of stories. He didn't reject it, either; he appreciated the others and kept his own counsel. This is a guy who loves to go home and help his mom. He spent last winter on the family place in the Trinity Alps of northern California, helping her remodel the house. He's an accomplished carpenter—he grew up wearing a tool belt and helping his father, a builder—and he dreams of building his own house in the woods. Dustin had paddled beautifully today. I could see where he'd earned his reputation as a graceful and efficient kayaker. No wasted movement. Never scared. He spoke the way he paddled, straight to the matter with the least words. He had told me earlier, "If you're scared, something's wrong."

I take it back—he's less like Clark Kent than like Jimmy Dean.

. . . .

Johnnie sat by the fire and told me that when he and Willie were children in Massachusetts, there were heaps of split cordwood out in the yard, and they'd help their father stack it. He'd come home from his job selling heavy commercial trucks, and all he wanted to do was mess around with his three sons. Dad would encourage the kids to climb the trees in the yard, to push their limits. Willie sometimes went too high and got stuck, and he was the one who took the rap when the flowerbed got torn up or the garbage was tipped over, whether he did it or not. If it was warm, they'd all go down to the local swimming hole and roughhouse in the water. The boys clambered over their father, who moved through the pond as unencumbered as a Percheron.

Johnnie said that when their dad died of a heart attack a year after their mother left the marriage, he and Willie reacted in different ways. Willie got angry. He started smoking pot and skipping school. "I became a geek," Johnnie said. He focused harder on his classes and became an A student.

Different as they were, in the late 1980s, Willie and Johnnie shared a passion for paddling and for the brand-new sport of squirt boating. Basically, you got into a handmade fiberglass microchip of a boat that could barely float. That was the idea; you were going to take kayaking from two dimensions—staying on the surface of the river—and transform it into 3-D. You were going to go up—spearing your stern into the water and launching your bow to the sky—and down.

The first boats had names like Vulcan, Prodigy, Jet, and Bigfoot. Many had bows and sterns so flat you had to stretch your legs out and squash your feet into painful contortions. No shoes; there was no room for an extra half inch of rubber. In profile, the boats looked something like the side view of a serving tray, with a saucer of a cockpit rising up in the middle. But they made up for knife edges and anorexia with flashy colors and iridescent spangles. The custom squirt boat makers outdid themselves with cosmetics. A renaissance of kinetic art flowered in fiberglass sheds in West Virginia and North Carolina and Colorado. There were crimson glitter flames on aquamarine decks, Union Jacks, and schools of mica fish. The stodgy wood paddles evolved into futuristic weapons with blades shaped as asymmetrical hourglasses or teardrops. Nothing less radical would do for a vocation that proposed to leave the surface and plumb the depths of a river's currents, and in so doing challenge the paradigms not only of kayaking but, it seemed, of everything else as well.

The high priests were the Snyder brothers of West Virginia, Jim and

Jeff. Jim was a kayak philosopher who wrote a book called *The Squirt Book*. It became a cult classic and a bible for the Kern twins. "Squirtists should reflect on the spirit revealed in the history of our subsport," Jim Snyder wrote. "It is indomitable and inimitable, a rock in time, a stroke for all. It is the one point central to all squirt development."

After the first foray on the Tsangpo, as he sat by the fire, Johnnie quoted a Jim Snyder motto: "You gotta be big enough to be small enough to let the world be awesome and it will."

All metaphysics aside, the apogee of the squirt boater's art was called the Mystery Move. In it, the kayaker used the opposing currents shearing along an eddy line to become a submarine. Because two currents pass each other going in different directions, eddy lines often develop whirlpools that spin from the top of the eddy near the rock or jutting shore and travel downstream until they dissipate. You, the paddler, use your weight and edge control along with a powerful sweep stroke to knife your bow into one side of the eddy line or the other, letting the current piling against the bow sink it. Then, as the whirlpool spins you, you rock over and edge your stern into the water and let the current sink that. Then you rock subtly and gyre, with your paddle moving in a circle of sweeps on the surface and then helicoptering slowly over your head as you sink—and the kayak and you . . . disappear. Completely under the water. You become, in essence, your own downward-spiraling whirlpool.

Willie took to squirt boating like a loon. He would sink his leading edge and spin down, break through the violent shearing surface current into a quiet, almost still world, down and down as the light dimmed—10 to 20 feet under the surface. "You look around, and the big whirlpools generated off the eddy line are funnels of light—they capture the light and twist and string out into beautiful tornadoes, twisting funnels with squiggling tails that roll down through the dark water. They're all around you, rolling away, spiraling toward you," he said as he sat by Johnnie in the firelight. He said he would grab a rock in the eddy on the bottom and just watch the vortexes.

I could imagine young Willie down there, sitting his kayak as if it were a beloved horse, attached to the river bottom and enthralled with the patterns of light and water, letting them wash his grief and cool his anger.

Charlie, who joined us, said Willie would submerge like a U-boat, "and then you'd see his paddle pop to the surface. And then just his hand. That's all you'd see. The hand would grab the paddle and go back down!"

In the maelstrom of the Tsangpo, it would be useful to be that comfortable underwater. The holes at the apex of the U-bend rapid that morning had been huge. They could take one of the big Grand Canyon pontoon boats, fold it like a taco, and swallow it whole.

Squirting wasn't the only or even the best skill when a dragon hole opened its jaws. Each of these guys had done their share of freestyle competitions. Freestyle, or rodeo, kayaking is essentially trick riding in a big hole. The river pours over a rock or ledge and dives for the bottom. This creates a trough, a dip or "hole" in the surface water that slides back upstream to fill in the vacuum. Downstream of this can be a wave—the back side of the trough—and if the trough is steep enough, the wave collapses on itself, continually falling back into the hole in a crashing foam pile. It's the same action as an ocean wave hitting a beach, walling up until it's too steep to hold its form and then breaking. The foam pile in a hole does the same thing as the break of a comber: It creates a breaking wall of white that can stop anything trying to bust through. A comber pushes a surfer ahead of it, but in a kayak in a river, the breaking action of the curler pushing you back upstream is counteracted by the swift current, or "green water," pouring downstream.

A hole can be deadly because these two forces can hold and pummel a boat in the trough. Just as a boat launching into ocean surf from a beach can be upended and trashed by a breaking wave, a kayak dropping into a hole and hitting the wall of churning white backwash can be stopped dead, upended, and cartwheeled. Out of control, it can be capsized and recirculated in the trough like a log held and hammered beneath a dam. There are stories of river runners whose bodies recirculated in holes for many hours before they could be retrieved.

The retentive quality of a hole can also be a great opportunity for play. It allows freestyle tricks that make rodeo kayaking a cross between surfing, bull riding, and gymnastics. A freestyler strokes out from shore or an eddy along the side, slots into the trough, and, riding up on the foam pile, suddenly catapults forward in a series of fast end-over-end cartwheels, rotating over one edge of the boat or another. This is called throwing down or swapping ends. Each linked end of a cartwheel scores technical points. The competitor has three minutes to post the highest score. If the hole is the right shape, he might throw in a loop—a complete frontal somersault—or an aerial loop—airborne—or a "Helix," which Steve Fisher invented: an aerial horizontal spin combined with a midair roll so that by the time the kayak slaps back down in the churning hole, it has rotated 360 degrees on two axes. There are "Blunts" and "Split Wheels" and "Pan Ams." All the time, the crashing hydraulic is bouncing and kicking and breaking over the boat, trying like a bronco to have its way with the paddler. Watching a truly great freestyler like Steve or the American Eric "EJ" Jackson is an exercise in constantly suspended disbelief. You just can't believe a person in a little boat is going from water to air and back, describing figures that would challenge a porpoise.

EJ, a two-time World Freestyle champion, told me once that rodeo kayakers also make the best all-around river runners because they have become intimate with every feature of the river, throwing their tricks in holes, against rocks, and down swirling eddy lines so that when they hit those features in a dangerous rapid, they have many more instinctive options for maneuvering. If they get stuck in a very retentive hole, for instance, they can "play" their way out of it—throw ends to either side, feel for a thread of water pushing through and downstream, get airborne, or slice the bow or stern under the crashing pile and out. A rodeo kayaker can even maneuver a capsized boat with underwater strokes; it's routine.

I'd already seen the guys use some of the same techniques in the past two days. Sitting by the fire, I said, "I can see why EJ says freestylers make the best river runners."

Scott's head came up. He had the brow-furrow, incredulous look of a kid whose favorite baseball player has just been dissed. "It's just the opposite, bro!" he said. "None of those guys can hang with us. The guys that just ride holes are worthless on the river. We all practiced those moves, but it's the experience on big water." His mouth compressed and his head shook a little.

I stood corrected. It's funny how, even in a sport as esoteric and beautiful as kayaking, there is a battle to claim dominance in one specialty or another, to divide up the pie. Maybe it was like poetry, another esoteric discipline full of passionate intensity. You haven't seen go-for-the-jugular competition until you've sat in a writers' workshop seminar with 35 young poets in black.

The next morning I got another lesson in cutting up the pie.

. . . .

It happened as the ground crew were shouldering their loads. I had just buckled on my pack, picked up my spring-loaded trekking poles, and stepped onto the trail. It felt good to move. Dawn had broken with 25-degree cold and frost on the tent fly. I climbed the rise above the creek, and Sherab stepped out of the trees on the river side of the path and made a gesture of prayer with his hands, pointing them toward the river. I cocked my head, confused. He did it again, emphatic. I followed him. We came out onto an open rock shelf, and there were two stacked-rock stupas overlooking the Tsangpo, with two old prayer flags. On one stupa was a tablet of rock engraved with a symbol called a double vajra, and on the other was a carved mandala, and there was Scott with a camera, along with Ken and Tsawong. When I stepped into the light, Scott's face tightened, and Ken looked like he had gulped down a cup of lime juice. They looked at each other and shook their heads. Fuck 'em. I was pissed. They didn't want me to know about this lovely and sacred spot; it would erode their "investment." Sherab had seen my little copy of the Buddha's book of wisdom, the *Dhammapada*, and noticed my questions about all things Buddhist, and he clearly thought it would interest me.

He showed us another double vajra inscribed in the flat rock of the ground and said it was thought to have arisen by itself, that it was very old and made this place sacred. The double vajra is a pair of lightning bolts that represent the power of compassion in action, but to me, they looked like two halves of an avocado placed side by side.

Sherab spoke shyly in front of the camera as Tsawong interpreted: "This stream, during eighth century, Padmasambhava came here to control the devils and evils. At that time, Achkubo came here to make control those devils. In this area is one place very important for pilgrims—they came here to visit Pemakochung. In five days and four days they can arrive in this place. Some time if they don't have luggage, it is three days to Pemakochung. . . ."

Tsawong interrupted himself to add his own commentary. "Padmasambhava—Guru Rinpoche—in eighth century came to fight devils. The fourth king of Trisong Detsen, he wanted Guru Rinpoche to come here to fight demons." Then he went back to interpreting quiet Sherab: "During '93 with Ken, travel in the Gorge, they had lots of sacred place, lots of camps for meditation. In the route is Father and Mother time, in the area is very sacred place for Tibet and all of them. Pemakochung is one of the very holy place for Guru Rinpoche in the eighth century."

"What does the place, Pemako, mean to him?" Scott asked.

Sherab paused. Then he spoke softly, and Tsawong said, "He say that place is the very important place to him—very sacred place for him. Last night talking with some Sherpas—they make fire with plastic in this area—weather will be very quick to change."

Ken explained, "A foreign substance in the fire will activate the gods to change the weather."

Sherab walked over to the small mandala. He said through Tsawong, "Nobody can rebuild Pemakochung. Double vajra usually for the throne for the highest lama—the most powerful man. In monastery they have double vajra and make a throne." He led us back to the one inscribed in the ground. He squatted and signified with his hands that it appeared by itself.

Tsawong said, "For normal people, if they stay by double vajra, they will bleed from the nose. Difficult for normal people to stay here."

The sun was breaking over the upstream ridges and lighting the water. I could hear it chortling as it slipped by the low bluff of sacred rock. Sherab stood and looked back toward the camp, and he was very serious. "Every morning, the porters put tsampa on the fire, make an offering. Here in this village they have snakes, tigers. They make offering for a safe journey. Three or four days after Gyala, you can have snakes, tigers, lions. Pemakochung they usually have tigers. They also have yeti."

Sherab in the end had spoken of what was uppermost in his mind—the Sherpas had committed a sacrilege. Also, the way into the Gorge was full of dangerous wild beasts, and it was necessary to walk with care and propitiate the gods. This was no joke to Sherab. Nobody went where we were going anymore. Pemakochung was in ruins, and pilgrims turned back well shy of it.

I had heard that where we were, on the flanks of Namcha Barwa, rare mountain tigers hunted to altitudes of 12,000 feet. Down in the Lower Gorge, on the other side of the Senchen La and some 20 miles below the confluence of the Po Tsangpo at the apex of the Great Bend, tigers were a terror. Whatever the actual range of big cats in the Upper Gorge, Sherab and the porters feared them.

Sherab and Tsawong went back to camp to get their packs. Scott and Ken and I stood on this ancient holy ground, and Scott packed his camera in its watertight case with concentrated fury. I could almost see the burn working down the fuse. "You said back at the hotel you would respect Ken's privacy, and now you're going back on it."

"I'm not. Sherab made a prayer sign and invited me up here. I took it as an invitation from a local."

"No! You gave your fucking word."

Maybe Sherab was right when he said that if a normal person stands next to a double vajra, his nose will bleed. Right then, standing there, I felt a kind of hemorrhaging of decency.

Scott said, "How would you feel if you spent 10 years invested in the place, a journey, and someone came and scribbled it all down?"

I said, "This is about the book. You can have the book; I don't care about it. *You* spend a year and a half in a room writing it. Or you, Ken, you'd be good. I love the guys on this trip. I want no competition. You write the book—I just want to get through here. I'll write an article."

Scott said quickly, "I'm not saying that."

They both agreed that I should write a book about the trip. Then Scott said he'd been this way with everyone. "I want everyone a little on edge. I want no fuckups. When Johnnie paddled ahead of everyone alone yesterday, I hammered him right away. Look, bro, I don't resent you. We should all just chill and think about this on the way to Gyala."

Then he grabbed me and hugged me. "I don't resent you. I want your hip to be okay. I want you to make it. No hard feelings, okay? Okay?"

I left them and hiked on. I jumped across open rocks and under a cut cliff and into a shaded oak forest of green glossy leaves. Moss covered the rocks and grew up the trunks of the trees. The trail snaked through glens of tall fern, some 10 feet high, and I stepped over scattered bones where a Himalayan chukar had met its end in a flurry of feathers. There were silver pines and tall cedars. Through the trees off to my right was the snowy flank of Namcha Barwa. From the left came the sound of a thin tributary falls spilling in across the river. When I heard it, I noticed that there were tears streaming down my own face.

Do you pray in hope of reward? . . .
Jorie Graham, in "Evolution."

Yes, I do. We never get it exactly the way we want it. Now I was going to have to fight for a story when all I wanted was to open my heart to the people and the place. I was more like Scott and Ken than I wanted to admit. Like them, I wanted love, simple friendship, and glory. And I wanted a stable home. And a life of raw adventure. The whole pie. Buddha's second Noble Truth is *The cause of suffering is desire.* And I wanted to be both in and out, journalist and expedition member; to tell the story, with everybody's flaws, and bond with them as an integral member of the team. The roles were incompatible.

I could understand why Scott wanted so badly to make another film, a parallel film with Ken, to give range to the spiritual aspects of this place. I didn't have a monopoly on the story—Scott would tell his in a movie, but he would be constrained by the hour time slot on NBC, which, with Chevy ads, would comprise some 46 minutes of film. Forty-six minutes out of what must at the end of this, whatever happened, seem a lifetime of stories. I could see why they were protective of that story. But it was my story, too.

I lied to those two when I said, "You can have the book." I am equal to them in ambition, and if they are greedy, so am I.

I listened to the little waterfall and prayed for grace.

. . . .

If Scott were to tell the whole story of his Himalayan quest, it would include the four great rivers that flow off a sacred mountain in eastern Tibet called Mount Kailash. One is the Tsangpo. The others are the Indus, the Sutlej, and the Karnali. Scott was drawn to Mount Kailash as he was to nothing else. It occupied a place in a landscape that shimmered between two realms, an earthbound and a mythic geography—not just for Scott but for almost anyone who lived in the region. For Hindus, it was the throne of Shiva, destroyer of evil. For Buddhists, it was a great stupa that houses many families of gods. For practitioners of Bon, Tibet's oldest religion, it was the central axis of the world. On its summit, say Buddhists, the yogi Milarepa culminated a terrific battle with the Bon sorcerer Naro-Bonchung and knocked him from the peak. For a Buddhist, the merit a pilgrim gained by circumambulating the mountain, a high, exposed trek that took four days, expiated the sins of a lifetime.

The four rivers flow off Mount Kailash in the four cardinal directions; Scott considered this auspicious. They had everything he wanted. The extreme sections of three of them had never been run; they were at the edge of what a human could challenge with a boat, and they were charged at their headwaters with spiritual power. They flowed almost literally out of another dimension. Also, with him being the fighter that he was, I think Scott took them personally. They were the biggest, meanest dudes on the block.

Between 1999 and 2000, Scott methodically knocked off the Sutlej and the Karnali. His film *Liquid off the Throne of Shiva* is an account of his Karnali expedition with Willie, Charlie, and another radical paddler, named Mark Hayden. They got into some very steep, cliff-walled water, and 20 miles in, one of the paddlers pulled out and started walking. Scott stayed on the river. It was a battle he was not about to lose.

Scott and his brother, Dustin, had acquired their fighting stance when they were teenagers. Their father had come up from Texas, where he'd grown up as a cowboy, herding cattle and horses on horseback. He'd been a Marine, enlisting at age 17, and sold cattle feed when the boys were growing up. He was tough, a man suited to a world that was sliding into the past. Their mother worked for a title company, then became an auditor. The marriage broke up just after Scott started school, and for the next 10 years the brothers moved a lot, shuttling between their father and mother, who followed work all over California. They lived mostly in lower-middle-class tract homes. They attended a dozen or so schools in 12 years, so many they lost count. That's a lot of mornings walking through the big double doors of a strange school as the new kids. They were picked on. They got a reputation for making bullies back down, and they had to watch each other's back.

Both boys were naturally and exuberantly athletic. Scott was an excellent soccer player, and they became superb skiers and skateboarders. They were also good at finding trouble. Scott was a hardened fighter, a brawler. An old friend, Todd Stanley, tells the story of a classic weekend party he had at his house in Rockland when his parents went away.

"There must've been 300 people at the house, a kind of bring-your-own-brew kind of party. Scott had his beer in the refrigerator. These guys kept drinking it. He came up to me a few times: 'Those guys are drinking our beer!' All of a sudden, out of nowhere, Scott with one punch laid this dude over my parents' couch—he landed on the glass coffee table and leveled it. A fistfight broke out. The house was destroyed. The brick retaining wall got trampled down. Two double doors got broken off the hinges. All of my buddies and me, we managed somehow to get everybody out."

When Scott was 15, he moved next door to Todd's brother, Doug Stanley, who happened to run a Grand Canyon guide school. He agreed to take Scott under his wing. Scott said to Dustin, "I'm through with the delinquent shit. This is what I want to do." He went through the guide school with a furious passion and, at 18, became the one of the youngest guides on the Grand Canyon. He took up kayaking around that time with equal intensity, and soon he was plunging down some of the hardest runs in the Sierras.

In the summer of 1992, when Scott was 20, he went to work as a river guide in Idaho, where he met Charlie Munsey, then a 24-year-old extreme kayaker and one of the youngest paddlers to master the complex and dangerous North Fork of the Payette. The two struck up an immediate friendship and decided to head to Nepal that fall. That trip would change Scott's life. In the Himalayas, he encountered rivers of a volume and ferocity he had never imagined. He began to knock off all the classic runs; three years later, the two ran the Thule Bheri, the last big first descent left in western Nepal.

In '92, Dave Allardice also gave Scott a berth at his rafting company. "The first trip," says Scott, "was a nightmare." It was one of the first commercial rafting trips on the Kali Gandaki River. Heavy rain caused the river to flood, and it became a torrent, too much for rafts laden with clients. One flipped and dumped all the passengers. Scott ran after the loose boat for miles in sheeting rain. He stopped to drink out of a ditch. "I was sick for three months," he said. "Full body rash and everything." But he was hooked. He returned to paddle for part of almost every year after that.

In 1995, the famous adventure filmmaker Roger Brown asked Scott to shoot some footage for him on the Thule Bheri. Afterward, Scott bought his own Hi8 video camera and shot his first extreme paddling movie, *Good to the Last Drop*, with a bunch of friends. Brown saw the film and hired him as a cameraman on three more movies, one of which garnered Scott an Emmy. He was launched. He thought kayaking was starting to place too much emphasis on what he saw as effete, balletic freestyle competition, and he wanted to shift the focus back on the hardcore adventure of expedition paddling and extreme river running. He would use a movie camera to do it.

Back in California, he began to meet paddlers and skiers with similar internal engines: smart, adrenaline-pumped explorers. He and Dustin met Andrew Sheppard in a skateboard park in Banff, and together they skied harder and harder terrain in California and the Canadian Rockies.

Scott hooked up with Willie and Chuck Kern and Dustin Knapp on the Little White Salmon River in Washington.

Scraping by on savings, driving beater cars, Scott traveled all over the West and boated cutting-edge rivers with his new companions; he filmed the runs, and the footage was riveting and sometimes magnificent. He began to do first descents of creeks in the Sierras—Upper Cherry Creek, the Royal Gorge of the Upper North Fork of the American—that were series after series of granite cascades, and he paddled them with a 22-pound Bolex movie camera between his legs in the cockpit. Scott and his friends were redefining what was runnable in a kayak. He and Dustin Knapp and two other friends formed an extreme kayaking video company called Driftwood Productions, which later morphed into Scott Lindgren Productions. Scott began to sell his videos to an emerging market of young paddlers who wanted to pump themselves up by watching death-defying feats in kayaks. Movies like *Spawning Grounds* and *Liquid Lifestyles* became cult classics. His aggressiveness in getting a good shot was legendary. He routinely ran first and alone down horrendous virgin drops in order to shoot the other paddlers.

During his seasons in Nepal, he ran rivers with two intrepid young sons of empire who did the most brutal stretches of remote rivers as if they were on a jaunt to a rugby game. They were Mike Abbott and Allan Ellard. Meanwhile, Charlie told Scott about a gorge in Tibet so deep it was said that there were tropical jungles at the bottom—and so remote that Shangri-La, or a place that inspired the myth, lay hidden there. A river called the Yarlung Tsangpo ran through it.

That was the beginning. Scott stole a copy of Kingdon Ward's *Riddle of the Tsangpo Gorges* from the Auburn library and devoured it. The book told a tale that made Scott almost sick with desire.

CHAPTER FIVE

KINTUP THE TAILOR

In the 1870s, at the height of the British Raj in India, the tailor Kintup stitched clothes in a shop in Darjeeling and guided British officers through the beautiful hills of Upper Sikkim. He was unschooled, unable even to write his name. But he had an active mind and a memory as sharp as his shears. He was thickset and displayed a determined energy that caught the attention of the officers. Bent over the dress uniform of a Bengal Engineer, mouth full of pins and wide-set eyes focused on the fine stitching of a buttonhole, he could not have fathomed that the deepest river in the world, lost in her thundering chasm, was drawing him to greatness.

The British in this period were in a frenzy of imperial surveying and mapmaking. They had launched perhaps the most ambitious topographic project that had ever been undertaken. Royal Engineers of the Great Trigonometrical Survey (GTS), lugging plane tables and theodolites, had thrown a mesh of topographic triangulations over nearly all of India. "Imperialism and mapmaking intersect in the most basic manner," noted Matthew Edney in his book *Mapping the Empire*. If you're going to govern a territory, it's a good idea to know where it is. The British were having a ripping successful time of it, but some outlying areas were proving troublesome, even intractable. Fierce tribes slaughtered every second survey party that came within their borders. One of these areas, the far northeastern district of Assam, lay just beyond the southeastern corner of the Himalayas. Here the stately Brahmaputra debouched out of the jungled hills. A tribe called the Abors lived there. The men wore almost nothing but scraps of cloth and sporty thatched helmets, and they were masters of jungle warfare.

Assam also was at the center of a debate that had been raging not just in the colony but also in the august halls of the Royal Geographical Society and in the parlors and game parks and estates of the military men and explorers and geographers of empire: What happened to Tibet's great river, the Yarlung Tsangpo, after it fell off the face of the map? Were it and the Brahmaputra one and the same?

The Tsangpo was born on the sacred slopes of Mount Kailash in the far west and flowed almost 1,000 miles eastward across the Tibetan Plateau, paralleling the Himalayas and gathering the runoff from their northern slopes. Then it dropped into a lost world unknown to the West. Did it somehow plunge south through the mountains and join the Brahmaputra? Or did it, as some insisted, work farther east to become the Irrawaddy, which ran down through Burma?

If it became the Brahmaputra, explorers would have something else to ponder, something astounding. The Tsangpo flowed through the Tibetan Plateau at 10,000 feet. The Brahmaputra came out of the Assam hills (it was named the Dihang at that point) at an elevation of 500 feet. For the Tsangpo to become the Brahmaputra would require a drop of more than 9,000 feet in something less than 150 miles. This hypothetical plunge excited visions of a vastly deep-cut gorge, ground-shaking cataracts, and possibly a hidden waterfall the size of a Niagara or a Victoria. The *Proceedings* of the Royal Geographical Society smacked its stylistic lips and theorized "a scene of wonderful sublimity—one of the last, and perhaps the grandest, of nature's secrets"—meaning that the Tsangpo might hurtle over one of the greatest falls on Earth.

The problem was simple and twofold: One had to trace its course either upriver from India or downriver from Tibet. Going up, one soon ran into fierce Abors armed with aconite-tipped poison arrows, spring-loaded skewer traps, and rock-chute ambuscades. After one rout at the hands of the Abors in 1858, the Raj sent troops and elephant-drawn Howitzers with the purpose of "inflicting such chastisement as will teach these savages to respect its power." The forces were ambushed and re-treated in disarray; they lost three officers.

The second option, going down the Tsangpo, meant dealing with Tibet.

. . . .

Even in the mid-19th century, when the Raj was in the fullness of its splendor, the Land of Snows was still a country of mystery and guarded secrets. China had sealed the region's borders tight in 1792, rightly fearing encroachments from the south by the British. As late as 1851, the Brits still did not know the exact location of Lhasa, a city only 300 miles from Calcutta. The Himalayas were the Great Wall of the frontier. But no Hi-malayan barrier was going to stop the British Empire. It had maps to make.

In 1851, Captain Thomas George Montgomerie, Bengal Engineers, came to India to work as first assistant for the GTS. While the British were barred from entering Tibet, he noticed that north Indian merchants and pilgrims were being permitted entry. Montgomerie had a stroke of genius: train a few Indians in surreptitious surveying, send them into Tibet disguised as Buddhist pilgrims, and let them do the survey. But how would they take the myriad measurements of distance and direction and elevation without exciting suspicion? What he developed was one of the most spectacular programs of clandestine intelligence gathering ever.

The Pundits, as they came to be called (*pundit* means "learned man" in Sanskrit), were trained to walk a uniform 2,000 steps per mile, even over rough ground and steep mountains. That's two feet, seven inches per step, which they could maintain through thicket and over rock and snow. Their pedometers were strings of prayer beads modified from the traditional 108 to 100. Every 100 steps they'd drop a bead; every 10th bead was a larger nut: half a mile. They spun handheld prayer wheels as they walked, chanting "*Om mane padme hum*," ("Hail to the jewel in the lotus"); inside the prayer wheels were prismatic compasses and note-taking implements. Hidden in hollow walking sticks were thermometers for measuring the boiling point of water in order to derive hypsometric altitude readings.

They chanted because that's what good pilgrims do, and it was found that a chanting pilgrim was most often left alone to his own geographic devices. The Pundits were trained to gauge and note the width of a river, its direction of flow, where its tributaries joined, the names and populations of villages, and the locations of forts and monasteries and roads. They were to take note of crops, local politics, and mountains. They were given cryptic code names in official reports—G.M.N., A.K.—to ensure their anonymity, although many of the results of their reports were widely published in journals like the *Proceedings* of the Royal Geographical Society and were avidly read from London to St. Petersburg. The penalties for being discovered as a British spy were cruel and terminal. Once unmasked, they would have sundry body parts chopped off and be left to die. Simply for aiding a Pundit, the Sengchen Lama of Shigatse was sewn alive into a yak-hide sack and lowered into the Tsangpo. The Pundits prayed every prayer and undertook every step of their survey at pain of death.

Montgomerie's two most dearly held missions for the Pundits were the precise triangulation of Lhasa and proving that the Tsangpo met the Brahmaputra. In 1866, Pundit Nain Singh—a.k.a. "No. 1"— accomplished the first goal by putting the Forbidden City on the map, for which he received the Royal Geographical Society's Gold Medal. The second objective proved to be more elusive.

. . . .

In 1878, Lieutenant Henry Harman of the Survey of India was dispatched to Darjeeling and put in charge of mapping Assam. Continuing the work of Montgomerie, he sent a lama named Nem Singh over the frontier. Harman was perhaps a bit too eager; it was already August, and Harman, loath to lose a dry season, dispatched Nem Singh without complete training. The Tsangpo was calling, and Nem Singh's mission was simply to follow and survey it from Tsetang as far as possible, down into India if he could. Harman also assigned the tailor Kintup, who had already earned a reputation as an amateur explorer, to go along as Nem Singh's assistant.

Even under the best conditions, on established routes under blue skies, the Tibetan Plateau is a harsh land. It is arid and windswept, subject to gales of sand and dust. Snowy mountains muscle out of the steppe, raising barrier ranges across the roads and pinching them into high passes, where travelers are vulnerable to killing storms. Where streams do run, they tend to cut steep gorges. The trails follow the drainages and cling to the walls until they lose all purchase and abandon the river for higher ground, often detouring many miles around a canyon. Villages can be days' journeys apart. In the barren reaches, under swarms of stars, marauders can have their way with visitors. This is true today, and it was especially true in 1878.

Nem Singh (code name G.M.N.) and Kintup toiled north to Lhasa, where, according to Kingdon Ward, they spent "considerable time" feting Nem Singh's old friends in the monasteries, presumably at Her Majesty's expense. Kintup would soon learn, to his considerable detriment, that lamas love to party. They followed the Lhasa River down to the Tsangpo and turned east. G.M.N. bent himself to the task of a Pundit, but he conducted shoddy survey work, mixing up dates in the log and exuberantly depleting mission funds. They made their way past the lowest explored point on the Tsangpo at Tsetang and continued downstream, sticking bravely to the river when the traditional route veered away to the north, to avoid the smaller gorges. They pushed some 280 miles into almost unknown territory, following the mammoth Tsangpo, whose bed in the wider valleys was a mile across. Then they caught a view downstream that would burn itself into Kintup's mind and forever change his life.

It probably can be stated without hyperbole that whoever sees it can never be the same. The Tsangpo, having meandered placidly northeast for more than 100 miles, suddenly struck a wall of rock and snow mountains and vanished. Towering over these summits were two giant peaks, standing separately but close enough to seem like sisters. They were in fact the highest peaks in the eastern Himalayas, Namcha Barwa on the south, 25,446 feet, and Gyala Peri, 23,462 feet, on the north—the breasts of Dorje Pagmo, the Diamond Sow, consort of Buddha, who, according to a centuries-old myth, embodied the Tsangpo Gorge.

The lama and his assistant made haste to the mouth of the canyon and, as the walls closed in, climbed to a high terrace and looked downstream. To their astonishment, the river did not detour around the two mountains but cut right between them. The summits of the peaks, each rising out of a huge massif of snow and ice, are in fact only 13 miles apart. The two awestruck spies had discovered the great portal; they were looking into the jaws of a gorge at least 15,000 feet deep. And where upstream the river had stretched lazily, almost like a lake, below Gyala they could see it breaking into torrential whitewater, barreling between walls only 100 yards apart.

The Pundits were at the end of the road. The Gorge looked impassable and frightening, and Nem Singh was in no mood to confront the robbers who lurked in the area. They hastened home.

Harman welcomed them back, excited that they had pushed the known world of the Tsangpo some 300 miles eastward. Then he took a look at the survey data. G.M.N's measurements of the altitude of the sun were "very doubtful," he wrote drily. The astronomical figures were garbled, and the record of their route home was incomplete. Harman sent him off for proper training.

Kintup didn't get off so easily; Harman knew talent when he saw it. The tailor was immediately outfitted for a second attempt on the Tsangpo. He was given his own code name, K.P.; a shortened string of prayer beads; and a Mongolian lama. He would have been much better off without the lama.

. . . .

Because Kintup was illiterate, Harman needed to send him with someone who could keep records. The two were to continue where Kintup had left off, penetrating the Gorge and following the Yarlung Tsangpo all the way south into India. In the event that the canyon blocked their way, Kintup was to prepare 500 specially marked logs and, on a prearranged date, throw 50 a day into the river. Harman would set lookouts on the Brahmaputra. When they retrieved the logs Kintup launched into the Tsangpo, that would settle the debate once and for all.

It was ingenious. Such a simple and elegant plan. Only a lapsed lama could mess it up.

The two men made it without incident to Lhasa, where, for six days, the lama feasted former colleagues in the Sera monastery on mission funds. By mid-September 1880, they were following the Tsangpo eastward over the desolate plateau. The lama fell ill for three weeks, and Kintup served him like a handmaiden. The lama recovered, and they traveled on to a town called Thun Tsung. There, Kintup waited while the lama had a four-month affair with the wife of their host. The lama had depleted their funds in venery and high living, so when he was discovered in strenuous tantric practice with the wife, Kintup had to use his own money to pay off the husband—25 rupees. They continued east to the point on the Tsangpo where Kintup had earlier turned back, and struggled 15 more miles to the ancient monastery of Pemakochung. Two miles from there, according to Kintup's report, the Tsangpo "falls over a cliff . . .

from a height of about 150 feet." (This single line fired 30 years of geographical lust for the Great Hidden Waterfall. Too bad it didn't exist. K.P.'s dictated report was garbled in translation, and it took more than a quarter century and Colonel F. M. Bailey to discover the mistake. The 150-footer was actually a small tributary that spilled in below Gyala. The falls near Pemakochung on the main river, later named Kintup's Falls, dropped a mere 30 feet.)

The pair traveled back upriver to get around the twin peaks, then stayed at the house of the local official of a semiautonomous district of Tibet. There, the lama, who was flat broke, sold Kintup into slavery for a pony and rode off.

. . . .

Kintup worked in drudgery while the great river flowed uncharted through its gorge, and the dates assigned for launching the logs came and went. He was a slave for 10 months. Finally, on March 7, 1882, he escaped. Any ordinary slave would confirm his freedom by returning home. He chose instead to carry on his mission of charting the river. *Kintup* means "Almighty One" in Sanskrit, and people have a tendency to grow into their names.

He struggled on down the Tsangpo, over high passes and into the sodden jungles of the Lower Gorge. Fearing capture, he steered clear of villages, and he slept in caves and on open ground. Alone and unarmed, he lived in peril from Bengal tigers. Leeches bled his bare feet. He starved. Disguised as a pilgrim, he *was* a pilgrim, a traveler whose devotion to his mission passes all understanding. Nearing the Indian border, he came to a monastery at Marpung just as the posse caught up with him. Throwing himself at the feet of the head lama, Kintup said he was an orphaned pilgrim sold treacherously into slavery. The lama bought him for 50 rupees.

Slavery again. But here, at least he could live peacefully among the chanting monks, the butter candles, incense, and chiming prayer bells and work his craft as a tailor. After 4½ more months in captivity, Kintup received permission to go downriver on a pilgrimage. He ignored the holy sites and went directly to a remote monastery called Giling 10 miles downstream. Telling the monks there that he was searching for salt, he went directly up into the woods and began cutting and limbing his 500 logs. He had been given 500 tin tubes to drill into the wood, but the special auger provided for this purpose had been lost along the way. Kintup improvised by lashing the tubes to the logs with strips of bamboo. He stashed his logs in a cave—all 500 of them. If you've ever worked in the woods, you know how long it takes to cut, limb, and buck a tree and to move the wood. Your shoulders become chafed and bruised. It's slow, exhausting, hazardous work—and that's with a chainsaw. Kintup would have had to thrash through dense undergrowth just to get to his tree, then pull away clinging vines to clear enough space to swing an ax. The official report of Kintup's mission states that he returned to the Marpung monastery "after an absence of one month and four days."

Now the problem was getting word back to Harman to set a new date for launching the logs. Kintup worked for his master in the monastery for two more months before asking leave to go on another pilgrimage. It was late autumn in Tibet when Kintup hightailed it all the way back to Lhasa on foot, hundreds of miles, sleeping in caves or on the snow-covered ground. He arrived in December and dictated a letter to a Sikkimese judge who was visiting the monasteries. He asked the judge to deliver it to the explorer Nem Singh (G.M.N.) in Darjeeling. The letter read:

> Sirs—the Lama who was sent with me sold me to an official as a slave, and himself fled away with the Government things that were in his charge. On account of this the journey proved a bad one. However, I, Kintup, have prepared the 500 logs according

to the orders of Captain Harman, and am preparing to throw 50 logs per day into the Tsangpo Bipung, from the 5th to the 15th of the 10th Tibetan month of the year called Chkuluk.

Ringing understatement was apparently not the sole province of the British.

Kintup trekked across Tibet and back into slavery, serving his master for nine more months. The head lama finally decided to set him free. Clearly, the lama thought, this was one devout pilgrim. "I am glad to see you visiting the sacred places, so from today I give you leave to go anywhere you like," he said.

In mid-November of 1883, Kintup threw his logs into the Tsangpo. As he had been told to do, he tossed 50 a day over 10 days. But he wasn't done. His mission was to continue farther down the Tsangpo, and so he did. As he moved through Abor territory, the tribesmen looked on him with increasing suspicion, and he turned around. Kintup reckoned that he had come within 35 miles of British territory.

Captain Harman never received the letter. He had left India the year before and died soon afterward. No one was on the Brahmaputra to watch Kintup's logs float by. Day and night, carrying the little tubes lashed with bamboo, they bobbed past the British military outpost at Sadiya, mute and sodden, heading for the Bay of Bengal.

After an odyssey of $4\frac{1}{2}$ years, Kintup made it to Darjeeling and gave his report. Nobody much believed it. He didn't have proof.

He worked as a guide on a few more survey trips in upper Sikkim and then went back to tailoring in Darjeeling. It would be more than 30 years before the British confirmed his observations of the Tsangpo Gorge.

CHAPTER SIX

GYALA TO DOUG'S LEDGES

On the third morning, after only an hour and a half of walking, the long line of ponies and donkeys and the scores of men carrying loads came into a field just above the village of Gyala, where they fanned out and dropped their packs. They began making fires and brewing cans of tea.

Dave said, "Tsawong, ask them what they're bloody doing. It's a bit early for lunch."

Tsawong said, "Actually, they say they want to camp."

Dave looked across at his dispersing army, at the village of Gyala and the trail climbing steeply out of it. Gyala was the last habitation in the province of Kongbo at the brink of the Gorge—a small cluster of stone houses, one whitewashed and flying tall, tattered white prayer flags. It was the last human habitation before the Tsangpo went 10-7 ("incommunicado" in Talkabout speak) and plunged into the Gorge. A warren of trails wound through the low stone walls stacked high with firewood that surrounded the compounds of the houses. Cut into the walls were wide gates painted with flowers and mythical animals. Gyala Peri blazed down on the hamlet like a crystal mountain. Out in the field, under four giant peach trees and a 30-foot prayer flag, was a chorten—a hollow stupa like a small kiva that was blackened inside from offering fires.

"Bloody hell," Dave said.

He gathered the head porters together beside a boulder in the field. I walked off to take a leak, and when I came back, they were sitting in a powwow circle. A good crowd had gathered, and Dave's voice was hitting a register of anger. "You lied to us! We will not camp in Gyala. That is *one* hour's walk. That is *not* a day's work."

The faces around him showed no emotion. They were an impressive bunch, with broad, sun-burnished cheeks and liquid dark eyes. Many smoked cheap Chinese Panda brand cigarettes. They watched Dave as he lectured them.

"In the last three days, we've gone eight hours. We're not stupid. We know where we are and where we're going."

The devil once hurled arrows at the Buddha meditating under his tree, and he turned them into flower petals. Dave's harangue was having about as much effect.

"A day's work is six hours minimum. I've had 20 years' experience working with porters. In Nepal, Pakistan, India, Tibet. We're going on. One hour ahead. Camp early, dry stuff out. Tomorrow we start again and do things right. You're getting 100 yuan a day. That's good money. We'll take care of you, but we've got to work together."

With that, Dave stood up, shouldered his pack, and stalked up the trail through town.

All the time the labor dispute was taking place, Tsawong interpreted calmly—he seemed to have recovered a certain Buddhist detachment—and the police official from Pe smoked quietly and listened. He was a handsome man in his late twenties. His name was Ching Mi, and Tsawong had said he had come along to help us with the porters. "Most are good, but some are bad," Tsawong had explained.

Looking back on it, that was quite an insight. This wasn't the sort of place you wanted to go with bad men.

. . . .

I sat to write some notes, and a family sitting at a fire nearby offered me tea and dried yak meat. It was midafternoon and bright and warm in the sun. There was some tension developing with the porters, but person to person, I found generosity and warmth. It was like anywhere else: There was politics and then there was breaking bread.

All the while, the kayakers were drifting down to a landmark of Himalayan exploration. Just below Gyala, looking through the trees and across the river, I saw it: a granite wall cleaved by a side creek and broken by a spilling waterfall. Where the stream coursed out into the river, both sides of the rock gateway were adorned with prayer flags. This was Sinji-Chogyal, the 150-foot cataract that had launched the Great Hidden Waterfall rumor. Kintup had stood on the very trail where I was now digging in my pack for my GPS and water bottle. His mistranslated report declared, "The Tsangpo is two chains distant from the monastery (Pemakochung) and about two miles off it falls over a cliff called Sinji-Chogyal from a height of about 150 feet. There is a big lake at the foot of the falls where rainbows are always observable." Here was the "lake," the flat Tsangpo coursing through a narrowing gorge, and there, in wetter times of the year, would be the spray at the bottom of the falls that would refract the sunlight into constant rainbows.

Sinji-Chogyal is a traditional destination for Buddhist pilgrims. Below the trail, tied to a tree, was a large dugout canoe for ferrying them across. Behind the falls, if you were worthy, you would see the image of a demon-god chained to the rock. Tsawong said the god was Yamantaka, "an emanation of Buddha, holds the wheel of life. If you pray, if your heart is pure, then you can maybe see Yamantaka."

The kayakers paddled to Sinji-Chogyal and climbed out. A rickety bridge crossed the creek above. The falls flew off the cliff in two stages. Wild peach and apricot trees grew alongside it. Below was a hydro-powered prayer wheel. We heard about it when Willie's excited voice boomed over the Talkabout: "There's a statue behind the falls where a demon is chained to the rock, and a prayer wheel in a little house turns in the water!"

. . . .

It was late afternoon, and we hiked on. We could see downriver, and it didn't look thrilling for a man on foot. At the end of the "lake," a sheer rock buttress swooped down from the right, and the river seemed to end, to yield to the vertical imperative of the squeezing mountains. Passang Sherpa turned to me and said, "Looks like the river flows *up* there, into the mountains." It was the same kind of awed impression Kintup must have had as he stared downstream from about the same place.

I replied, "Nobody can turn a river back to its source." It was a verse from one of the Dynasty poets, and Passang smiled.

That evening, we made camp in a grove of leafless alders overlooking a long, sandy beach and the long straightaway upriver. We could just make out the pilgrims' dugout crossing back to the right shore.

A lovely, peaceful evening. The Sherpas made a fire. The smoke drifted up through the shade and out into the sunlight over the beach. The porters were nowhere in sight. The Sherpas were frustrated; they wanted to start on sweet tea and dinner, and the porters had the pots and all the food. Stout Kannuri took up a length of rope and disappeared. In a few minutes, he came back with a load of lime-green bamboo stalks tumped to his back. While the kayakers paddled down the long flat in the last sun, Passang rapidly split strips of the tender bamboo with his belt knife, and Kannuri deftly wove them into a sturdy pack basket called a *dhoko*. It was meshed with a pattern of uniform hexagons like a cane seat and rimmed with a tough roping of strips at its oval mouth. The Sherpas would divide up the weight of Kusang's pack, and from now on, he would carry the kettle and tea fixings and anything else they'd need to start on dinner.

The porters came out of the woods and filed in a long line down the beach and into camp. The donkeys' bells clanked, and their hooves rustled in the leaves. The paddlers hit the beach in pairs and were thronged by porters, who insisted on carrying their kayaks up to camp. Dave laughed. He said he'd overheard the porters talking among themselves. "The translation is: The kayakers have a big cock and balls!"

Johnnie, inspired by Kannuri, took some of the bamboo strips and sat on a rock, fashioning some camp shoes. He fed the bamboo through a pair of pink rubber soles he found along the river and made airy, adjustable thong sandals. The Sherpas prepared dinner: *Dal bhat*, a delicious lentil gruel, with rice, roasted potatoes, and a banana pie.

The paddlers described seeing redstarts and swallows darting in and out of the falls and small flocks of doves swirling in the canyon. "Below the top was a cave," Mike said. "I tried to get in there, eh? But it was cliffed out. The little bridge looked like it was made of twigs."

Before dinner, the kayakers hopped down to look at the rapid below camp. It was long and straight, with big ledge holes. A classic, clashing minefield. At the end, the river jarred into a tight left bend and disappeared. A 2,000-foot rock wall crowded it from the right: the sharp end of the Musi La spine. There was no way around on dry land. The ground crew would have to climb over. We were on the brink: Once the paddlers were around that corner and the ground team over the pass, we would be beyond help, with no easy return in a place few people had ever been.

From the maps and from Kingdon Ward's journals, we knew that after the Musi La, the river changed character. It lunged into the chasm as if released from a dam, incising its gorge with a will and a fury. The flanks of the mountains closed in even more tightly, and the Tsangpo, unleashed from the torpor of this backed-up "lake," burrowed for the bowels of the earth.

. . . .

Dave examined a young porter wife who stood in her long skirt and green army cap, holding her jaw. She was suffering badly from an abscessed and rotting tooth. She stood patient and trusting. Dave was clearly distressed. It needed to be pulled, and nobody there knew how to do it. He discussed it with Charlie, who in a previous incarnation had thought he might become a doctor, and gave her ibuprofen.

Night settled over the canyon, and we sat at the windy fire. Ken told us that in 1950, there was a great cataclysm, the Assam Earthquake, 8.6 magnitude, the most powerful in the 20th century. This is what supposedly destroyed the ancient monastery of Pemakochung, but Ken said he thought the Chinese actually wrecked it. As one of the remotest monasteries in Tibet, it must have been a potent symbol of refuge. He said that most pilgrims stop right here, at Sinji-Chogyal, because they aren't equipped to go farther. "You see the porters don't have the gear," he said. "That's why everything becomes about appeasing the gods."

Through the wind, I could hear Kannuri chanting in the cook tent, and Tsawong was talking about the D.L. He said, "They don't allow us to hang pictures of the D.L. in the monastery. So we hang Avalokiteshvara. Actually, D.L. is emanation of him. He has four arms, two normal and two in prayer."

The kayakers reached for the battered kettle at the edge of the fire and poured tea into enamel mugs. They cupped the mugs in both hands and blew on them and sipped while the temperature dropped below freezing. Willie talked about his early kayaking days.

"Growing up, it was all about swimming holes," he said. "Then we did the Allagash—we were 13 or 14. Chuck went to a summer camp with kayaking, came back, and said, 'Guys, you gotta try this!' We each got a kayak. We started doing big drops—maxed out at 40 feet. It was *pencil*. That sensation—you go in, and the water would close all around you, and then you just changed directions and shot up." He laughed. "We definitely accordioned some boats."

Forty feet is four stories. Johnnie and Willie were young teens and didn't really know how to kayak. I could imagine them, holding paddles that were much taller than they were, the bigger boy with his curly hair spilling out of his helmet, beside himself with excitement, and the slighter child in glasses, containing his own enthusiasm as he deliberately analyzed the drop. The two standing side by side, leaning over the bank at the lip of the falls like some perverse Norman Rockwell painting, both completely without fear. Chuck would have started college by then, and the twins had a lot of catching up to do if they wanted to paddle with their older brother. The twins had a book called *Waterfalls of the White Mountains—30 Trips to 100 Waterfalls*. It's an excellent guide for tourists. The Kern boys used it as kayak map. They knocked off the falls one by one.

Mike said he got his start launching kayaks off diving boards. "I worked up to 10 meters. I went over vertical on the 5-meter board and the water hit the spray deck and it about castrated me, eh?"

The others winced. Everybody knew the sensation. Kayaks have much bigger cockpits now than they used to, for safety—it increases the ease and speed of escape. The neoprene sprayskirts stretch over these openings to seal the water out. They are flexible and stretchy, and they're the only thing between the elements and your lap. All of us had had the breath knocked out of us when a big wave collapsed—*thump!*—directly on our groins.

When river runners get together, the talk inevitably comes around to rivers.

Steve said that for him, the most dangerous part of learning to kayak were the hippos in the Upper Zambezi. They could take down a kayaker like a trout hitting a fly. Also crocs. Steve said, "There're some rivers in South Africa where the crocodiles are a real problem. Some I won't run. There's one called the Cunene River—my friend made the first successful attempt. He towed a little buoy behind him because they come from behind, in the pools between rapids. He had 27 contact attacks in two hours."

Mike was fingering what looked in the firelight like a huge claw. Somebody asked him what it was. "Came off a tiger," he said. "A 13-footer, nose to tail. Man-eater. Killed 150 people. My granddad shot it." He held it up. "I showed it to the Nepali boys and they started eating it! Peeling off bits."

Mike told how his family had lived in India, where his grandfather was a famous tiger and leopard hunter. Once, the locals asked Mike's granddad to come kill a notorious man-eating tiger. "He used a girl as bait," Mike said.

"Was she alive?" Willie asked.

"She'd been attacked and was going to die anyway. Her family suggested it. So he made a hide in the tree and put some bells on the girl—he had a rifle, high-power, with a light on top of the rifle. He heard the bells rattle, turned on the light, fired a couple of shots, and blew the bulb off—didn't know if he'd hit, so he had to sit in the tree the rest of the night. When the light came, the tiger was dead where he'd last seen it." And the girl, too, I gathered. God.

Ken said, "When we climbed up on Namcha Barwa from Churasi, they shot the gun off every half hour to scare the tigers."

I take it back—when expedition river runners get together, the conversation *usually* comes around to rivers. Sometimes it's tigers.

. . . .

The next morning, the paddlers hung out by the fire and played Shithead with a deck of nude Chinese playing cards someone had bought in Chengdu and waited for the sun to warm things a bit. All they had to do that day was plug the one big rapid and drift around the corner. For the ground crew, it was a different story.

Soon after daylight, the wives of porters led the ponies and donkeys in a line up the long beach, and the ringing of the halter bells was lost to river sound before they were out of sight, heading for home. From here on, the way would be too rough for horses. With Sherab leading, we went straight up the side of the ravine into black stands of pine and spruce clinging to the slopes. We picked our way around blowdown and found footholds on chips of rock, pulling ourselves up on roots and the stalks of bushes. Sherab climbed steadily and chanted under his breath. After climbing 1,000 feet from camp, we entered a clearing of tufted dry grass. Thick bamboo forest raised high walls of green above us, and giant old-growth hemlock, spruce, and fir—granddaddies with trunks five and six feet across—towered over the forest. The Sherpas pulled out their long machete-like knives and waded into the wall of bamboo, completely at home. We climbed steeply, up through sections of snow, and were soon at the top of the Musi La, which my GPS put at 11,500 feet. We had climbed 2,000 feet. It was just after noon.

I had expected snow at the top. So had Charlie's porter, a solitary, good-natured young man who had woven a bamboo ring and slipped it over the toe of his sneaker to act as a kind of crampon. But there were only patches of snow on the way up. I smelled sulfur. *Musi* means "sulfur," and at one time, beneath a cliff on the Gyala side, locals mined it here.

We took a break, and the wind feathered the bamboo. This was red panda country, the small raccoon-size creatures that survive only in the remotest high forest. It also was home to little musk deer and the powerful takin, *Budorcas taxicolor*, a rare wild bovine put on Earth for the Monpa and Lopa peoples of the Tsangpo Gorge to hunt. This is what the Monpa and Lopa believe. The animal is low-slung, measuring at most four feet high at the shoulder, and dense, weighing as much as 800 pounds. It has small, heavy horns and the long, dour face of a moose. Ken said it was related to the musk ox and that the species separated when the glaciers pushed them down into the gorges of southeastern Tibet and western China. Beyond the barrier of the Musi La, we began to encounter more and more sign, and sometimes we could see the dark creatures grazing on a slope across the river.

When Padmasambhava brought Buddhism into the Tsangpo and defeated the Bon demons, the takin might have gotten a reprieve, for Buddhism forbids hunting. The Monpa, hunters from eastern Bhutan, adopted Buddhism after they migrated up into the Lower Gorge some 200 years ago. But when they saw the muscle-packed creatures, they couldn't help themselves. The takin was a gift from gods, and the Monpa would have to make an exception. The same went for the goral, a red, goatlike herbivore. Even now, although the Chinese had outlawed hunting in the Gorge for the people of Pe, whenever the porters saw a takin—and they could spot them on the farthest ledge—a shiver of excitement went through the porter train, and all forward progress stopped while the men sighted down their walking sticks and clustered in excited groups.

Takin helped pacify Wickliffe Walker's surly porters in the fall of 1998, after Doug Gordon died. During a daring rescue trek over the shoulder of Gyala Peri to reach the three surviving kayakers and lead them out of the river-left side of the Upper Gorge, Walker and his team experienced increasing difficulties with their Monpa guides, until the Buddhist hunters spotted a herd of takin and managed to kill five. For the rest of the trip, the Monpa were content.

Sherab and the Sherpas slashed at the bamboo stalks, some almost an inch thick, and opened a way that dropped off the saddle, 2,500 feet straight down. There was no trail here. We were falling through the gateway to the Gorge proper. It must have snowed recently, because the ground was sodden and slick and quickly turned to greasy mud. We skidded and skied, and every stalk that had been cut was a sharp punji stick. We ran across the tracks of a large beast that, like us, was skidding down the pass. When we stumbled out of the bamboo, I walked 100 feet through wispy, waist-high brown grass and under a scattering of alders and stood stock-still.

A current of cold air poured off the river. The river was wide and calm, smooth as polished turquoise. All around us, the sides of the canyon soared thousands of feet, dark with thick timber and scarred by landslides. Shreds of mist spumed off the spines of buttress ridges. Slender waterfalls flew off black cliffs. Just downstream, in the mouth of a side canyon that cut into the opposite wall, a perfect pyramid of mountain rose 1,000 feet off the river, bristling with ancient pines and layered in streaming clouds like a T'ang Dynasty landscape. Beside it, a glacier poured down a side canyon, shoving ahead a chaos of rock and earth. And all along this side of the river, from beneath the bench of alders and purple-stemmed willows, a margin of smooth sand curved gently downstream. The beach ended in a pile of boulders where a slide tumbled down from the right wall, constricting the river. The thunder of a rapid filled the whole canyon. I dropped my pack and jumped down to the beach. As I walked downriver, I realized I was following the tracks of a big cat and two cubs along the damp sand at water's edge. Probably leopards. No human being had been here for years.

The kayakers came in a group around the corner to look at the rapid they would run tomorrow. They tossed their paddles up onto the bank and hopped onto the rocks. The boulders were the size of houses. And then there was the rapid itself. It was terrifying—the first really big drop, a plunge of 30 feet or so over a quarter of a mile, with the entire volume of the Tsangpo cascading into a single channel 40 yards wide. The sound bespoke the fury: You had to shout, inches away from another's ear, to be heard. The Tsangpo was picking up speed. Below this, it would tilt to unheard-of steepness, 100 to 150 feet a mile, a white freight train charging down a staircase. No one in history had ever successfully paddled this combination of water volume and gradient. It was just a few miles below this that Doug Gordon had died.

Even as the kayakers jumped from rock to rock, their eyes went to the water, and they began to trace out possible lines. Johnnie yelled, "Sweet! Look at that girl!"

Steve hopped onto an elephant-size rock and scanned the drop.

In whitewater, there are three kinds of bad rapids. One is so mean and ugly, so sure to end in a wreck, that a kayaker simply picks up his boat and portages around. The second kind of bad rapid looks a little like the first, only with an excruciating thread of possibility. A scouting kayaker shudders, shakes his head, and then begins to piece together a possible way through the mayhem. Ninety percent of him wants to shoulder his kayak and walk around, but the other 10 percent of him thinks, "I could make that move around the boulder and probably punch through that 10-foot pile of collapsing foam." It's the 10 percent that makes him different from most people in the world. His excitement takes hold, and he begins to visualize every paddle stroke.

Then there is a third kind of bad rapid. It's exactly like the first, a death drop, except there is no way to walk around it, no way to go back upstream, and no way out of the canyon. Damned if you do, damned if you don't. It's every expedition kayaker's nightmare, and it is what these seven would strenuously try to avoid—paddling around a corner and going past the point of no return.

Steve studied the exploding white flume below him with the air of a master golfer lining up a 20-foot putt. I had put this rapid in the un-runnable, instant-portage category.

"No worries," he said.

One can tell a lot about a person in the first moments he ponders a big drop. Little Dustin Knapp was even quieter than usual, perhaps because he'd been feeling poorly the past couple of days. "I hope it's not the norm—this is the worst kind of rapid, a little gnarlier and it's an obvious portage. This is right on the edge."

Willie, on the other hand, was exuberant. "*Burly*. Yessir. Looks like a carnagefest to me. Looks fucking *heinous*." Willie possesses such a surfeit of inborn energy that his hands shake and quaver. Small tasks like threading a grommet with cord can become a Class V move for him.

Scott claims he is chemically imbalanced. But here, as he pointed out possible lines and pulled at his beard, Willie's hands were rock steady. The river calms him; it's the music to his beast. And looking at some of the worst whitewater he had ever seen—whether he ran it or not—made the afternoon solid gold in Willie's book.

Standing beside Willie, tall Allan raised both eyebrows and grinned, his dreadlocks sticking out from underneath his helmet. Mike pursed his lips.

Allan: "Bit dodgy. Hmm."

Mike: "Terrifying, if you ask me. Bit of a line along the left."

Johnnie leaped and hopped from boulder to boulder, never taking his eyes off the water. He'd stop and squint, getting another angle, then move on. Steve hopped down closer to join Scott on a high rock farther downstream. Scott stood holding his paddle vertically, propped against the granite like a spear. Steve squatted, helmet in hand, very still and focused in his bright yellow drysuit.

Down the middle of the drop, it looked as if a typhoon had concentrated all its fury on a single quarter-mile swath of sea—jaws of foaming holes, one after another, probably formed by a series of ledges buried in angry white froth. Out of the question. The routes on the right side, our side, among the big boulders, all fed into the middle. No chance. The left side, on the other hand, was intriguing—if you had, say, a terminal illness with two days to live. There was no riverbank to speak of; at the top of the drop, the canyon wall was composed of sloping slabs of granite at an angle low enough to stand on, but they gave way to steeper, darker cliff as soon as the rapid unleashed itself. The water falling into that side of the constriction was also solid, thrashing white, but it threaded down through a cluttering of boulders, left of a pile of rocks that could be considered a very small island, over a couple of short ledges, and launched over a 15-foot ledge waterfall. Part of the current then charged straight into the cliff wall. Another part, out toward the middle, fed into a mean comber maybe 10 feet high. No place anybody would want to end up.

The kayakers went back to their boats and began to paddle back up the expanse of flatwater to camp. They'd had an eyeful. The Kerns were seriously considering a run, because they were the Kerns and considered everything. But Willie was also on-river safety coordinator, and he'd be balancing the risks.

Back in camp, Scott walked up from the beach in his boating gear and looked at his expedition. We were all here but for one glaring exception: no porters. It was almost 5 P.M., and we'd been here an hour and a half.

Scott asked, "Who's with them?"

His brother said, "Nobody."

Nobody but Tsawong, who had no radio and for whom the porters were developing an increasingly noticeable antagonism.

Scott reached down unconsciously and loosened the buckles of his life vest. "Really?" he said. "What happened here?" The thought crossed everyone's mind that the porters might not show up, that we would have to spend a freezing night in thin bivy sacks beside the fire. That they might refuse to continue to Pemakochung. I began writing in my journal, "Could be critical. So much depends upon . . ."

"Whaddaya think of the rapid, bro?"

While I was thinking about survival, Dustin was asking Scott about the river.

"It's big. It's doable." Scott paused. "I'll probably haul my boat down the right side, though." Everyone laughed. He turned to Johnnie. "Give me a cigarette. If this was roadside . . ." He looked up. If the same rapid were beside a highway in California or even within reach of a helicopter, with easy access to rescue, they'd run it.

Willie smoked. He said, "So, Fisher, whaddaya think when you look at that?"

"Holy shit."

"What are you gonna do?"

Everybody looked at Steve. "I'm gonna run down to the left of that island. Get all cluttered in the rocks there. And get out and have a look."

Willie said, "Left of the big hole at the bottom?"

"Yah."

Steve had already decided to run.

. . . .

With evening closing in, the first two porters straggled into camp to a lofting of cheers. They looked done in. Willie hopped up and unloaded their packs while Andrew Sheppard lit cigarettes and handed them to the dismayed Peians and clapped them on the back. A few minutes later, improbably, Tashi showed up with the spare yellow Gus kayak, beaming modestly. He carried it on his head like any long-portaging kayaker, with the stern angled up and his head against the padded strap that braced the kayaker's lower back, taking most of the weight on his forehead as with a tumpline. How he had shoved and wedged it through all the bamboo was anybody's guess.

Tsawong arrived looking like he'd just seen the eighth ring of Hell. I could imagine he'd been prodding and cajoling the men up and over and through their numerous tea breaks, feeling greatly outnumbered. All 68 were accounted for, including the policeman and his assistant and fat Babu, Tsawong's boss. With all the women gone, it had a less festive, decidedly more military feel.

The porters tugged on the cigarettes and looked around. Most of them had never been this far in. I didn't see how any of them could have brought enough food in their small sacks for the weeks ahead. If the weather suddenly changed, they'd be in trouble. Tuli delivered my drybag and insisted on helping me set up my tent. He didn't seem that tired. He was born the same year I was, 1959, the year the Dalai Lama fled the Land of Snows. He must have witnessed scenes he'd rather forget.

Before I turned in, Charlie asked me in a confiding tone how my hip was feeling after the Musi La. It seemed like a thoughtful gesture. I told him it was okay. "Hurts, huh?" he said. I admitted it did, and he thought for a second and said, "You could take a porter, you know, and hike out."

"I don't think so, Charlie."

"Just so you know that if it gets bad, there are options."

Charlie speaks in a soft tenor. He has a kind of Ritchie Valens face, high-cheekboned and boyish. His smile is offhand and almost self-deprecating.

"Thanks," I said. But no thanks. I crawled into my narrow tent and turned on my headlamp. My hip throbbed, and I visualized healing. In kayaking, as Johnnie said, your head follows your eyes, and your torso follows your head, and your boat turns. You learn to focus on the clean line of current that threads the rocks and holes, the one you need to take. Now I imagined Himalayan mountain water coursing in veins and working into joints, cushioning. Then I popped another Celebrex.

. . . .

Steve did what he said he would do. He and Scott drifted down. Above them, along the slope of the bristled mountain, two birds gyred, probably Himalayan griffins. When they were still a safe distance above the horizon line, according to Steve, Scott said, "Have a good run," and headed for the right-side portage.

Steve swung left and booked for the far bank. Dustin Lindgren leaned over a video camera on a tripod atop a boulder and yelled, "He's going for it!" The only reason I heard him over the thunder was that I was beside him.

Just at the brink, Steve hit the left bank. He arced up into an eddy beneath the sloping granite slabs and jumped out. He hauled his boat about

10 feet up from the water to a shallow ledge where it would stay put and then hopped down to a good vantage. He studied the tongue at the entrance and then worked his eyes down through a maze of rocks along the left, the violent pourover ledges and tight channels. You could see him puzzling out a line. He lifted his arms and mimed a sequence of strokes. A mistake here at the top and his life was worth a heap of sand. Then, abruptly, he turned and climbed up the rock and squeezed into his boat.

He stretched on the sprayskirt, picked up his paddle, and shoved off. Seal launch. His yellow-green "Big Gun" sledded down the granite and hit the eddy. He leaned back as the boat skipped over the pool, and he allowed the eddy swirl to turn him upstream. He used the momentum to break the eddy fence and get his boat clear into the fast current, and it grabbed his bow and turned him downstream. His paddle went in almost vertically on the left, drawing the water off his bow and tightening the arc. And then he was heading straight down and rocketing between the first two boulders.

All of this in one smooth, seamless S-turn. He was totally committed.

He came down through the rocks like a swallow taking bugs, with the same tautness of body and precision of motion, all miraculously relaxed and smooth. His back was straight, his eyes on the next move. He threaded two narrow chutes, hooked into a tiny suggestion of eddy at the edge of a little island, and was out of his boat and pulling it onto the stones. He took one step, still holding his paddle, and looked downstream.

It was almost perfunctory: As his eyes traced his next line, he nodded once to himself. There was no urgency. He was setting his pace; he'd felt the rhythm of the river.

The problem was a waterfall. Just below him on the left, a good chunk of the main current squeezed between a boulder and the wall and thundered over a high ledge in a 12- to 15-foot cataract. All Steve would see from above would be the waves tossing their heads in the line of his approach, and then the horizon line of the lip and billowing spray. Beyond that was the dark rock wall angling into the river.

Steve stood on his island, a rock about the size of a lifeboat, in the middle of the raging river, completely alone. He looked very small. Spray leaped all around him. He stood tall, leaning into the drop, getting as much of a view as he could, his paddle propped into the stones at his feet like the spear of a Masai. Above the cone mountain, the razor edge of the summit of Gyala Peri hung in the sky, sharp as cut stone, unfurling a banner of snow. He nodded once more, got back in his boat, and launched again.

Within seconds, he was hitting a wave and adjusting his angle for takeoff; he had found the thread of current he wanted for his flight over the falls. Then his boat hit air, and he plummeted and disappeared in the storm of froth. When it emerged, he was upside-down. He tried to roll—one, two. He tried again. He was being swept downstream on a stormy ramp, and he wasn't rolling—and then he did. He came up paddling. The jet of water rocketed him toward the wall on his left. It didn't look good at all. Many kayakers have died pushed up against walls, where they are beaten against the rock and eventually flipped and pinned. Along this cliff there was a shallow, carved-out pocket. It was less an eddy than a cliff-trapped vortex where a vicious, circling current swirled upstream almost as fast as the main current swept down. In the frenzy of opposing currents, the eddy was a maelstrom of colliding sheets of water, whirlpools, and chaotic waves. The eddy fence, a curb of fast water at the eddy line, was a foot high, maybe more. The runaway train was taking Steve into the wall, and he went with it, planting one good, hard guiding stroke as he hit swirl, and was instantly spun upstream. His boat rocked into a reaction surge caroming off the wall, and he was bobbled hard. He struggled to maintain his balance and was shoved up against the black cliff. His kayak bobbed and scraped the rock. Somehow he shoved off, and a whirlpool caught his bow and he was flipped again.

There is no more terrible place to Eskimo roll than in a violent eddy against a wall. So many currents collide. As soon as you begin to roll up, a monumental force backed by tons of moving water can grab your bow or stern and force an edge and flatten you. Steve rolled. I don't know how he did it. He came up, took a couple of strong strokes, aimed for the exit door at the top of the eddy, and then was gripped by another gyre and flipped again.

It was then that it occurred to me, to all of us, that he might die. The capsized hull of his boat, the color of an unripe lime, flashed out of the turbulence. The black wall loomed like a tombstone. He was on the far side of the river, against smooth rock, far beyond help.

He rolled in the tumult. He scanned for a way out, set his angle, and powered—a few strokes; the surges hit and jostled him, but he held the angle, then he sprinted through the eddy line, broke free of the vortex, and was clear. The main current picked him up and swept him downstream like a leaf hitting a fan. He was careening straight toward the monster hydraulic. He dodged left of it, crashed through a breaking wave, and stroked left into a green eddy behind a jut of the wall where Willie was idling as a safety boat.

Dustin jumped up from his camera. "Yeah!" he yelled. "That's what we brought him for! Test dummy! He's the loosest man in a kayak on the planet!"

In the eddy, Willie grinned and stretched his arm up in a high five, and the palms of the two men—Steve's as cold as an ice pack in his glove—clapped together. "Way to go!" Willie said.

"I got pretty worked," Steve said, panting. "I got squirreled in the eddy."

The two ferried across the river and got out on the right bank, where the rest of the expedition was watching. Scott was hopping down the rocks. As soon as Steve was standing, Scott was on him. "Never do that again!" he yelled.

"What?" Steve said. "Nothing happened. I got a little bit worked."

"*Never* do that again! You put the whole trip in jeopardy. That could have ended it." Scott turned and walked away.

Steve looked shocked. Scott had wished him a good run above, and he thought everyone knew what he was doing. He turned to Mike. "It looks like everybody but me got a fright on that rapid."

"Yeah," Mike said. "Maybe that wasn't the best thing to do."

. . . .

Part of the problem was that the margin of survival was further narrowed because the Tsangpo eliminated the kayaker's equivalent of a parachute. If unable to paddle out of danger or to roll up after a flip, he has only one option: pull the cord on his sprayskirt, slide out of the cockpit, and swim for safety—usually a throw rope or the stern loop of another paddler's kayak. In the drastic rapids of the Tsangpo, however, there was little chance for a team member in a kayak to rescue a swimming paddler. Had Steve swum, Willie might have been able to get close, but the charging main current fed into another set of drops. Willie couldn't have chased him for long without dropping blind into life-threatening rapids. Even if Steve could have grabbed hold of Willie's stern loop in the Tsangpo's main current, Willie wouldn't have been able to tow him to shore through the maelstrom. And a throw rope from the bank could make it only a fraction of the way across the river. Despite the moral support of running in a group, here on the Tsangpo, each kayaker was essentially on his own when it came to rescue.

The equation was simple: A swim meant almost certain death. And so the team had come to a grim understanding. "We talked about it," Johnnie had said. "We decided that out here, you drown in your boat. Swimming's not an option."

There are few other men who could have recovered from that place against the wall. Maybe none. Steve's experience playing in holes the size of semitrucks on the Zambezi had given him unique training. His skill at freestyle—all the twirling and cartwheeling—gave him a constant aware-ness of his boat position, so that even upside-down, getting thrashed, he knew at all times where he was and could collect himself. His performance today was astonishing and heart-stopping.

In Scott's book, though, it was an A-1 fuckup, and it changed the rules of engagement for the rest of the expedition. Steve had cowboyed down and made it—but he might not have. Communication hadn't been clear among the paddlers; there had been no plan of attack.

They wouldn't dwell on it. The seven had their hands full. Judging from the topo maps and the report of Walker-McEwan, the river ahead barreled through fast-falling rapids without letup. The Gorge tightened. About two miles below, Doug Gordon had attempted to run a ledge and been swept away. Just below that, they would pass the point directly between the peaks of the two mountains—the spot that defined the deepest river gorge in the world, where the torrent ran so far beneath its shouldering peaks that Colonel F. M. Bailey called it "one of the world's dead ends."

The next stretch of whitewater was big and pushy, with giant boulders scattered down the riverbed, and they found a good spacing between boats and ran in a line. Read and run: challenging, muscular whitewater they could scout from their kayaks. It was the very best kind of paddling. They caught eddies behind the rocks, scanned downstream, saw a good line, and went for it. They hit horizon lines, and as they eddied out at the lip, they could see water flushing out from the bottom. An experienced paddler can tell a lot from the speed and color of the current emerging from the base of a drop. If it's foamy and slow, there's probably a gnarly hole there. They paddled to the edges of these ledges and shot for the fast green water in the run-outs. Sploosh! The first man over, the "probe," would nod or shake his head just at the lip to signify whether the place and angle he'd chosen were safe and clean.

When they came to the next significant horizon, they pulled out on the left bank, sat on the smooth, sun-warmed back of a mammoth boulder, and held a meeting. Scott was furious, and Steve was still smarting from his reprimand, but they came together. They vowed to forgo wild-hare impulsiveness and work as a team. That meant moving slowly and methodically, communicating constantly. Scott said that from now on, they would move downriver in pairs or more. "Good call," Steve said. "We should've planned on that from the beginning." Then they launched off the rocks and into what was probably the steepest 15,000-cfs stretch of river that has ever been kayaked.

Meanwhile, the ground team ran smack into a black cliff. I thought it was one I had read about in Kingdon Ward's account: the sheer end of another spur, the Tomtom La. Our porters dealt with it the same way Ward's porters had: they made a Himalayan ladder. After cutting down a young spruce with their long knives, they hacked off the limbs, leaving stub ends for rungs, and propped it against the vertical rock. Twenty feet up, the slope of the cliff lessened a bit, and the Sherpas and Andrew scrambled and found a crack that angled left to the top, some 35 feet high. The Sherpas pounded stout sticks into the crack, and Andrew ran a climbing rope along it, hitching the rope to the stakes for a handline. They threw two more ropes straight down to the rocks below for hauling.

Kannuri stood on a bit of exposed rock where the handline ran out, completely relaxed, and gave each porter a strong pull across and onto the ledge. A cluster of porters, eight in all, gathered at the base and tied the loads onto a hemp rope bridle, craned their heads back, and yelled. Andrew, his long blond hair in a ponytail beneath a cap set backward, began to pull. He reeled up the 80-pound baskets and bags hand over hand without pause, like a kid hauling in a fish on a handline. We began to call him the Canadian Winch. He looked like a different animal from the punk on the plane in the flared gangster pants that dragged on the ground. Here he wore polypropylene long underwear and mountain boots, and with his broad shoulders and long legs, he looked like the top mountain athlete that he was. He pulled up loads that would have worn out two men—one after another, like a machine. The Sherpas took turns on the other line.

Then the rope went slack in Andrew's hand. A strap had snapped. A basket containing the heavy Pelican box with the first-aid kit cut loose and fell three stories. The eight porters were all bent over, their heads in a small circle, tying another load. The leaden bundle fell like a cartoon piano. Andrew didn't have time to swear when he heard the impact. The basket missed all eight heads by a few inches and exploded on the rocks. The ABS plastic–armored first-aid case shattered. The porters jumped and fell over each other. They looked at the wreckage, then looked up and blinked.

Silence. You could hear the deep rush of the river below. It was the second time today that someone had nearly died. Andrew breathed. "It landed in the only spot where there wasn't a head." He hopped down the cliff like a mountain goat and tied on the rest of the loads himself.

Below us, out of sight, the kayakers were battling the most relentless whitewater they'd ever encountered.

· · · · · · ·

The mood of the Tsangpo kept changing. With the walls on either side narrowing the riverbed, as well as their options, the water fell as steeply as a steep creek run, with many of the same characteristics. But people can paddle steep creeks precisely because they have relatively little water pouring down them; the current doesn't have the push and charge of a bigger river. The boys had never seen anything like this: The Tsangpo had the volume *and* the rocks *and* the gradient. Massive boulders made getting out difficult, so scouting from land was not a sure bet. Boat scouting, on the other hand, was almost impossible. As soon as they got on the water below Steve's Rapid, giant waves blocked their view downstream. When they could see ahead, the river simply plunged out of sight.

Coming over the top of a wave in big Class V water is a little like being at sea in a violent storm. For a split second, you get a view downstream: It's chaos. Steep waves much higher than your head break in a continuous crash, and the sound is like the tear of surf on a gale-ripped shore. Giant rocks loom, and lateral waves pile up and roll off them much like the bow wake of a ship. You see shaped humps—big rock pourovers just under the surface, backed by killer holes that can trap a kayak and become a paddler's watery grave. Rooster tails jet up from sharp rocks like sawdust off a rotary blade, marking potential "pin spots"—rocks shaped in such a way that if a boat collides with one, it's likely to stop dead, vertically or upside down. Patches of bubbling slackwater pattern out of the havoc, signaling eddy lines, the treacherous shears between opposing currents that can catch and flip a boat in an instant. Survival depends on a flow of constant recalibration. One mistake—a decision to go a foot too far to the left, or allowing yourself to get shoved six inches to the right at the wrong moment—and your life may end. There may not be another sport that requires the processing of so much data so fast.

They ran in groups of twos and threes, always with one of the video cameramen in the first heat. Steve hung back, filming the others from the bank. When he ran back to his boat to run a drop last, he was glad to see Dustin Knapp idling in the eddy, waiting for him. Dustin wasn't feeling his best. He was tired, and he itched all over. When he'd put on his boating gear that morning, he'd seen that his body was covered with spots. The rash bubbled up on his neck and back and crusted on his scalp. Naked, he looked like a raspberry pancake on legs. But you wouldn't know it to look at him on the water.

Scott and Johnnie went for an eddy along the left bank. It was a swooping airplane turn on the side of a big, pillowing rock. Johnnie hit the eddy line, and a whirlpool opened up like a gurgling mouth and grabbed his boat and flipped him. He tried to roll and was swept around the corner. Mike and Willie, waiting in an eddy below, saw the boat coming over a wave upside down and thought somebody was swimming. Then they saw Johnnie try to roll in the big, fast water, miss it, and try again as he was being drawn into a section of river he hadn't scouted. Below, to the left side, was a humongous killer hole. Willie and Mike bolted out of the eddy. They were right behind Johnnie when he finally came up on his third attempt, and they screamed, "RIGHT! GO RIGHT!"

"He pulled to the right," Mike said. "No worries."

. . . .

They had all been a little anxious about this section, because they knew it had killed a man. They were surprised and relieved when they found they could move down it piece by piece. They estimated that, counting the two portages they had to make, they were kayaking about 80 percent of the rapids. "It was actually really nice whitewater," Steve said. At the end of the stretch, they stopped and sat on a large boulder and had a moment of silence for Doug Gordon.

I had met Doug when I was a teenager, a beginning kayaker, and he was a legend and on the U.S. Kayak Slalom Team. It was a hot June day on the bank of a Colorado stream called the Crystal. The river was flooding, a steep narrows of sluicing white. I was nervous, and he told me to follow him, to lean forward and dig into the crashing waves and paddle through them. Five of us put in, and it became immediately clear that this was fast-water Class V. One of the experts swam. I capsized and managed to roll, and in all the speed and chaos, I saw Doug disappear over a scary pourover. I somehow sprinted and hit the thinnest eddy along the shore, grabbed a root, and crawled out. Then I saw Doug's paddle, the very top of it, vibrating on the other side of the hump, and I knew he was caught in a hole and surfing. His paddle blade slid left and right, trembling. He was hanging in, working to the edges of the hydraulic. And then he was free. I ran down the bank and saw Doug paddling happily on downstream. Later, he complimented me on having the presence of mind to keep it together and find a way to paddle out. Praise from Doug. Life couldn't be better.

Somewhere in here, on this stretch of the Tsangpo, Doug had lined up for his plunge over a drop and at the last second surprised his teammates by going directly over the big ledge rather than running the safer chute closer to the left shore. He was sucked into the hole at the bottom, flung on end, and chundered upside down, then made an attempt to roll and missed it. He was swept into the main current and never seen again.

The boys did one last stretch before camp and looked back upriver, and then they knew just where the accident had occurred. They had all seen the awful footage that Tom McEwan had shot of Doug going over the ledge, and now they could see the rock that formed it. "Yah, that was definitely it," Steve said. "It had the same look."

They pulled out of the river, propped their boats in the boulders, and climbed up into dense woods to look for us. It was nearly dusk, and a gentle rain sifted down through the dark trees. Someone with a GPS announced that they were now directly between the two peaks of Namcha Barwa and Gyala Peri. They were in the deepest spot of the deepest gorge in the world, and just below camp was a huge rapid.

CHAPTER SEVEN

DOUG'S LEDGES TO THE SPUR

On a September afternoon on a little river in western Sichuan, in what was once Tibet, I paddled around a corner raucous with new-forming waves. I was on a whitewater expedition assignment for *Outside*, and I was concerned: There was heavy rain upstream, and the river was rising. I came around the bend in my kayak and passed a ledge with a big hole beneath it and saw the empty raft cartwheeling in the backwash. It was sickening. I sprinted ahead, looking for swimmers, saw a helmeted head, and paddled through the tumult, yelling, "Grab my stern! My stern!" He didn't hear, or didn't understand. I got a glimpse of his face: one of our young Chinese guides. He was being pulled away from me, and we were both being swept fast into a big logjam piled against the left bank. I stroked as hard as I could and hit the shore, jumped out, grabbed my throw rope, and ran. He was helpless. He washed into the logs, and I saw his helmet jam against the helmet of someone already pinned there. I ran along the rocks, falling once, and I thought, "This is how people die."

I clambered out onto the logs, and Scott Heywood, an outfitter from Sheridan, Wyoming—an expert paddler, and one of three kayakers on the trip—was right behind me. We grabbed the shoulder straps of the man's life vest and hauled him over the floating trees. He was gasping, probably hypothermic but alive, and we left him there. We scrambled out to the other man. His head was just above the water, with his face turned away from me. We hauled on his life vest, but he didn't budge. We adjusted and tried again, as hard as we could. Nothing. I knelt down and lifted his head, and then I saw it was Dave, a 38-year-old banker on honeymoon with his young British bride, Fiona. He was breathing. "My left foot," he said weakly. We tried again and again. We used a rope and pulley system called a Z-drag. The river was rising fast. I knelt and held his head out of the water, but more and more of it splashed into his face. We took turns. The river rose over him. He died in our arms, and our hearts broke. That was 1989.

. . . .

While the Sherpas made dinner and the porters lit their fires in the intermittent rain, I walked down through the woods to the boulders of the bank to say hi to Doug Gordon. Standing on the shore, I didn't feel grief. Or I did, but I didn't feel the accident was tragic. Doug had lived well, had touched and inspired people, and I have never thought longevity in itself is a virtue. But I did think that this was a very long way from home and that the cost to his young wife and his five-year-old son is probably beyond measure.

"Thinking about your mate?"

It was Dave. I tapped my pipe out on a rock and smiled.

"I didn't know him that well," I said, "but I liked him."

"Funny who the river takes, eh?"

"Yeah."

Dave leaned against a rock. "Hellacious through here. Look how bloody steep it is."

"I figured it out. Our last camp was 9,230 feet by my GPS. Here the river is 8,800 feet. Two point one miles as the crow flies, so I figure about three river miles or less—420 feet of drop in three miles; that's at least 140 feet per mile! At 15,000 cfs."

Dave gave me one of those looks of mixed admiration and pity that a jock gives to a geek in physics lab. "That's a bloody record," he agreed. "It's big-water steep creeking."

I met Willie on the way back to camp. "Incredible day," he said. "My best day. The river's definitely showing"—he flexed his arm—"'I'm *this* strong.' A day of humility. Either the rocks are getting bigger or we're getting smaller."

Willie wanted to hold a short service for Doug, but Scott nixed it. Maybe he didn't want to jinx his own trip by lingering over a death. *Don't look back.* The sticks in the fire popped and hissed. The river sent up its white, pulsing rush. The wind in the trees sounded like spectral surf and thrashed down gusts of leaf-held rain.

. . . .

At breakfast, Charlie Munsey diagnosed the rash plaguing Dustin Knapp as chickenpox. That's not just a rash; there can be fever and nausea, and it puts the brakes on your system like any other bout of illness. But Dustin never once complained, and you wouldn't know he had it unless you happened to look at him.

There was a happier rhythm to breaking camp now. Today was bright and warmer yet than the days before. The summit of Gyala Peri hung over us like a floating island. Cheered by the sun, the ground crew wound in a long line steeply down through the trees and onto the boulders that formed the bank. The challenges of this boulder jumble seemed more fun than dangerous.

It was dangerous, though. Jumping along the backs of the rocks, you could be 8, 10, 15 feet off the ground at any given moment. You leaped like a gecko onto a steep shoulder, hands and feet slipping on the water-smoothed rock and smearing for purchase, and you had to rock climb carefully to the top. A slight misjudgment could mean a broken leg or cracked skull. We were doing it with loads snugged close to our bodies, the weight distributed from shoulders to hips. Tuli was carrying my bed and notebooks, so I had less than 30 pounds. The kayakers, when they portaged, were doing the same thing, only with 50-pound teetering boats humped onto their shoulders. Often, they had to carefully lower their boats into a crevice, climb down, prop the boats against the next boulder face, climb up, and haul the boats after them. It was time-consuming and exhausting work. Poxed Dustin Knapp had to do those moves, too, but he often made a dicey leap across the void because he didn't want to spend the energy on a safer transfer, seal launching off the last rock into a Class VI rapid. But that was the good part. "I feel best when I'm in the river," he had told me. "Don't think about itching. When I'm in camp, I look down: 'Hey, I'm falling apart.'"

It took the ground team two hours to cover 1.2 miles of bank, and then we ran smack into another high cliff slabbing a steep spur that jagged up into the mountains. I don't think it even had a name. It looked scary to me. The porters dropped their loads, started fires, made tea, and thought about it.

We'd run out of boulders. A little ravine, trickling and wet, of exposed mossy rock—more of a waterfall slide in wetter months—ran straight up into the hanging woods behind us. In front of us, the Tsangpo rolled through an easy run of big haystack waves. One was breaking, and Allan paddled down, hit the white curler and spun against it, and threw his boat into a vertical cartwheel; the whole crowd of porters gathered at their fires on the rocks raised a cheer. How completely alien it must have seemed to them. Their experience with boats was probably limited to a tippy dugout canoe crossing flat water to a place of prayer. I thought that our porters must look at the kayakers the way we might look at a Buddhist monk who sits through a Tibetan mountain winter in a cave, wearing nothing but a light cotton shift and practicing his inner-heat technique.

The kayakers had done exactly what they said they'd do: They ran the first steep drop after camp and portaged a section along the left bank, then put in and paddled a very tough, ledge-stuttered stretch.

That last sentence is casual, to say the least. It's like writing, "They opened the hatch of the moon lander, climbed down to the dusty surface, hit a few golf balls, and flew home." To give an inkling of what it was like in there, we should do an experiment in tele-transport. Close your eyes—

hey, wait, forget that, you need to read this. The room you are in now—fill it with thunder. Not the distant rumble of a coming storm but the layered boom and crash, the thresh and sift of big surf, the kind that shakes the sand under your feet and drowns your words. That sound is not coming from in front of you; it surrounds you on all sides.

Now the chair you are in begins to rock. It is shoved up and back on a surge of bubble-infused current, bobbles, and slides forward again. Any normal person would get dumped in a second, but you're a pro now, you're a Steve Fisher or a Mike Abbott, and this surging motion is the impatience of a wild horse being reined back: You are merely in an eddy, facing upstream, and you are completely relaxed and barely conscious of the shifts and half spins. Your hips adjust and readjust reflexively, and your paddle touches the water without thought and keeps you aligned. Your attention is over your right shoulder downriver. Just below you, sticking off the right bank, is a rock. It is a beautiful, smooth ivory-colored boulder swirled with darker grain like an exotic wood. It is exactly twice the size of a UPS truck—at least the part you can see. A third of the river's current, tearing downhill at something like 15 knots, slams into it, piles up eight feet, and crashes back on itself with a gnashing you can hear beneath the general roar.

Another thing: You can tell by the shape of the pillow that millennia of rushing water have hollowed the rock so that its bottom portion slopes back, overhung. Should you miss your line and not generate enough speed to paddle around the rock, you will slam into it, and when your boat hits the undercut, the current will shove you back under the boulder, down beneath the surface, and pin you there. A horrible but common way for a kayaker to die.

Nor do you want to overshoot the move and go too far to the left, because just left of center is a giant ledge. Half the river seethes over this drop in a gush of aerated white, and beneath is a violent, clashing line of white froth, parallel to the ledge, perpendicular to the current, with a trough in which you could comfortably park Greyhound's express bus to Endsville.

Plus, a five-foot-high, curling diagonal wave feeds off the big boulder toward the center of the river, angling down and across the main onslaught like a giant, sucking funnel. But don't worry. There is a safe passage, a tongue of water six inches wide. Your boat is wider than that by two feet, so you'll need to center the kayak precisely on the tongue. Ready?

You dart out of the eddy with a full-on sprint and shoot across the gush, and just as you are about to clear the rock, you slice your paddle into a bow draw on the right and spin your boat to face downstream. You hit the diagonal wave, and it breaks over and buries you completely. It surfs you just far enough, as you knew it would, and as you break into air again, it lands you on the center of the tongue, your one precise passage through this very real Scylla and Charybdis. Digging in to get precisely enough forward motion to overcome the slide, you break over the wave and charge right, tucking in behind the boulder into a big green swirling eddy. You glide across it, sliding sideways, and your boat bumps gently up against another kayak. It is Dustin Knapp's, and he turns toward you and smiles that mild smile, and you feel the joy and the adrenaline surge through you. They are the same thing, and the surge of the great river is the same, and your spirit rushes outward in an expanding wave. The universe, somehow all of it rushes in, and you know that you were put on the Earth for that moment.

And that's just one move.

Willie said after that run, "We peeled out, and all the water was screaming, piling into and under a 60-foot-wide boulder. Just above were all these holes. Turbulent boiling water. We had to put in some fucking Ninja strokes and make the power ferry out to the middle and around. . . ."

This is the difference between Willie and you in your storm-tossed chair: He loved every second of it.

. . . .

Watching the paddlers, it's still almost impossible to believe how tiny their boats look threading the rocks. The rocks are like asteroids, moons,

132

planets. The ledge holes are white cataclysms, like storm surf that would crush a 55-foot fishing boat.

For the ground crew, this next spur didn't look like much fun either. Ken tucked his water bottle back into his pack and said, "Well, I guess." He looked up and tightened his mouth, settled the bush hat back on his head, and picked up his pack. What kind of man comes *back* to the Upper Tsangpo Gorge? A passionate one, certainly. I liked Ken, even if he had become in some sense my adversary.

We went straight up, first on the moss-wet rock of the creek, scrambling with hands and feet for holds, placing each foot gingerly on the greasy stone, then hauling ourselves up on small trees and pushing through the woods until we broke over into a cupped bench of blackberry thicket beneath a dihedral of black rock cliff.

It was a relief to be suddenly on the near level, until we tried to push through the thicket. It was some 10 feet high, dense as a hedge, and defended by prickers. Ken and I took turns hacking at the brush with our trekking poles. We forced through three-foot-high openings that looked like takin highways. The thorns tore at our clothes and scratched our hands and faces. I thought I heard Ken curse. Just once. I might have been wrong.

I heard thrashing behind us and loud gasping, and when I wheeled, there was fat Babu. That's all I knew about him—his name. And that he was Tsawong's boss at the Tibetan-owned travel company called Windhorse Adventure. And that Tsawong needed to impress him on this trip to get his mountain guide's license and the opportunity to lead more lucrative tours. Babu had a head the size of a grizzly bear's. He had the high cheekbones of a grizzly, and the small ears. He carried his own pack, and he wore good mountain boots and gaiters. And he had a gut. Babu's stomach was so big and solid and shapely, so utilitarian, it didn't look like the burden of excess but rather like the chief of the whole operation, as if it commanded his legs and head and arms to take it wherever it wanted to go. Whatever opening we thrashed out of the thorny mesh would accommodate only a mere sliver of Babu, who must have been taking a beating at the edges. He was Wide Load. I was gasping from the effort. It was amazing that the big man was staying with us. I wondered if Tibetans get heart attacks.

I said, "Babu, this is tough going. Where did you get so strong?" He half closed his eyes, half smiled, then half nodded and said, "*Ruugh.*" What the hell was he doing here? I found myself fighting a prejudice—that any Tibetan who had gotten grossly fat under Chinese occupation must be a collaborator.

When the Chinese invaded in the 1950s and began their systematic devastation of the country, they had a tough job—not the destruction of a sect or dogma but the rooting out of a country's very soul. Buddhism is not merely the official religion of Tibet. It is the country's blood. It runs through every activity, every thought and emotion of every Tibetan. Before the Chinese took over, the country had been governed by monks. In one of the most violent corners of the globe, it had elected not to field an army, and for centuries, it had pacified invading Mongol kings not with force but with the sheer inspiration of its lamas. In Tibet, the national heroes were not athletes or movie actors but bodhisattvas. To the Chinese, everyone was suspect. Whoever did not flee—whoever stayed and survived—had to accommodate to some extent. To get a tour company license and lead foreigners to sacred sites around the country, I wondered how far one had to go; was there a line between accommodation and collaboration?

We got up to the base of the steep black slab rock. There was a notch in the spine of the spur above. We would have to climb up to get through it. One reason I took up paddling in college was that I realized—after five years of intense rock climbing—that I didn't like heights. We picked our way up the slab and edged along a fracture crack, coming out on a ledge of brown grass where Andrew and Dustin Lindgren were happily perched, looking over the river and the cliff like a pair of takin. They had to grab us and pass us by them on the narrow game trail. We turned and looked down and could see the porters just breaking over into the bench, and we laughed when we saw the smoke from tea fires rising into the clarified air.

The other side of the spur was like descending into a different season. We tromped down through bamboo and then a grove of leaved rhododendron with fat flower buds. The way opened and the sun poured onto slopes of feathery dried grass and tussocks of yellow moss. We could look straight downstream now, to the east, to a far distant wall of tall, snowy mountains running north-south. Ken said that they were the Pome Range. Jesus. That was the cradle of the Lower Gorge. We would have to walk all the way there before turning upstream into the apex of the Great Bend. Sometimes it's not good to see where you are going.

Above us on either side were the glaciated massifs of Dorje Pagmo's two mountains. Ken said that his trip through here in 1993 had been the first by Westerners since Kingdon Ward's in 1924. Nobody had been past Pemakochung in a generation. Since then, there had been only Walker-McEwan and the Chinese scientific survey in 1998. Ken said, "In 2000, some woman paid an exorbitant amount to come into Hidden Falls, but she came the other way, from Pelung." So perhaps three parties since Kingdon Ward had been this way, and a few pilgrims. No wonder the takin tracks were everywhere, and cat tracks, too.

That afternoon, we entered a camp cleared out of the woods, where the kayakers already had a fire going. The Sherpas arrived soon after and set up a kitchen tarp, and the porters surprised us by being right behind. The little generator purred as Allan charged the radios and laptop. He said the kayakers had run about five major rapids today. They could have been at camp half an hour after the first portage but had to wait hours in the cold wind for us to catch up.

Allan stood and unwrapped a sucker and was about to toss the plastic in the fire. Charlie said, "Hey, trash in the fire is supposed to bring out the yetis."

"Whoops," Al said, and put the wrapper in his pocket. "There're gonna be a lot of yetis waiting for us at the top."

"Remember, run downhill," Mike said. "Apparently they have huge breasts and they topple forward. If you run uphill, they throw them over their shoulder."

Scott drained a can of Enlarge fortifier drink—he'd brought a personal case into the Gorge. He hadn't been eating much in the past month and was alarmingly thin. "Be Invincible," read the label on the can.

That night, 15 of the porters gathered cross-legged around one big fire, and Dave and Ken and Charlie joined them and asked Tsawong to relay some questions.

Tsawong: "Who among you has been to Pemakochung?"

Sherab: "Five times. A few others have been once."

Tsawong: "Who has been beyond it?"

Porters: "No one. Only Sherab."

Tsawong: "Do people still make *Kora* there—the pilgrimage?"

Porters: "No."

Tsawong: "Who has seen the falls?"

Porters: "No one. Not even Sherab."

. . . .

When Kintup's report was sanitized of militarily sensitive information and published in 1889, one detail caught the attention of explorers far and wide: the three lines about the Sinji-Chogyal cataract. Kintup described a waterfall that splashed 150 feet down into a lake, where rainbows played in the perpetual spray. Could this be another great wonder of the world? The last?

Captain Frederick M. Bailey of the Bengal Lancers heard the call. Tall, lanky, cool under fire, he marched into Lhasa with Colonel Francis Edward Younghusband in 1904. Bailey was a born naturalist who never went anywhere without his butterfly net. He was resourceful, charming, and had a good ear for languages and an eye for local nuance and customs. He was a keen marksman who loved nothing better than an upland pheasant hunt, and he was tough. (He also made a great secret agent. After the First World War, the British sent Bailey to infiltrate revolutionary Russia. Relentlessly pursued in central Asia, he was such a master of subterfuge and disguise that the Bolsheviks hired him to find and arrest the British spy—in other words, himself.)

Like Scott Lindgren, Bailey was obsessed the moment he read about the Tsangpo Gorge. He remained in Tibet for 3½ years and conceived a bold plan for penetrating it. He and one assistant would go alone, privately funded, without military orders or backup. But just before they set out from Chengdu, Bailey received a four-word telegram from his father: WARN BAILEY MASSACRE SADIYA. "It was an alarming message," Bailey wrote, "because it failed to say who had massacred whom and why. . . ." Sadiya was in the Abor hills of Assam, home of the pugnacious tribe that had repeatedly made hash of Her Majesty's Army. In yet another embarrassing loss, the British political officer in Assam, Noel Williamson, had sallied into Abor territory despite official warnings and had been killed with 39 of his men.

Despite the telegram, Bailey and his 16-year-old Tibetan servant boy, Putmandu, "proceeded with great caution," as Bailey put it in his memoir, *No Passport to Tibet*. They crossed the Yangtze, the Mekong, and the Salween rivers, topped snow-covered passes 15,000 feet high, and ran smack into a new conflagration between China and Tibet. In Lhasa, the hated Chinese Viceroy and 100 of his officials and servants had been massacred. The Chinese responded by razing parts of Pome, destroying monasteries, and murdering hundreds of monks. The residents of Pome, for their part, ambushed and killed 300 Chinese troops. In the beginning of July, at the edge of Tsangpo country, the local district administrator refused Bailey porters and ponies, convinced he would be killed by the Chinese for being a British spy or by the Poba for the hell of it. He had to turn back.

That was Bailey's first try. He returned to India and official displeasure at overstaying his leave. "At the age of thirty," he wrote, "I felt slightly aggrieved to be reprimanded for what appeared to me a matter for congratulations." Still, since the chance to make another attempt on his own nickel and timetable probably wouldn't come again for many years, he'd have to see "whether it could not be performed in the natural course of duty."

That opportunity presented itself almost immediately. In the winter of 1911–12, the army dispatched a battalion of more than 700 Gurkha Rifles skilled in jungle warfare, along with 3,000 spear-carrying coolies from the Naga tribe, who were blood enemies of the Abors. Their mission was to strike back at the tribe for the deaths of Williamson and his men. "Noel Williamson had disobeyed orders by crossing the Outer Line into Abor country without authority," Bailey wrote unsympathetically. "By being murdered he had forced the Government to avenge his death. It was very annoying and very expensive. But if it had to be done, the authorities argued, they might get as much value as possible for their money. For the first time for many years, the possibility of entering Tibet from the Assam side had opened up. A systematic survey was to be made. . . ."

Gotta love the Brits. Slaughtering natives *was* annoying, but it was a damned good opportunity to make a map. Nowadays, the whole enterprise would be called Operation Monsoon Justice; the Brits simply called it the Abor Expedition, and they rolled through the native villages like a Howitzer over a mouse. The bamboo-spiked pit traps and rock ambuscades that had worked so well in previous campaigns barely tickled the British lines and failed to kill a single soldier. How many Abors were killed was never recorded.

. . . .

Bailey wangled himself a position on the expedition as intelligence officer, with orders from the British foreign secretary that he "should be allowed as much scope as possible for the exercise of his talents as regards exploration." Bailey took this as "implicit permission for me to enter Tibet." He was the Ur James Bond, with a License to Explore. In Tibet, Bailey found his own paradise, where he could wander without a plan, "happy in the

knowledge that every place was unknown." He swatted at unnamed but-
terflies with his net, discovered the blue poppy that Kingdon Ward later
collected and named *Meconopsis baileyi*, and even squinted at curious ro-
dents. Passages like the following abound in Bailey's memoir.

> My friendliest visitor was a shrew, which came onto my table
> as I was working. I grew fond of it as a companion, and yet the
> more I looked at it the more I felt that it might be a species
> which had never been seen or heard of before. As a man I
> wished it a long and happy life; but as an amateur naturalist I
> felt that the interests of science came first, so just before I left
> I converted my friend into a collector's specimen. It proved to
> be a new species and was named *Soriculus baileyi*.

In February 1913, he accompanied a military detachment up into
the jungled headwaters of the Dibong, a tributary of the Brahmaputra,
where he heard about an isolated village called Mipi farther up the river.
Its inhabitants were reported to be Tibetan. Bailey had read of the 17th-
century prophecies of a hidden Edenic land called Pemako, where crops
would grow untended and where Buddhists would find refuge in times of
persecution. Ancient religious "guidebooks" placed the sacred valley
vaguely in the severe mountain fastness of the far eastern Himalaya. Now
here was a band of Tibetans who had traveled south looking for it. Bailey
saw his chance to find a route into Tibet and the Tsangpo. With a small
escort, he rode into Mipi and found not denizens of paradise but a terrified, beaten, half-starved remnant of the original immigrant group, sick
from the heat and low altitude and harassed by hostile Mishmis. Most of
the band had returned to Tibet in 1909, leaving the old and sick who
could not make the journey.

Bailey won the confidence of the headman, and over the next month
tapped him for all the information he could about possible routes north.

He'd need one other companion, a surveyor, to map the country they covered. He found his man in Captain Henry Morsehead of the Royal Engineers, a stalwart surveyor who seemed to be completely heedless of danger, leeches, and fever.

In mid-May, they headed up into the Lower Gorge. The coolies went snowblind on their first pass. They triggered avalanches, and Bailey slipped and fell. ("I thought [it] was going to be my last, but I saved myself with the handle of my butterfly net.") They pushed on into the Lower Tsangpo, up the left bank, and over 3,000-foot spurs that the translator of the Pundit A.K. had quaintly called "undulations." By mid-June, on the verge of the Lower Gorge, they were booted out by local officials who suspected they were agents of the Chinese. So they made an arduous and diplomatically dicey circuit around the Great Bend and down the stunning Po Tsangpo Valley. Floods caused another detour. Finally, in mid-July, they hit the Tsangpo opposite Pe and took a dugout ferry across the river.

Imagine Bailey's disappointment in discovering that the falls weren't on the main river after all. They saw the 150-foot tributary falls below Gyala and struggled on to Pemakochung, as we were doing now. When they got there, they found just above it the source of the mix-up, a falls on the main river that dropped 30 feet. Later dubbed Kintup Falls, this was the one that now had the kayakers so concerned.

Bailey found a few monks and caretakers at the monastery. "It was as if we had reached one of the world's dead ends. When we asked about the road down the river, they said there was no road. When I said, 'Then how do you get down the river?' they said, with some satisfaction, 'We don't.'"

But Bailey was too close to let the matter of a great hidden cataract go. They pushed on a bit downstream and explored the Sanglung Glacier pouring off Namcha Barwa. "We were both excited, because until this moment we had been largely following in Kintup's footsteps down the Tsangpo, confirming his information . . . and . . . what was most important of all, making a map." The thought of finding a Niagara or a Victoria "would have kept me awake," Bailey wrote, "even if it had not been for the pain and throbbing of the cuts in my knees."

He joined a group of Monpa in hopes that they would guide him, but at Clear Creek, the critical egress point for the climb to the pass and Luku, the Monpa ditched him. The way downriver was blocked by sheer rock wall. Bailey made it partway across this cliff, risking everything, for the price of the merest slip was certain death. His one porter, Anay, who was barefoot, made it all the way, but it was too much. The servant scrambled back. How could the captain know that the treasure he had been seeking was no more than a few thousand feet away? Rainbow and Hidden falls thundered through the chasm just around the bend.

Bailey turned back. He was down to almost no food, his blood was poisoned from the cuts, and the Monpa had destroyed every improvised bridge and log ladder in their wake. When he got back to Pemakochung, he found that the Monpa had robbed the monastery. That explained their strange behavior.

On his return to India, Bailey made inquiries in Sikkim and located the old tailor Kintup. The two explorers met and compared their journeys. Kintup confirmed that the 150-foot waterfall in his report did not exist on the Tsangpo. Bailey asked the colonial administration in India to give Kintup a pension. Instead, the government awarded him 1,000 rupees. He died at home soon afterward.

. . . .

Not much had changed here in the century following Bailey's expedition. Travel was every bit as difficult. Before we turned in, the porters around the fire said they feared there would be much snow up high on the Senchen La. Dave said that tomorrow we would go to Pemakochung, and there was a curious silence; the porters' faces were masks and their eyes gleamed, impassive and impenetrable.

CHAPTER EIGHT

PEMAKOCHUNG

In the beginning, there was only a quiet, meditative monkey and a rock-ogress disguised as a princess. She was very beautiful. The winds blew over the Earth, the seasons came and went with monsoon and sun and winter snows, and the monkey and the maiden were the only ones to hear and see. They alone smelled the rain and watched the blossoms drift out of the trees. The monkey lived in a cave and sat in meditation, content. He was a holy monkey. He was compassionate and kind, though there was very little in the world to practice kindness on, except the princess. She, on the other hand, was a Material Girl, lusty and greedy. Also very bored. Her womb ached. Her desire swelled. She moaned and screamed for sex. The monkey heard the cries in the night, and he felt compassion for the princess and went to her. They coupled and bore six children, from whom sprang the six tribes of Tibet.

This is how Tibetans explain their dual natures. To the monkey they attribute their kindness and compassion, their devotion, reflectiveness, and nobility. To the princess belong their avarice, lustiness, and duplicity.

. . . .

February 9 began as another cold and clear day after a night of misting, intermittent rain. I woke very early and saw beside my tent five of the younger porters, all asleep in a sardine line under one cover of overlapping blankets. A sheet of plastic was stretched over a rope, lean-to fashion, above their heads. So that's how they stayed warm without good bags—shared heat. A little later, as they made their tea fire, I saw the boys from Pe solemnly sprinkle tsampa and juniper twigs into the flames. Camp broke on time, with everybody picking up their loads on schedule and hitting the trail—or lack of it—at 9:30, which in Tibet in the winter is very early; Dave was pleased.

Rob Hind said, "So you think we'll make it to Pemakochung today?"

Dave swung up his heavy pack, which held some $30,000 worth of porter cash in Chinese yuan. "We'll bloody try, mate. The only certainties in life are death and an Australian nurse."

The ground team's climb up and over to Pemakochung would be brutal; there was a good chance we wouldn't reach the monastery by nightfall. The kayakers would then be on their own while we camped beside a sacred lake high up the spur. Set like a jewel in a hanging step of what must certainly be snow, the lake was called Tso Lamemba, which means Lake of Fire. Its waters were reputed to shoot flames at night.

For the first time on the trip, the kayakers packed their boats for self-support, stuffing the sterns with bivy sacks and enough food for two days, the amount of time they'd be without ground support if we got stuck up high. Steve's boat, made by the Canadian kayak company Riot, actually had a watertight bulkhead for dry storage behind his seat. The boat was called the Big Gun, and the round hatch cover on the rear deck had a jazzy cartoon graphic of a Terminator in shades, blasting away with a machine gun.

It would be a momentous day. In 1.6 miles, they'd paddle into the photographic territory of the satellite map. Then, at last, they could compare everything—the whitewater on the images with the actual rapids, and what they'd seen on Ken's videos of the river in 1993—and get a much better idea of what was coming up.

Pemakochung looked to be about three river miles away. The Tsangpo swung in a broad northern arc around a high, steep spur that bristled off

Namcha Barwa. On the eastern side of the ridge, a looming natural am-
phitheater cradled the ancient monastery. Along the way, just above the
ruin, was Kintup Falls. The boaters had a Xerox of a black-and-white
photo, shot by Ludlow and Sherriff in 1947, of a vicious-looking, river-
wide cataract taken from below. It wasn't encouraging. The photo was
stained with tea and tattered now from being passed around in camp and
studied by headlamp and firelight. It seemed to have absorbed a sepia tone
of gravity. The cascade looked to be pressed on either side by sheer walls.

Willie smiled out of his pointed beard: his warrior smile, generous
but fleeting, guarded, almost mischievous. "Today we'll get around the
corner and take a look—solve the problem of Kintup," he said.

Fifteen minutes after we began to clamber along the boulders on the
shore of the reverberating river, the porters dropped their loads, sat down,
had a smoke, and started making tea. We had gone half a mile.

While the Chinese seem to have no problem flat-out refusing you
and can even seem to delight in it, a Tibetan will rarely tell you no—to
your face. The porters wouldn't tell Dave outright that they weren't
going all the way today; they'd simply balk long enough so that it couldn't
happen. They knew they had us by the balls. They were acting nothing
like an Australian nurse.

It was already clear to Dave, from the pace of the porter train and the
shortness of the winter days, that we would not make it to the monastery.
Tonight we would camp in the snow beside the flaming lake. Fine by me.
There probably wouldn't be anything too terrifying to surmount today on
the ground. There were the huge rocks along the shore, but we were all getting better at negotiating them. They were a puzzle of their own, a varie-
gated, humped sea of water-smoothed stones. They were cool to the touch,
even in full sun. Down between them were gravel, smooth sand, cobbles
of smaller stone, and broken, bleached logs like bones. And bones. Here was
what must have been a takin, and there a bird, torn apart and scattered.

The crevices formed twisting, shadowed mini chasms, holes and shafts, passageways. Some you could walk through for a short distance; some echoed like chambers. Some were icy cold and cut with sunlight, and the floor of this netherland had its own patterns: runnels and little deltas in the sand from a heavy rain, banks of small stones that had been eddied into a corner. As often as not, to climb out of a crevice, you put your back against one boulder and your legs against another, or stemmed with your feet apart, and chimneyed up. A slight misjudgment, a fall and a broken ankle, could leave you lost to the world. Your cries for help would be drowned by the roar of the Tsangpo. It was best to stay atop the rocks.

The adjustable trekking poles were a boon. Now, as I hopped along with Andrew and the Sherpas, I lengthened them and used them like little vaulting poles. They had sharpened graphite tips, and I set them against the rounded flank of the next boulder, tested the purchase as I loaded the springs, and swung across the gap. It was a gas.

Steve said he had already made so many crazy jumps with his boat on his shoulder, onto sketchy edges and holds right above the water, that he didn't even think about it anymore. He said that it was probably one of the most dangerous parts of the paddler's day.

A few nights before, Scott and Willie had talked about seeing a mountain goat scaling the walls of the Grand Canyon of the Stikine in British Columbia. Scott said, "He shot up this gully, dude, that was 5.9, 5.10" (5.10 is extremely difficult on the rock-climbing scale). "It was unreal. This thing was a solid, 1,500-pound animal. It had like a full-on huge rack." Mountain goats didn't do so well on the river. At Site Zed, a notorious rapid, they saw the carcass of a mountain goat wrapped around a rock.

Willie nodded, excited. He said, "We saw this moose swim the Stikine. It was like he knew what he was doing. Every time he hit a wave, he'd blow and close his ears. Hit the back side of this eddy like he knew what he was doing, climbed up this slope. Flapped his ears forward." He brought his hands to his own ears and mimed the moose.

Thinking of that as I jumped to another boulder, I laughed out loud. It's the thing about river running that I've always loved the most: You go into the country on a natural magic carpet, moving at a speed that is normal to all its denizens, and if you are quiet—you can be absolutely silent in a way you can never be walking—and if you are on a wilderness river, you slip past scenes you would never, ever witness any other way. I've seen beavers building houses, deer and elk nosing the water, foxes and bighorns, alligators and tapirs, and once a couple of backpackers making love, all close enough to throw a pebble.

We climbed to a grassy lip that looked down at the gentle curve of the Tsangpo. Andrew and I chewed on desiccated berries from a lone tree. The ancient pilgrimage guides describe Pemako as a "celestial realm on Earth." It occurred to me that a single moment's complete gratitude— for the winter sun, for the smell of the warmed grass and the sound of the river and a handful of berries—contain within it all that is Shangri-La. It's the highest form of love, the crop that grows without tending, the milk and the honey. It's being most alive.

. . . .

Dave's voice was on the radio. Even flattened by the transmission, his frustration was audible: "The porters are breaking for lunch."

Andrew said, "Get 'em moving."

Charlie came on: "It's not that simple."

From where we sat, we could see the smoke of a council fire rising out of the trees at the base of the forested ramp. It was serious, and it was sort of funny. Sort of. The famous Everest climber and filmmaker David Brashears came here in '93 in an attempt to push through the Gorge. His porters abandoned him somewhere around Pemakochung. They stole his remaining food. Brashears, conqueror of Everest, crawled back out of the Gorge, defeated and near starving.

The kayakers, meanwhile, were picking their way down the first mile—serious whitewater. They were leapfrogging each other in groups of two and three, pausing in the green pools behind the biggest boulders, running the slots, clipping the edges of huge holes, getting buried, reemerging, making it. Scott came on the radio, totally jazzed. "Yeah, we barely got out of our boats. That section was sweet!"

They all pulled out right, just upstream of where we were sitting, and had a look. It was a typical Tsangpo quandary. All along the left cliff wall, boulders jumbled in a deadly, white-thrashed sieve, and on the right, a huge terminal ledge hole extended nearly across the river. Steve was obviously fully recovered from eating humble pie. He glanced quickly at the layout, squeezed into his boat, and seal launched off a high rock just next to the hole. That move alone would have given me pause; a flip or a dawdle could have resulted in getting sucked into the hole by the aerated towback he had just splashed into.

Steve darted into very swift water between the bank and big rocks offshore and slipped into a narrow slot, over another big ledge, and straight through—a sizeable hole. He shook water from his head as his yellow boat skidded across a big green pool off the shore. The others followed, and they gathered as a group in the eddy. They were almost directly below us. The river constricted further, all choked with boulders. Down the right side along the shore was a very technical maze of rocks— on-the-edge, big-water steep creeking. Anywhere out in the center or left fed into a massive diagonal hole that funneled everything straight into a black death cave in the left wall. Yuck.

Rob arrived on the bluff, sweaty and huffing. "I never want to see another porter again," he said. He sat on his pack and dug in the pocket of his fleece jacket for a cigarette. "They said they don't want to camp in snow; we said, 'Okay, then we go all the way to Pemakochung tomorrow.' They said, 'Yup.' They said they know the distances and we shouldn't keep pushing them." Rob sucked on the cigarette hungrily. "Then they sat down and fed us tsampa and yak meat and yak butter tea, just like that! Some of them are really friendly, and some are a bit—" He waved the hand holding the butt.

Suddenly we noticed the whole pack of porters filing out of the woods, eschewing the ramp that was the planned route and that we, the lead group of the ground team, had already taken, and coming along the river boulders. What now?

Scott, on the radio: "Looks like the whole crew is coming right at me!"

We could see the paddlers coalesce into a knot on the rocks.

Scott then reported: "We've decided to camp with you guys tonight, then take off tomorrow with today's supply of food."

Charlie on his radio: "Good call."

I noticed that Dustin Knapp was in his boat on a shore rock and picking up his paddle. He launched straight into a tiny, rock-guarded slot. He hit the bottom and sliced almost 90 degrees left into a sluice no wider than his boat. The sharp turn and the current pushed him up against the rock, and for a breathtaking moment, he looked stuck. He shoved off and paddled onto a ramp of current that took him toward the deadly center of the river. Stroking hard, he slid off the jet to the right and grounded on a colossal flat exposed boulder that was periodically awash with surges. Jesus. We laughed out loud. It was a completely creative egress from death whitewater—except that now he was dry-docked up on the rock, a paddler on a pedestal, shoved by the surges washing over.

He began to push along on his hands, and then he was right at the lip, rocking his weight forward over it. He plunged off the back side and was in the current again, swiftly arrowing into one narrow slot after another, the last one just the width of his kayak that dropped him eight feet into a green-water pool at the bottom. Pretty good for a young vegan with chickenpox.

Allan was there in the pool, in his boat for safety, and we saw the two high-five. Then Dustin hopped out and took out his camera to film the rest. Meanwhile, the newly mutinous porters just dropped their loads on the bank and sat down to watch. I couldn't really blame them. This was like watching Baryshnikov dance or Jordan drive in for a layup.

Big clouds swept over and threw the river in shadow, and the afternoon wind came up. It was already 1:30. The cold shadow would make the run more difficult psychologically for the other paddlers. Willie launched and ran the line. Steve came right behind him, got stuck for a minute in the first slot, rocked out of it, and nearly collided with Willie up on the flat rock. The surge shoved Willie off, and then Steve was perched there alone, comically. Holding his paddle vertically, he did the hand-push across it. When he fell off the other side, he was caught in the current and nearly shoved sideways into boulders below, but he took hard strokes left and cleared himself into the next chute. Scott ran clean and fast, straight-backed but leaning forward a little, as if projecting his intention into the next move, charging into it.

Now they were facing a river-wide dam of boulders with a big green tongue barreling through it just left of center, the strongest part of the river. The tongue crashed into a hole with a giant breaking comber that made your bowels churn if you just glanced at it from a quarter mile away. You wouldn't take a destroyer through there, or a triple-hulled ice breaker. You'd take a picture of it and put it on your fridge if you were serious about curbing your appetite.

"Steve looks keen," Dave said.

As usual, Steve was idling in an eddy, farther out and downriver from the rest, checking it out, eager to go.

He broke back to the shore and conferred with Allan, sitting in his boat. Then Mike, in his red kayak, flashing his orange paddle, stroked up the big green eddy and out toward the center-left current. He paddled out behind the last guarding rock and paused, craning his neck. He looked ready. Steve detached from shore and paddled up toward him; here came Allan behind Steve, and then Mike broke out, wanting to run first, laying into a strong drive upstream and across, gliding out across the aerated, milky current. He arced into a broad peel-out and went for the tongue. It picked him up and hurtled him downstream toward the wall of terrible white froth like a Clorox bottle on a tsunami. He aimed for the right side of the tongue and, paddling for his life, nipped the edge of the hole and ran right into a pool along the shore. Allan followed. He timed his slant down the right side of the tongue so the big current did all the work, and he landed next to Mike without taking more than a few hard strokes.

"*Right* on," I heard Andrew, the mountaineer, murmur in awe.

The rest cleaned it and then ferried in a safe spot across the river to scout down and run the left side of the next rapid, which looked just as big but more open. We picked up our packs and headed across the grass bluff to a precipitous landslide gully that poured out of the cliffs above. The sun was already down behind us, and the wind was in our faces.

The problem now was that this gully plunged straight to the river, and we had to cross it. We knew the porters would be making their way along the bottom, and it was nearly impossible not to kick rocks out of the loose dirt to hurtle down out of sight as we delicately picked our way. A porter feeling a little mutinous might not be appeased by being turned into a bowling pin. The other problem was that every barely solid-looking slab of a rock you stepped onto might be your sled ride into the Tsangpo. No ropes, no protection, just Dave ahead of me, stepping and muttering, "Ho, touchy girl there, think we'll give you the go-round."

. . . .

The fire was struggling. Dense gray smoke wafted out of the pile of broken and damp rhododendron limbs. Passang Sherpa squatted and spun the bellows, a six-inch metal flywheel in an aluminum housing that he worked with a crank on the side. It whirred like a loud hummingbird and harmonized with the thrum of the generator. We were camped at the base of the ravine we would climb to the fire lake tomorrow. It was dark and wet, a cramped little bench of dead leaves and moss-covered rocks. Vines of tiny tiger-striped leaves climbed the trunks of the trees. Many of these plants were still unnamed, this vine possibly among them. And there were rhododendrons 20 feet high, hundreds of years old, their leaves drooping and dark and shiny. A few tall ferns spread new fronds. We were dropping so fast, we were lowering ourselves into a new season.

Kannuri, the gentle lama who I now believed Knew Everything, made a whisk out of bamboo so he could bake us a Dutch-oven cake. He cut four perfectly rectangular slots in opposite sides of a hollow bamboo and inserted interlocking crossed fins. He set the device in the batter, rolled it between his palms, and frothed the batter as fast as an electric mixer. His brother Jangbu, Everest climber, started making pizza.

The porters continued to straggle in. I got up to meet Tuli, who brought over my bag and helped me clear a space for the tent, chopping out a stump with a borrowed knife. I gave him a dip of Copenhagen. I showed him how to tamp it between his cheek and gum, and he clenched his mouth around it and smiled tightly. I think he swallowed all the juice. Having watched the various porter negotiations, I knew he was considered an elder and did a lot of arguing with Tsawong—and then he showed this warmth. The princess and the monkey. Or maybe it wasn't that. Maybe the porters were just being consistently practical; they did know the distances, they did know that with the gear they had, it was impossible to camp safely up in the snow. Maybe we weren't listening hard enough, respecting their situation. It was easy to just roll your eyes and get pissed off at the delays and draw a line between us and them.

Kusang handed me a cup of sweet coffee, and I took it down to the creek and stripped to take a bath in the icemelt and wash my socks. I took a deep breath and did a pushup in the little pool, and when I dunked my head, I got an instant brain freeze, what the boys must have gone through every time they flipped or submerged in a breaking wave. I put the same clothes back on, but it felt good to wash off the dried sweat.

Back at the fire, the maps and photos came out. Tomorrow they would paddle into the territory of the satellite map. Kintup Falls was on everybody's mind. Mike, Allan, Willie, and Ken bent over a zoomed-in satellite image of the Pemakochung bend and Kintup Falls and compared it with the two Xeroxed photos taken by the British botanist Frank Ludlow, who was in the Upper Gorge in 1947 and recorded 30 species of rhododendrons. The falls looked mean.

The porters gathered in excited groups around the big laminated sat map. They had a surprising grasp of the country and were quick to orient themselves on the big photo. Dave said it was because they were used to looking over the landscape from the vantage of high ridges. They pointed out Pemakochung.

"Senchen La?" they asked. Their tone seemed to be asking, "We're going that far?"

Dave pointed and said, "Po Tsangpo—Pelung." We were now in the lower left-hand corner of the image; the Po Tsangpo was a world away at top center, across dark cliff, splashed snow, and threading river. The porters looked at each other. One pointed to a spot across the map, on the other side of the looping Great Bend, the Lower Gorge, and said, "Luku." A simple statement, his finger dead-on the exact location. It would prove to be prophetic.

. . . .

Before I turned in, I sat on a moss-free rock and wrote. One of the porters, Tu Chu, came over to watch. He was young, maybe 25, with a wide, friendly face. His friend Pin Zo, one of the boys who had offered me food outside Gyala, crowded behind him and looked over his shoulder. They watched the pen skim over the pages of the notebook in silence, following the movements the way one might follow a figure skater. I closed the notebook and pulled two books out of my pack. One was my little *Dhammapada*, the sayings of the Buddha. On the cover was a photograph of a Buddha statue, candlelit and golden. I showed it to Tu Chu. He blinked and took it in both hands, bowed his head, and touched it quickly to his brow. He passed it to Pin Zo, who did the same, and he handed it back and nodded. Then I showed them a collection of Hemingway stories. (I had also brought a slim volume titled *100 More Poems from the Chinese*. Hemingway, Buddha, poetry. Discipline, wisdom, beauty—protein, fat, and carbohydrates.) They were even more inter-

ested in the Hemingway. On the cover was a painting of two men in a
canoe entering choppy water on a river in spruce-fir country with blue
hills in the background. Where I live, I explained. The boys studied it and
talked and pointed. They argued. Their faces lit with smiles.

It was telling: A photo of the Buddha inspired instant reverence and
awe. They handed it back quickly, as if it were too hot to hold. But a little
boat on a river, they loved it. They were hashing out the fine points of
the paddles and the gear. They had dugouts in Pe that no doubt looked
similar. The kayaks were a little over the top, but they could relate to this.
It occurred to me then that paddling wasn't such an odd and alien en-
deavor after all. Nor was hoping to save your soul.

. . . .

Snow and ice filled the gully not far above our camp. We wished the
kayakers good luck—they were going to paddle loaded again and camp
on their own—and we climbed into it. Andrew kicked steps where he
could with his big mountain boots. As we climbed, 1,300 feet straight up,
the snow deepened, and when we broke over the top, we slogged into a
scene of magic. The tall rhododendrons were in full leaf, a solid green
forest of twisted limbs hung with tattered flags of Spanish moss, and underneath, unbroken winter white. It was eerie, like a Louisiana jungle
transposed to the Arctic. And silent. A light breeze stirred the shags of
moss and glimmered the dark leaves, and for the first time on our trip, we
could barely hear the river.

Wallowing in the snow, we followed the trail of the Sherpas out
into a wide, level clearing. Set in the snow was a black lake, unfrozen.
The sacred lake of fire. As we skirted it, each footprint in the snowy,
spongy tundra filled with dark water. I could imagine the awe or terror
of this place when at night the lake flashed with light, and I wondered,
being a Westerner, if there was a scientific explanation. At the far side

of the lake was a scorched fire pit set against a giant fir, the char climbing the red bark; a crossbar on forked sticks to hold a kettle; and a single, threadbare blue prayer flag fluttering on a sapling. The loneliest hunter's camp in the world.

We climbed straight up into the woods. The snow was waist deep now, and there were giant blowdown and looming trees, some eight feet across, and a lower green canopy of 20-foot-high rhododendrons. Another 1,200 feet up. Dustin Lindgren and his old friend Andrew, the two ski models, loved it. Fighting to keep up with Dustin, I asked him why he didn't wear a watch. "Aw, if I had a tattoo, I'd lose it. I tried. I can't keep anything—watches, sunglasses." We climbed over a log and caught our breath, and I looked at his feet. Evidently he had lost his boots, too; he was wearing sneakers in the deep snow. When I mentioned it, he said he'd given his boots to his porter. "My feet love this," he laughed. "They're blocks. It's like they've got a brain of their own and they shut down."

When we finally topped out on the ridge, I took one look east, down the Tsangpo Gorge, and sat down.

Straight below us, 1,400 feet down, were the wooded bench and the meadow of the old monastery pressed against the river. The current was a maelstrom of white. The Tsangpo twisted left around a sinister black cone mountain that vented sulfur—the seat of the Protector, Dorje Draksen. I could smell it. Brimstone. Downstream, the river disappeared between soaring walls, twisting through layer after layer of steep spurs and drainages cutting in from either side, marching eastward into a distant haze.

"We're going there," I thought. Through that corridor. All the way. This was already as remote and wild as I'd ever been, and we were going . . . *there*. It looked impossible, and I could now see why Kintup turned back, and why, when Bailey asked the monks at Pemakochung how they got down the river, they replied, "We don't."

Then I saw the little specks of kayaks just coming into view on the torrent of river, which drops steeper and steeper here, at the heart of the

Gorge, and the magnificence, the audaciousness—the sheer awe—of this project hit me.

Our radios filled with an excited voice.

Willie: "We're in the thick of it now!" Then nothing.

We dropped straight off the cirque. Too steep to walk, not steep enough to rock climb. It was a controlled slide. Slipping and butt sliding, gathering speed, scrabbling to slow down. At one point, Ken recovered from a near spill, turned to me, and said, "This is what wrecked Brashears. He said it was the hardest climb he'd ever done." Ken said that when he got home in '93, his knees didn't stop hurting for months.

At the bottom, we careened out of the woods onto a tumble of sharp, rough moss-covered stone blocks that had fallen off the ridge. Dave and Charlie had charged ahead to get a look at the river from ledges, and again the radios came alive.

"David, we're in heaven. We went on a little nature walk, checked out a bunch of takin and potential cat tracks, and now we're walking back for the boats—this was a full day, David." It was Willie. He sounded charged and exhausted.

Dave: "What do you think of the sneak chute far left?"

Charlie: "It looks good."

Dave: "You could get a couple of Greyhound buses in the hole."

Charlie: "And then some. It all comes straight into the wall, and then there's a spiral—looks pretty terminal."

Dave and Charlie were evidently looking down at Kintup Falls. They were on different outcrops high above it, scouting the lines. That must mean it was possibly runnable.

The rest of us filed into the site of the old monastery, wet and beat. An open grove beside a swampy meadow, tall rhododendrons and some gnarled, leafless fruit trees, and a 10-foot-high stone wall were all that was left. Scattered along the old foundation were stone bowls and ancient bronze lanterns corroded green. We all looked around, quiet. I could tell that the Sherpas were deeply impressed. Every Buddhist in this part of the world knew of Pemakochung. Passang nodded. He said, "Pema, a famous monk, he was born here. Just before the Dalai Lama."

Dustin Lindgren found a two-foot-high statue of the Buddha with the head knocked off. I picked up a small bowl half covered in leaves. It fit in my two palms. I started: I was holding the top of a human skull. I showed it to Tsawong, and he said they were used as special offering bowls for an alcoholic drink called *bali*.

Willie's voice came over the radio: "Just upstream from that cobbled wall is a giant cave, with a creek coming out the mouth."

Charlie: "I came that way, almost fell into it." Pause. Then, "There's a good line this side."

Willie's voice was cheerful but serious: "Okay, you first, bud."

Charlie persisted: "There's a Class I chute right against the wall; then it's all green water." It must have been hard for Charlie, I thought—scouting these mythic drops. For him, too, it was the first time he'd been on the bank as an observer and not in a boat. And he had run rapids as difficult and remote as any that had ever been done, until now.

Pause. Then Andrew's voice. He sounded happy and respectful. He must've been on yet another overlook. "You all are hanging out; someone thinking of running it?"

Willie: "Actually, the boys are tired. We're just kind of having a moment."

Andrew: "I'll give someone five bucks to run it."

Willie: "That's five Canadian? For the sneak or the meat?"

Andrew: "The sneak."

Willie: "How much for the meat?"

Andrew: "Five American, and a copy of the picture I take."

Radio silence for a few minutes. I looked at my watch: 5:07 P.M. Then Charlie again: "Dorje Draksen's fortress is spewing steam from vents, and we smell sulfur." Silence. Then again, with a new tone of excitement: "Dustin's gonna run river-left."

So one of them was going to run it. It would be mild-mannered, chickenpox-speckled Dustin Knapp, the quiet kid who ran more than anybody.

. . . .

The Sherpas set about making dinner, and the rest of us sat on our pads, picked off wood ticks and leeches, and caught up on our journals or read paperbacks. I was talking to Ken and Andrew when a rumble like thunder shook the air, followed by loud cracks and clatters. For a moment no one spoke, everyone's ear turned to the sound. Silence. Then another gunshot trailing off. It was an avalanche loosing out of one of the gullies above us, the third so far this evening. The cracks and clatters were big rocks hurtling into the boulder piles below.

Ken said he and Andrew had been perched on a little rock outcrop at the edge of the woods, looking straight down to the river, and they saw Dustin stroking down the left bank for the falls. "It was wild. He came down, flipped when he hit the first wave at the bottom of the falls, was getting sucked back in—the hole was maybe 200 feet wide—then he rolled back up and pulled it out."

Meanwhile, Andrew had found a limb that stuck straight out over the 200-foot cliff to the river—and started doing chinups.

Ken said, "He thought it was Chinup Falls."

Andrew grinned. I was beginning to think that if he didn't get his minimum daily dose of adrenaline, he might wither up or, worse, turn into a normal person. He said, "Duster was just trying to take the chicken out of his chickenpox."

Dustin told me the next morning that the decision to run had been simple. He was feeling sick and exhausted—he couldn't bear the thought of heaving the boat onto his shoulder again for a long, rocky portage—so he just got back in it and paddled through Kintup Falls.

That night, in their tiny bivy sacks on the swampy ground, under the watchful eye of the Protector, they slept as they hadn't slept all trip.

At dawn, February 11, four porters drew their pay quietly and quit. It was too much. I didn't blame them. Right ahead of us downstream, on river-right, was the scariest-looking obstacle yet: the spur running down from the Namcha Barwa massif called the Kondrasong La, several thousand feet high and so steep it was mostly rock cliff—a sheer buttress that fell right to the water. The porters had waded through the waist-deep snow above the ruins, and they knew that the Senchen La was much higher and steeper. That left 64. "Good riddance" was Dave's attitude, but there was a nagging anxiety among all of us that a trickling away of a few porters might turn into a tide of desertion, à la Brashears.

Everybody needed an easy day. The kayakers were camped below us and in radio contact, and a consensus decision was made that morning to head only about a mile and a half downriver and camp just at the base of the Kondrasong La. That would give us an afternoon off. The river here, just after Kintup Falls, catapulted almost due south in a thrashing straightaway into a tight U-bend around the black fortress mountain. The Tsangpo hugs the mountain, doubling back north on the far side, and then "skids round the Sanglung cliff and plunges away towards the north-east, interrupted by occasional violent jerks to the north and south." The words of Francis Kingdon Ward. He and his companion Lord Jack Cawdor, the Fifth Earl of Cawdor, along with two guides and 20 coolies, were here, moving downstream from the monastery, on November 22, 1924. Their mission was to botanize, collect new and rare seeds, and penetrate the Gorge farther than any Westerner yet—to discover the great falls if they could. Describing this part of the Gorge, Ward wrote:

As the river, rushing like a lost soul between the hot hell in the heart of the Himalaya and the cold hell on the wind-swept peaks which guard the Gorge, grew more dynamic, as the scenery grew harsher, and the thunder of the water more minatory, the touch of Nature came marvelously to the rescue. Everywhere, by cliff and rock and scree, by torn scar and ragged rent, wherever vegetation could get and keep a grip, trees grew; and so, from the grinding boulders in the river-bed to the grating glaciers above, the Gorge was filled with forest to the very brim. 3000m of forest coloured those cold gray rocks of tortured gneiss; and when the summer rain weeps softly over the scene of riot a million trees will flame into flower and strew their beauty over the ruin.

The geologic hell part I could relate to. I was limping now, using the trekking poles like crutches, letting them take all the weight off my left leg. For the paddlers, there was one beefy stretch of rapids down to the next left-turning corner, easily scouted from slabs of mossy granite that the ground team would hike.

. . . .

Willie stood on a slab overlooking the thrashing rapids. It was mid-morning, and the world was blue and white and black-gray. The sky was a depthless winter ether, with stray barkentines of fluffy clouds moving east across it as if under sail. The granite slab was covered in dry black moss. The sun was high over the bristling peaks to the south—Namcha Barwa and, now visible farther along the river, the secondary peak of San-glung, over 23,000 feet. A great frozen river poured down between them, and the sun turned the Sanglung Glacier into a dazzling tide of chopped snow and gleaming ice. A huge fracture line ran across the steepest part. For an undisciplined second, I thought of last night's avalanches and of what might face us on the Senchen La.

160

The river was also white, and very loud. There was a bit of green, too, creamy and aerated with millions of tiny bubbles, in the occasional startled eddy pool behind the biggest rocks. Willie stood in his paddling gear, squinting. Two takin grazed high on the opposite canyon wall, seeming to feed on rock; a single fleck of burnt red was a goral, the mountain goat–like beast, moving in and out of the fir trees.

Willie hummed to himself.

The Tsangpo tumbled down this straightaway toward the Kondrasong La cliffs at the corner as if being sucked down a giant drain. A big orange boulder jutted from the middle of it, and there were nasty holes to either side.

With no holds for hands and feet, Mike and Allan friction climbed to the shallower angle of rock that formed a sort of ledge and joined Willie and me shoulder to shoulder. All the porters sat along the slab, waiting as if for a kickoff.

Willie said, "There's a route." He held out his left hand and made a swooping F-16 jet turn, feeling the acceleration of the right arc that would be activated as soon as he hit the crashing diagonal wave with the whole left side of his body and a hard left stroke. He planned to bounce off the collapsing pile. He would use the diagonal like a powerfully breaking ocean wave to catapult himself right—across the corner of the hole below and into the safety of the eddy, where Charlie stood on a boulder with his camera, looking small. It would be a radical, jarring move.

Willie said, "That's our line."

Allan whistled out his breath. "That's a big rapid."

Mike said, "Right of the big flat orange rock, swing wide in the eddy water and move right."

Willie said, "Hey diddle diddle." He never took his eyes off the water.

Here came Johnnie, hopping nimbly over the slab in his blue drysuit and life vest and all his gear. He joined us, took a deep breath, and looked over the river. He spat, and I saw he had a chew tucked into his upper lip.

"How's the sneak line look, boys?" he said.

Willie slid his eyes toward his twin, a little smile working on his mouth. "You tell us," he said. "We won't say a word. See what you come up with. Take your time with it. She's dotted."

Johnnie cut Willie a look that held a whole lifetime of play and mischief and deep collaboration, ever since they were young teens leaning out over some ridiculous waterfall on their scenic tour map. Johnnie cleared his throat. He began to sketch out a left sneak and stopped himself. "But it pushes you towards the ledge hole," he said.

Willie said, "Uh-*huh*. Now look more toward the middle of the rapid. Spend a little more time with it." Willie was talking to Johnnie as if he were six. "Sorry, I'm coaching you. Sit here and look at it long enough, you can see everything. Almost too much. Nice little camp access right there, though."

Johnnie had told me it was never competitive between them. One day someone might not be feeling 100 percent and walk a rapid; another day it would be somebody else. They'd been doing this, on and off the river, their whole lives. After their father died, Johnnie buckled down in school and became a wickedly proficient forward in lacrosse. Willie did drugs and skipped school and shoved a teacher—without meaning to — and got expelled. Two years later, Johnnie attended Gould Academy, a prep school in Maine. Willie went to a little boarding school, the Hyde School, also in Maine. It changed his life. The Hyde School is a last resort for many kids who have bounced in and out of other institutions. The academics are serious and challenging. The most minor infraction might result in doing hundreds of pushups or cleaning bathrooms with a toothbrush. Community and sports and the out-of-doors are stressed. And perhaps most important to Willie and the fractured Kerns, the school requires that a student's entire family attend a multiday workshop in which they make a commitment as a unit to the student's growth and education.

With this solid expression of support from his family and within the unshakable structure of the curriculum, which scheduled almost every moment, Willie thrived. He was asked to redo his sophomore year. He joined the football team, and, big and strong as he was, with his great heart and the fuel of his anger, he found himself to be a formidable asset. "It was the first time I began to think of myself as an athlete," he said. He did his homework and enjoyed his classes. Soon he was building an Outward Bound–style ropes course with a few teachers and other students, and he became an instructor and safety monitor high in the treetops. He went home on breaks and in the summers—his mother had moved to southern New Hampshire—and fed a growing passion for kayaking with his two brothers.

Johnnie graduated from high school a year earlier than Willie. That summer, Johnnie decided to take a postgraduate year at the Hyde School. He would essentially redo his senior year with his brother to strengthen their relationship and heal the family. The following spring, they played on the same lacrosse team, and they moved in sync like clockwork, Johnnie attacking and Willie defending. No one could stop them.

. . . .

Now Dustin Knapp joined everyone on the ledge. He stood in a little circle of his own complete calm; if he'd had a jacket on, his hands would have been in the pockets cozily, as if he'd just stepped out of a tea shop on a brisk day. His eyes moved slowly, left to right, occasionally pausing for an extra second, moving back up and over a particular spot. "Looks like if you don't mind getting wet, left of center looks okay. Looks like it'll beat you up a little." He sounded about as concerned as if he were trying to decide which corner would give him the best odds of hailing a cab.

"There's the rub," Willie said.

I turned to see that Scott, his brother, and Ken had joined us. Scott carried his helmet and wore, even in the balmy sunlight, his articulated neoprene paddling gloves. He looked up at the glacier. "There's gonna be quite a bit of snow on the Senchen La. We've got snowshoes. We'll send a crew up to pack it out." Faced with this mighty rapid, Scott was already leaning forward into the days ahead.

Dustin Lindgren stuck his chin toward the Kondrasong La. "That doesn't have a lot," he said. "It's about the same height."

Scott turned on his brother and said aggressively, "You think you can get over that bad boy, Dustin, with a kayak on your head?"

Now Steve, the last paddler, hopped up to the overlook and took a 30-second look while Willie showed him the line. "Yuh, good," he said almost to himself, then turned and walked back up to his boat.

They ran. First Allan, then Steve, Willie, and Mike in a spaced line. They bounced down over the entrance waves and swung wide to the right of the orange rock as they'd planned, then worked a bit left in the slower current behind it to set up their charge. They wanted to hit the two viciously curling diagonal waves at the perfect angle and the right momentum. The first lateral crashed over each of them and hurtled them precisely into the slot between holes. It was some of the hugest water I'd ever seen anyone run. When they barreled into the second wave with their left shoulders, it picked them up, crashed over them, and then flung them down, slinging them to the right and perfectly into the next slot, just as they'd planned. It was like getting shot out of a cannon. Willie flipped and rolled fast. They fell into the very corner of the terrible hole they were worried about, but they had so much momentum from the force of the wave that they easily burst through and skated into the eddy behind Charlie's rock. Damn.

Scott stood beside Dustin Knapp, who was filming beside him. "Nice run," he said. "It's all pushing through, bro. Shall we go?"

Shall we go. Into the jaws of Hell.

THE KONDRASONG LA TO KONDRASONG LA FALLS

We camped on a narrow, grassy bluff above a steep bank of huge boulders that tumbled 100 feet to the water. It was 5 P.M., and Dave was sorting loads on the big blue tarp. He looked uncharacteristically grim. Tsawong stood nearby, holding his notebook and pen, counting loads and checking them against his list. Despite his tight, official expression, he seemed lost. Nineteen porters had just announced they were leaving us.

Dave had dug a brick of cash out of his pack and counted out the 100 yuan per day per porter—eight days so far. Then he had added the half pay for return days that is the standard porter formula in the Himalayas, the rationale being that the men had to walk out the way they came and should be compensated for their time. I wouldn't have wanted to walk back out the way we came for any amount of money. It had already been the toughest trek I had ever made.

I worked out the accounting in my head. The return pay meant four extra days at 100 yuan, for a total of 1,200 yuan per porter—$144 American. A fortune for a farmer living in Pe. Times 19, which meant $2,736 out of Dave's bank.

As Dave told me this news, a few porters started leaving—planning, I guessed, to make their own camp back in the ruins. Dave barely looked up. The 45 remaining porters seemed unconcerned. They took turns paddling the extra yellow kayak about the little camp with a stick, with others pushing and dragging them, to much laughter. They nearly scattered the tea fire. Tuli tied a set of takin horns to the front of the Gus, and the men made snorting sounds. They gave each other enders and up-ended one poor guy, who had a rash all over his body that we had deter-mined was not chickenpox. They pitched him past vertical and held his hanging torso over the fire while his laughter turned to cries for mercy and the hilarity of the rest drowned out for a moment the rush of the river.

Scott squatted, chewed a stem of grass, and looked downriver. "The biggest thing now is just making the comparison" between the sat images and actual river. "It's reiterated the fact it's still really hard to tell gradient on the map, but we can tell some of the big rapids. More importantly, we know what's coming up all the time—and that we're not that far from Clear Creek. Once we portage past that one bad section, it's just gonna be a hoof." He was talking about what they called the Northeast Straits, the longest, most constricted blown-out piece, obscured on the sat map.

"It might take us a few days to get over that thing with all the boats." He was still thinking about the Senchen La, as he had been that morning. "Especially now we're down to 45 porters. Hope they all stay now. Orig-inally we thought we could do it with 45—we didn't really have the budget to employ 64."

Willie dug in the pocket of his cargo pants and pulled out a pack of cigarettes. He handed one to Scott and cupped a match and lit Scott's be-fore his own. Scott's hand was red and chafed, with small cracks in the creases. Willie's butt trembled like an aspen leaf. "The other thing that's interesting is that Ken and those guys said that Kintup Falls had changed," Scott said, "which is wild. I am guessing it was only a 15-foot falls.

"One thing I'm still getting used to are the edges on the Gus," he continued, turning the subject to boats. "And that scoop." This was a groove Johnnie had designed into the center of the boat, running along just below the waterline, that was supposed to help the boat carve like a ski. It was catching water and flipping them. Johnnie had designed the

Gus with two challenges in mind: steepcreeking, in which the water is low-flow and you run a lot of waterfalls, and the Tsangpo, where you needed speed and enough volume to pack gear.

Scott said, "I'm putting nothing up front. I'm going full stern-guy. When I sit back, too, it's easier for me to turn. I just think there are two different boats—there's a big-water boat, and a big difference between a big-water boat and a creek boat. The more I paddle big water, the more I like a dynamic, freestyle, play-boating hull."

Scott was talking about the flat-bottomed planing hulls that began to appear in plastic play kayaks in the early 1990s. I remembered seeing the first one on the Gunnison in Colorado, just downstream from where Chuck died. The bottom was as flat as a skillet and looked about as river worthy. The sides of the boat were pretty much flat, too, which made the transition from the bottom to the sides, the chines, square and boxy. "Uuugly," I thought. I asked the owner if I could paddle it out on a breaking surf wave. It skimmed on top of the water and could spin without fighting the water it sat down in. I slid into the trough of the wave, was picked up onto its face, and began to carve back and forth. It's a lovely sensation, like flying, with all the river hurtling underneath you as you skip and veer down the front of the wave, held in place by its steepness. Dang, the boat was quick. I did a couple of doughnuts, like a teenager in a snowy parking lot. This part of the wave was a curling hole, and it had much less boat to grab on to. Rather than sitting down in the water and letting the white pile of the hole build up over the usual rounded "displacement" hull, this boat sliced right into it, under the pile. I surfed back to shore, gave the kayak back to its owner, and said, "Weird." The next week, I bought one.

For the same reasons, kayaks got shorter and shorter over the years. Less length meant less boat for holes to grab, quicker turns, less end to broach and pin. The boats on the Tsangpo were half the length of the original kayaks—the ones developed centuries ago by the native peoples of the Arctic. Those boats were perfectly suited for hunting on the open ocean and landing through surf. They were made of skin stretched over light, rugged frameworks of wood. Bone was used at strategic points for flex. The paddler sat in a small cockpit sealed with a skin sprayskirt. Inuit paddlers were said to surf shore break for fun, dexterously maneuvering through the crashing walls of water.

The first Western designs were ingenious derivatives of the Eskimo boats. The most popular were called foldboats, or folding kayaks, and the first commercial designs were manufactured in Germany by Klepper, beginning in 1907. The company is still thriving today—I took two of their boats to sea kayak in Cuba a couple of years ago. The early frames were made of interlocking and jointed strips of wood, and the skin was rubberized cloth and canvas. The skin could be peeled off, the skeleton folded, and the whole affair bagged for a ride through the Alps on a train.

Foldboats were among the first kayaks launched on whitewater rivers. The men and women who piloted them were brash. They often wore no helmets or lifejackets, and any sharp rock could shred their hulls. I say "piloted" because the kayaks turned with the agility of an oil tanker. In 1938, three French paddlers—one of them a woman, Genevieve de Colmont—paddled foldboats on the Green and Colorado rivers, making it to Phantom Ranch, halfway through the Grand Canyon. In the next few years, Alexander "Zee" Grant Jr., of the Appalachian Mountain Club, took his foldboat all the way through the Grand Canyon and down other runs that would become Western whitewater classics, like the Middle Fork of the Salmon in Idaho. When you paddle these runs in a modern, hard-shelled kayak specifically designed for whitewater, freed by the evolution of materials from the native paradigm of skin and bone, you realize how brave those foremothers and forefathers were.

My first kayak was made of fiberglass and Kevlar, and I seamed the deck and the hull together and laid up a seat in the winter of '79 in a poorly ventilated shack by the Connecticut River in New Hampshire. At

Dartmouth's Ledyard Canoe Club, we'd never heard of OSHA; the fumes sent us stumbling out into the snow, giddy and light-headed, and slayed brain cells by the millions. The result was a 13-foot hard shell and a C in calculus. The boat had a shallowly rounded displacement hull and a peaked deck to shed water, sleekly tapered and pointed at both ends. A tennis ball was duct taped to the bow for protection and the safety of fellow paddlers. I thought it was the slickest craft on Earth.

The boat I paddled every afternoon in a play hole in the summer of 2003 is made of super-linear plastic, is six feet long, with a flat hull and sides and squared-off ends, and looks like nothing so much as a teal-colored brick. It's designed specifically for freestyle playing in waves and holes, but I've taken its seven-foot progenitor comfortably down easy Class V rapids.

Johnnie's Gus had a "moderately" planing hull, not quite pancake flat. Allan and Mike's boats, on the other hand, called the H2 Zone and made by the British manufacturer Pyranha, were two inches shorter and had true planing hulls. Willie said, "Yeah, I watch Al and Mikey surf and think, 'Yeah, it'd be fun to surf like that,' but if I put my gear and my 200 pounds in that boat, I'd be sunk. And with those little rails underwater, a big function of that is knowing when they're gonna grab. It's an evolution. It's gonna go from here. This is by no means the end. This is Johnnie's first go, took a lot of thoughts from a lot of people, made a great boat. He's got a couple more boats on his contract—it's awesome."

Scott returned like a terrier to what was most on his mind. He said, "We're not gonna have enough porters to carry the boats over the pass. We're gonna have to carry them."

There was a respectful pause in the rhythm of the conversation as everybody considered that prospect.

As the sun set behind the Namcha Barwa massif and haloed the highest ridges with fire, Dustin Lindgren and Andrew came into camp carrying a bouquet of huge rose-red rhododendron blossoms. Ken pushed his glasses up his nose and said, "It's early spring in the Gorge." And I thought again of the cold melt creeks pouring off the glaciers into the Tsangpo and how the boys had better hurry up and run whatever they were going to run.

. . . .

On Day 10, after breakfast, Dave called a meeting. The porters gathered in a rough semicircle, fingering their prayer beads. Tuli, who knelt on one knee, was the oldest. His puttees were wrapped neatly up his calves, and he looked clean and fresh. Behind him, standing, was a group of boys probably not much older than 18. One wore a pink knit sweater vest and a cheap pair of Terminator sunglasses propped in his curly hair.

Dave began speaking. In a measured voice, in the cadenced Kiwi accent that rose at the end of his sentences, he explained that some porters had left, which was all right because they had been going through the heavier food fast. But now they were pushing on into the most serious part of the Gorge, and he needed a commitment from the rest that they would go all the way through now, to Pelung at the end. He said that we were making history and that the only way the expedition would succeed was if we all worked as a team. He said that we would take care of them and that if they went all the way, he would give them a bonus.

Tsawong pushed his hair out of his face and interpreted. When he finished, Dave's fine speech—clearly morphed and sounding less conciliatory from Tsawong—hung in the air. Some of the porters nodded. Then Tuli spoke, low and fast. Before he finished, a dozen other voices tumbled over his; Dave held up his hands for them to wait, and it had begun. In the rush of comments, Tsawong tried to interpret one and then another; then he gave up and, his voice rising indignantly, started arguing with them on his own. The kid in the pink sweater hissed, vehement.

Dave yelled, "One at a time!" and bent his ear to Tsawong, who had literally gotten his back up: He stood erect, blinking, ruffled. The gist was that the porters wanted tomorrow off, as it was Tibetan New Year.

Fine. Done, Dave diplomatically agreed. Cultural sensitivity and all that.

They also wanted extra half pay for every day they worked at the end. *What?*

They wanted half-days' return pay. An extra 50 percent.

Dave held up his hands as if trying to stem a breach in a levee. Whoa. "You will take a bus home from Pelung. Three days at most. We'll pay your bus fare and for those three days."

They didn't want to take a bus home. They wanted to walk back through the Gorge! Therefore, they wanted full return pay. It's what the 4 who quit at Pemakochung got, and the other 19 who left yesterday; fair is fair.

Dave shook his head. "You're not walking all the way back through the bloody Gorge. That's ridiculous."

Yes, we are, they said. We could start right now.

Now I understood why none of the porters had looked concerned when the others quit and were paid off. It was a bonanza. The Teamsters had nothing on these guys. It wasn't a strike, exactly; it was sophisticated labor relations.

The expedition hung in the balance. Dave straightened himself and said, "Fine. You'll get return pay." Immediately, the porters broke and began collecting their loads. Rob told me later, as were making our way up the rock face, that he and Dave acceded because they had to. "It's fucking highway robbery is what it is," he said. "We'll sort it when we get to Pelung. They'll get what's bloody fair."

I thought, "Really? A deal's a deal, isn't it?" Dave and Rob had just made an agreement in poor, if not bad, faith. On the other hand, I probably would have done the same thing.

171

. . . .

Willie Kern was screaming. His yells carried no farther than his waving arms and were overwhelmed by the crash of the river. Without looking, he leaped across a five-foot gap between high boulders on the bank, keeping his eyes fastened on the orange hull of his brother's boat as it was swept upside down into the maw of a death rapid.

The kayakers were now in nearly the narrowest and steepest part of the Gorge: Walls of broken gneiss thousands of feet high fell from the back side of Dorje Draksen's fortress and from the Kondrasong La spur.

The rapids fell in a steep triple drop. The first objective was to get across the river, right to left. The target was the lower edge of a rock on the opposite shore; just behind it was a safe eddy. Between the men and the eddy was all the unleashed fury of the Tsangpo, barreling through this narrow inner Gorge. After they ferried, they had to break through a high wall of wave that curled off the rock and fed like a funnel into the center of the river. Out from the edges, the main current was so powerful and deadly that you entered it only as the last option.

Johnnie was following Scott and Dustin in the must-make sprint to the far bank. In a ragged line, the three paddlers poured on their most powerful strokes, crashing through breaking waves and skirting deep, gnashing holes. Nobody wanted to be there. Here the river dropped so steeply, it simply fell out of sight: From a kayak, you couldn't see more than 20 yards ahead.

Scott blasted through and splashed safely into the pool. Dustin hit the foam pile of the lateral and his bow dropped; he was thrown vertically, did a perfect pirouette, and, facing the hole, slammed down onto his hull and paddled in. But when Johnnie hit the wave, it surged, exploded, and tossed his kayak like a toy. Upside-down and airborne, it landed back in the main current.

Willie was all motion. He remembered that Johnnie had not gotten out of his boat and scouted the rapid on his own. He was therefore now paddling blind. If he rolled up—*Fuck a duck, Johnnie, ROLL UP!*—and then survived the violent thresh of the breaking wave that would hit him next, Johnnie would see a slackening of current to the left. His instinct would be to work his way to the left shore.

But what Johnnie could not see from river level was what had Willie screaming: The flattening left side of the river cascaded over a broad ledge and into a maelstrom of backwash that no man would ever come out of alive. In a few seconds, Johnnie would paddle to his death.

Johnnie rolled up, slammed into the seething white pile of the next wave, and disappeared. He was spat out the other side and rolled up again, terrified. He shook his head clear, saw the deceptively inviting line ahead of him down the left, and began to turn his boat. Just then, for no apparent reason, he glanced at the right bank, directly at his brother. Willie was cutting the air wildly, both arms up and straight, palms facing, frantically mouthing the word *CENTER!* Allan was behind Willie, doing the same. Johnnie growled, spun his boat back to the right, aimed it straight down the river's throat, and dug in. He ran the next horizon line blind and caught an eddy.

Steve came right after Johnnie. He hit the lateral and got rejected as well, thrown into the middle of the river. As he roller-coastered over the second of the 10-foot waves that fell into the giant breaker, the blade on the right side of his paddle came unglued. Steve hit the wave with his one good blade. The curler buried and flipped him. He rolled inside the pile, fought through it, and became a possessed canoeist. It's very tough to use only one blade sitting down in a kayak. Stroking with all his skill, the paddle shaft vertical as he dug in, Steve went over the next drop and fought with half a paddle over to a shore eddy off the right bank. He barely made it. Dustin, who'd seen Steve's paddle break and pulled out to chase him, said, "You knew he was okay when you saw half a paddle go flying into the rocks. He was yelling. He tore the Riot sticker off his boat and cut it in half."

. . . .

Once, in the Adirondacks, I was biking back from swimming with my girlfriend in the local swimming hole when I saw a station wagon collide with a pickup on the country road. After the violent sound of impact and the sudden silence filled with the ticking and hissing of the engines and the falling of one last piece of glass, the crickets resumed and the cooling evening breeze flowed out of the woods. One of the drivers was dead, the other unharmed. I ran into an outfitter's shop across the road, and within minutes, the evening was filled with flashing lights, officers, the staticky voices of emergency radios. The next morning, there were glass, debris, and stains on the tarmac to remind us.

A death on a river is somehow even more disturbing. One moment the water tumbles around a bend, raucous with waves, pillowing around rocks, lapping and ripping the shore, and paddlers descend in bright boats. The next moment a boat is upside-down, pressed into the sieve of a downed tree or undercut rock, the hull piling with current, gleaming in the sun. You retrieve the body, however long that takes, and you stand in shock on the shore, and the river flows just as it did. The rush and sift and gurgle. The rapid looks the same; it is innocent, as beautiful as moving water always seems. What is cleaved is your own heart, and the past from that moment, and the sense that you can ever relive anything.

Willie wrote blithely in his journal that after Johnnie recovered from being swept by the main flow, he was "shaken but not stirred." That nonchalance was Willie's protection. He knew as well as anyone that a different outcome had been a hairsbreadth away. Had Johnnie been anything less than the ice-water-in-the-veins, superb kayaker I had seen here and in movies, or had Steve been unable to fight through his line with half a paddle and a single blade in what was approaching a Class VI rapid, death would have come as swiftly, as simply, as this: a kayak swept upside down over the next horizon line.

When the ground team broke out onto the rocks of the bank, we found the kayakers huddled around a small fire in a nook of cliff, eating a pot of curried couscous and drinking tea. They were unnaturally subdued. Not dazed, exactly, but shocked into reticence. Scott had the keyed-up inwardness of a man who has just been in a brawl. Charlie, ever sensitive, said gently, "You guys all right? Looks pretty tough up there. . . ."

Kayakers are like fishermen, and the story will out. Steve frowned. "The fucking glue failed," he said. He had continued down the river with Willie's extra breakdown paddle, which was for just such emergencies.

No one was in much of a hurry to get back in the water. The sixth inning had been pretty rough, and the seventh-inning stretch was attenuating into a . . . well, baseball isn't such a good analogy. War is more accurate. This was Day 10 of a battle whose outcome was never sure. The clambering over two-story boulders, the scouting and portaging and constant uncertainty, as well as the ice-cold water and relentlessness of the rapids, were taking their toll. As was the power of the river. Altitude must have been a factor, too. For the first time, the river squad looked tired. They were marshaling their strength for the assault on the Northeast Straits. There wasn't far to go today. The sat map showed one more major drop, and then the river jogged southeast and eased off for about a mile, collecting itself before veering right-angle left into the blown-out corridor of the straits. So there was time for a break.

It occurred to me that now most of them had had scarily close calls. The only ones who remained relatively unscathed were Mike, Allan, and Scott. They were also the paddlers with by far the most experience on Himalayan rivers; I wondered if it was coincidence and didn't think so. They had gained maturity in the world's most adverse river conditions and probably unconsciously treated the Tsangpo with more respect. Steve was Achilles in this Iliad, the one with the most confidence and hubris, and I wondered if he, too, was learning the wisdom of moderation. He and Willie and Dustin—and now Johnnie—had all been grabbed by the river and shaken like Leda by the swan.

In Yeats's stunning poem, Zeus transforms himself into a swan, swoops down, grasps Leda's neck in his bill, and ravishes her. The last two lines read: "Did she put on his knowledge with his power / Before the indifferent beak could let her drop?" The question is central to what I wonder about the paddlers on the Tsangpo—and all of us, really—as we move through her Gorge.

. . . .

The paddlers ran over a horn of rock, threading death hydraulics, and down into a house-size wave that rocketed them to the far shore. Then they paddled around the corner and discovered a new waterfall.

Ken said it was new. They called it Kondrasong La Falls. There was nothing like it in any of our old photographs, and it roared like it was new in the world, like a rambunctious teenager, but of course it wasn't. It was millennia or even eons old, probably. It hadn't been written about because the other parties of the past century avoided the exposed rock face skirting the Kondrasong La and came over it higher up, the way Ken had in 1993. Or maybe it *was* newly formed, at least the current shape of it. Floods and earthquakes changed things fast in the Gorge. They had shrunk Kintup Falls from what Bailey described as a 30-footer in 1913. They created rockslide dams and then cut through them in a heartbeat to form Steve's Rapid up at the top. This was one of the most geologically active spots in the world, so anything was possible.

You didn't have to be a geologist to take one look at the thing and decide to walk around it, unless you were a Kern. The twins looked at it, squinting the way a kid studies the tall pine tree his brother has just dared him to climb. Willie stroked his beard, which made him look, technically, like an adult. Steve gave the falls a look, too, of course. "Ah," he said. "Yuh." Then, "Look at that too long and you'll have to piss."

It was the entire Tsangpo necked down to 30 yards of width and dropping in a ramp about 25 vertical feet. The boiling current crashed into a pile of rocks 40 yards farther downstream at about 30 knots. There was an eight-foot slot between two of the biggest rocks.

Willie said, "Good idea, pissing."

Steve said no, he had tightly scheduled piss stops. "I've got it down to no pissing at night."

"Wow—and none during the day?" I said. "Your drysuit has no fly?" (Most of them had added strategic waterproof zippers.)

Steve half turned. "Nope—I allow myself one piss in the morning and one in the evening."

Willie grinned. "Like an apartment-house dog."

He pointed to the gap in the rocks and said that's where they'd run it if it were roadside. But getting upside-down in the falls and not rolling up in time would plaster a boater against the big rock. I couldn't see how being roadside would add much to the chances of survival.

Meanwhile, the other four, who knew right away they weren't tangling with this monster, were—what were they doing? They were ferrying across the river and bouncing down through little ledges and boulders off the left bank. Then, at the very lip of the falls, they shot into a small eddy against the wall. It was ballsy. The eddy was infused with bubbles as if with a kind of hydrologic anxiety. Miss the eddy and get sucked over the edge and become jetsam, no question.

They got out and carried their boats onto a ledge of sloping, smooth bedrock 15 feet above the tailwater beneath the falls. The water was sliding fast in a black pan straight into an undercut wall that curved out from the left. One after another, they tucked into their kayaks and shoved off the rock platform. Like a high dive, airborne, hitting and buoying out and sprinting hard away from the long blank wall.

Dustin was third. He bobbled out of the water and began his sprint and misjudged. The river tugged him straight down into overhung cliff. Usually, in a rapid, he never looked like he was working too hard. Now he did. His paddle flailed at a blurring rpm. He wasn't going to make it. The wall was 100 feet across, and he was going to smack the middle. Where the water piled into the face, it formed a hump of "reaction wave" like a bow wake, a pillow of water curling back away from the rock. Dustin spun his stern into it—he was a few feet from his Maker for sure, and the wave picked him up and he surfed across it. He surfed just in front of the wall, gliding—like a bead on a string. I watched him, frozen. A loss of speed, a slight bobble, and he'd be plastered, shoved under the slope of the rock. All the way to the last jutting corner he flew, and the wall fell away and he paddled around it and was free. I yelled in relief. Tsangpo whitewater was maybe harder on an observer.

We made camp in deep woods below the falls, at the brink of the Northeast Straits. Tomorrow was Tibetan New Year and Tibetan Day Off and my 43rd birthday. The boys would try to scout the mile-and-a-half corridor of blown-out, photo-paper white.

. . . .

We were playing Shithead away from the smoky fire with the nude Chinese playing cards, and the younger porters were leaning in, very interested, but not in strategy. Scott was in a mood and sat off by himself and didn't want to talk about the day. Steve was talking about elephants.

Allan laid down an ace in a very partial sailor outfit and said, "Mrs. Willie Kern."

"Elephants," Steve said. "I paddled up to these two males wrestling full-on in the water. They stopped, looked at me for a moment, then kept going. They sniff you with the ends of their trunks."

Allan tossed down a four of clubs stretched out on a bearskin rug.

"My friend handed one big male his paddle," Steve continued. "He took it in his trunk, tasted it, and handed it back."

Mike said, "Hippos look cuddly, eh? But they're bad to the bone." Probably egging Steve on.

"Yuh, the worst." Steve told how they run canoe trips for paying clients on the Upper Zambezi in inflatable "ducky" kayaks. He said, "You've got to be really, really careful. The hippo can submerge for 20 minutes. But usually it's 5 to 7. So you've got to look 7 minutes ahead of you downriver. Always have someone out ahead with binoculars. They have two big tusks. Their upper teeth are molars and the tusks come up and they grind them against the molars. Razor sharp."

He said four of his buddies were paddling one day through a big pool, and a hippo came up and took his friend. Took him down like a croc taking a duck.

Everybody looked at Steve.

"He was pierced and drowning. My friend Paul paddled in to help him, and a hippo took him, too."

Steve studied the cards in his hand. Nobody moved. And?

His sleepy eyes came up. "He got a tusk through his body here and one that went through the bone of his arm. He got a prosthetic arm and later paddled the source to the sea on the Zambezi, 2,000 miles, through the huge whitewater. He and the doctor who gave him the arm raised a ton of money for getting rid of land mines in Mozambique. When you paddle the Zambezi, you don't wander off on the river-right side. There are a lot of land mines. Signs everywhere. You can hear the daily explosions, from the de-mining. They get 10 together and detonate them. Makes quite a bang."

That night before I turned in, I saw Tsawong looking up through the trees like a lost acolyte, unsure where to turn. I said hi. He said, "This very sacred place. Very special." He was talking about the whole Gorge. Then he told me that his wife was three months pregnant. Their first. They had lost two others to miscarriages.

"I'm sorry."

He tilted his head sideways, a nod half of thanks, half of resignation. I fingered the protection string at my throat and looked at him straight on before I realized my headlamp was blinding him. His blinking almond eyes were deep. His hands were long and slender. He looked too delicate for this rough country and for the abuse heaped on him from both sides. He reminded me of the androgynous bronzes of the bodhisattva Avalokiteshvara, except that he had two fewer arms and 10 fewer heads.

He told me that before he left Lhasa, he had asked his cousin, a religious painter, to make a *tanka* for his baby's protection. *Tankas* are scrolled hanging paintings of mandalas and of the Buddhist pantheon, commissioned for karmic merit and providence. When he was in the Lower Gorge in '98 with the Chinese, they were camped above the river, and he woke up in the middle of the night and heard Dakinis singing. A Dakini is a kind of Buddhist angel.

"Are you sure they were Dakinis?"

"Yes."

"What did they sound like?"

Tsawong closed his eyes and made a keening sound, high and wavering.

"Like Shania Twain?" I said.

Tsawong cocked his head. "Yes."

CHAPTER TEN

NORTHEAST STRAITS TO PINE CAMP

The takin did not want to be eaten, and neither did Charlie. The tracks in the mud of the steep slope were of a large cat and a takin. Each cat print measured four inches across. It was quite possibly the mountain tiger that hunts on the slopes of Namcha Barwa. The frenzied takin had skidded and scrabbled downhill, barging through dense thickets and breaking down small trees. The cat tracks were like neat punctuation. A dot-dash Morse code of mad panic and determined hunger. They were very fresh. Rough crumbs of dirt lay in them, unsmoothed by rain, and the musk smell lingered.

Dave and Ken were breaking trail halfway to the next camp. It was called Beach Camp, a river-level nook in the cliff of the right bank that marked the end of the Straits on the sat image. Charlie was moving along by himself as close above the river as he could. His was one of the hardest assignments. He was charged by the editors of *Outside* to get the action shots on his Nikon, and he wasn't in a boat on the river. It meant he spent a lot of time breaking away from the ground team and charging solo through jungle, down to wherever he thought he could get a good vantage. If we were trekking a couple of hundred miles and gaining 30,000 feet of total elevation, Charlie was probably tacking on an extra 30 percent.

He heard crashing in the trees above him and wondered why the other guys were making such a racket, and then Dustin Lindgren's voice filled his Talkabout.

"Dustin to Charlie: A cat's been chasing a takin at pretty close quarters downhill. Tracks real clear. So keep your eye open for a big cat eating a takin along the river."

Charlie froze. He keyed his mike. "Copy that!" The crashing was way too close. He did not want to see a tiger eating a takin anywhere when he was alone with nothing but $5,000 worth of camera gear to protect him.

On the river, the paddlers were beside themselves with excitement. While the Tibetans took a day off, the boys planned to scout as much of the straits as they could, then run the next day. It was the steepest section yet, and the most walled in, but they ran the rapid below camp without a hitch, and then they encountered rock bank along the left, beneath the cliffs. The low-water gambit was paying off in spades. The first thing Willie said when he appeared out of the trees that afternoon was "She's giving it up for us!" His hair was wild. He had left his helmet and life vest and sprayskirt in his boat by the river, and the arms of his drysuit were tied around his waist. "We're gonna be able to run the first three rapids!"

Passang Sherpa set a large pot of dal lentils on a tripod of rocks over the cooking fire. He said, "Maybe God is with you."

"Yah, that'd be the first time!" said Allan. Which wasn't true, or he wouldn't have been standing there.

. . . .

There was a renewed energy. After so many months and years of anticipation, the last dreaded section of the Upper Gorge looked at least navigable. Dave was happy. He'd had a day off from porter wrangling. Charlie had an air of gratitude about him. Dave dropped his lightened daypack and announced, "Charlie almost got eaten by a panther!" Before he could get a cup of tea, two of the porters, the pudgy one with the body rash and one of the boys, hovered beside him. "What?" Dave snapped. The sad, fat one lifted his shirt and showed his rash again and grimaced. The other held his jaw. Scott winced with irritation. "Give 'em antacid."

"Afraid that's all I can do you for, mates," Dave said. "I'm no doctor." He gave the porter with the rash antacid and the one with the toothache two ibuprofen.

The Sherpas brought four big pots of food to our fire. Jangbu had surpassed himself for Tibetan New Year. We had curried green beans and lamb, deep-fried whole potatoes, and noodles. Afterward, Kannuri brought out an apple-banana cake frosted with a layer of Scott's chocolate Enlarge drink thickened over the fire. A large emergency candle was stuck in the middle, and the boys sang "Happy Birthday" to me. It was just getting dark. Scott talked about money and time. He said something about Mr. Liang telling him that the road from Pelung was open only on the 11th, the 15th, and the 21st—which sounded like a load of bull, but Scott had to give him the benefit of the doubt. "The 11th is 26 days from now. If we go past that, I won't have enough to pay the porters. As it is," he said, "we don't have enough to get home. That's another phone call I have to make."

With LED headlamps casting a blue glow over the two poster-size photographs of the river, we went over the days from here.

One day to Beach Camp at the end of the straits.

One day to Pine Camp high on the bluff.

One day to Clear Creek.

Equals three days.

A couple of days over the Senchen La.

A few days to climb down and see Hidden Falls. Willie wanted to cross the river above the falls and explore the view from the steep ridge. "What a fucking historic opportunity," he said, "to look down a stretch of the Tsangpo no man has ever seen." He'd get a view of the "Ten-Mile Gap" that Bailey left unexplored and that Kingdon Ward missed; Ward had climbed up onto the Senchen La without ever seeing it. It was called in recent literature the Lost Five Miles, the part that had not been reconnoitered by trekking upstream from the confluence. No Westerner had ever looked into it. Scott and the paddlers were interested in scouting it for a possible kayak run, maybe splitting the team and sending a few paddlers along the river-right rim, but if anything above had been steep, walled in, constricted, and totally blown out on the photos, this thread of river was more so. It was Oreo—black cliffs, pure white filling. Such a total *taco*, as Willie liked to say.

As they talked, the wash of blue light circled and converged on the straight run of the Lost Five Miles, which stretched like a bead of acrylic caulk from Hidden Falls to the confluence with the Po Tsangpo. Most of the group thought we needed to concentrate on getting over the Senchen La. Scott said he didn't want to waste resources and time scouting a stretch of river that was probably unrunnable. Instead, he said he was leaning toward getting over the Senchen La to Payi and running the river from a cable bridge below the confluence down to Luku, about 20 river miles. I saw a decision forming: complete the historic run of the Upper Gorge at Clear Creek and then make an attempt on the Lower Gorge below the confluence. Time was a problem, and not only because they might run out of money and food; we were seeing more and more signs of the coming spring, which would pump the Tsangpo with volume. The rhododendron blossoms were reminders to keep moving.

But what about the porters? Why not relieve some at Payi and send them home? Rob pointed out that the rest of the porters would revolt when they saw they weren't getting the same deal as the ones who had quit at Pemakochung. The short-timers got return wages equal to four-sevenths of their total pay, while the others would get only half wages for the few days' trek and bus ride home.

Wait: Hadn't all the porters been promised return wages? Yes. The agreement had been made under duress, but it was still in bad faith. Sooner or later, all of this was going to come to a head, and it wouldn't be pretty.

The consensus was to keep the core group of porters all the way to Pelung. If local chieftains along the way insisted on our hiring their porters, a tradition called *ula* . . . "Well," Charlie said, "we've got 50 guys more. We've got an army."

Dave said, "I'm tempted to fuck off a bunch of our porters and make them walk back the way they came."

Charlie said, "They'd slit our throats at night."

On that reassuring note, we turned in.

. . . .

Valentine's Day, and the river was giving Willie some tough love. So far they had carried only six drops on the whole river, plus a few hops around ledges, and they had paddled more than 90 percent of the river. They had said back in California that if they paddled 50 percent, they'd be doing well. But this, the Northeast Straits, was a whole new ball of wax.

At the very entrance to the straits, the Tsangpo grabbed Willie in his boat, shook him, and tossed him aside like a bone from a dog's mouth. Four strokes into the first drop, he hit a crashing lateral wave; it was bigger than he thought, and it surfed him toward the tearing middle of the river, which disappeared over one horizon line after another. Exactly where no one in a boat should be. And just as he got there, the current grabbed and buried his stern and he was thrown into a giant back-ender, airborne. It launched him up and over two boat lengths farther to the right. *Shit, I'm getting shot over 20 feet before I have a chance to roll.*

They had scouted this yesterday, and he knew what the rest of the rapid was like.

He rolled up immediately. That extended his life for another minute. But when he rolled, he was surfing something, shoved sideways against a breaking hump of water—a hole? A breaking wave? Desperately, he braced, sculling his paddle blade against the collapsing foam pouring off the hump, trying to stay upright, and all the while the current shoved him higher and higher up the mound of water.

Johnnie watched his brother, helpless. Willie was alone. The Tsangpo, all of it, necked down into the narrow chasm and dropped away as it hadn't done before, with a reverberating fury unmatched by anything they had seen above. It dropped out of sight. In here, the Tsangpo was plunging 200 to 250 feet per mile—almost double the gradient of some of the record-breaking stretches above. The force of the river was shoving Willie higher and higher up the hump, and at the crest, he realized it wasn't a wave at all; it was the face of a giant boulder covered by current. He'd been surfing the pillow of a pourover. He looked straight down the back side into the afterlife.

The bottom of a big pourover is like the bottom of a dam, with massive, aerated towback pulling surface water into the rock. He was going to fall straight into it. In a flash, Willie saw that if he could make it back toward the middle of the river, back left, there was a ribbon at the corner of the hole, a thread of current pushing through. He was sideways to the river. As he was swept over the top, he took two vigorous backstrokes and landed smack on the ribbon and came through. Charged with adrenaline overdrive, he surfed waves back to the left shore and caught an eddy and his breath.

The others, chastened and educated by Willie's run, treated the first lateral wave with due respect and broke through it, holding a safe line down the left.

That was the first rapid.

. . . .

Ken and I climbed and traversed, loose dirt giving way under our boots, and came upon Dustin Lindgren sitting on the ground alone, nodding his head to music from his big headphones. He pushed back the headset, looking relieved.

"This is where the panther got the takin," he said. I could hear Monster Magnet pulsing from the headphones. "Tell you the truth, that's why I waited for you guys. I didn't want to be alone up here. That's when the big cat gets you."

So young Lindgren wasn't absolutely fearless. I didn't tell him that technically there were no panthers in the Gorge, just tigers and leopards. Then he said, "But if you gotta go, that wouldn't be a bad way. Get killed by a mountain lion. You'd be up in Heaven, sittin' around, and one guy'd say, 'I got killed in a car wreck.' And you'd say, 'I got eaten by a mountain lion.' It'd be cool."

If the kid felt fear, it was irrelevant. It's all about the story.

Scott's film *Aerated*, the one they'd completed just before the trip, begins with a sequence of a guy in a kayak lowering himself a few feet from the underside of the 750-foot-high Foresthill Bridge, near their office in Auburn. Then he releases the harness. Holy shit. A second later, he opens a parachute. With consummate skill, he guides the boat down into the ravine and splashes neatly into the water. It's elegant, unprecedented, and near nuts. Dustin said they practiced the release mechanism again and again from a tree in the backyard. Wonder who thought that one up.

I had just been telling Ken as we climbed that I thought the paddlers lived their lives weaving a tapestry of stories. Ken did, too, in a more periodic manner. In Minneapolis, when he was not at home taking bulk orders for Scrabble, he voraciously read the accounts of old explorers—another way of staying immersed in the narrative.

Modern-day adventurers do much of what they do in creation of story. The tales pour out at the fire; they are savored and added to. One man's episode becomes part of another's repertoire, and the stories multiply and intertwine. It seemed like a wonderful, archaic way to live. Who lives like that anymore? Hollywood subsumes more and more of that part of our consciousness and lures us into the gray smog of routine, of consuming and producing, of a mass-produced narrative. We need adventurers to create new, vibrant stories. It's the blood of our humanity. Dustin didn't want to be tiger food, but if it happened, he wouldn't bitch in Heaven.

He died to save us from a humdrum life. . . .

. . . .

The seven kayakers hugged and creeked down the left bank as they'd planned. Willie hit the last eddy off the shore. This was it. Just below, the left bank was pinched off by cliff. This was the must-make ferry across the Tsangpo to more rocky margin, across a 20- to 30-knot current right above the meanest rapid.

Willie went for it. He set his angle—a slight diagonal upstream—and laid into it. The ideal ferry angle, maybe 20 degrees, was guarded by a big hole just below. The trick was to drop below the hole and then ferry just in front of a 50-foot-wide rock in the middle of the river, maybe riding up on it a bit. Right in front of the rock there was a critical midpoint, a kind of continental divide; once he crossed it, the current sluicing off the far side would carry him around. But should he stall out and come up short, he'd get tugged around the near side of the rock, fall into a slot, and disappear.

The rest of the team swooped into the little eddy, boats knocking against each other, and watched. Willie charged across the first bit of current and got in immediate trouble. When he opened up the angle of his bow to drop below the seething hole, he lost momentum. He was being tugged right down into the left slot. A moment's hesitation, wondering if he should just give up, cut his losses right now, and try to return to the left shore before he got sucked into the gap. No, he'd go for it. Facing upstream, he slid across and hit the pillow of the rock and rode up on it. Yes! Maybe he could surf across it. . . . He windmilled his paddle; sprinting with all his might, inching across the pillow, moving right, he might make it—he was expending all his energy—*after the rock there was the rest of the river to cross*—the current pouring around the left side of the rock sucking him, fighting him, pulling him back left.

It's like a dream where you run as hard as you can and get nowhere. He didn't make it.

He was maybe one stroke away from breaking to the far side when he fell off, to the left, into the slot, and disappeared over the horizon.

Johnnie blinked. There was the boiling river, the hole, the rock, the gap. And no Willie.

They were out of their boats. It was automatic. Paddles thrown up onto the rocks. Rocky bank for a little ways downstream before cliff walled them in. Boats tugged and shoved onto the boulders. Standing, hopping, looking.

There was Willie on the bank, bringing his kayak to his shoulder, patting the top of his helmet: *I'm okay.*

He was alive only because he was that good and had the presence of mind as he was swept through the gap to spin and rocket back to shore, to the last tiny eddy that would save his life. He had seen it the day before, when the possibility of missing the ferry first entered his mind, and he'd noted the one escape route. Now there was only one option: to do it over again. There was no way out of the inner canyon but to ferry. He got right back in his boat. Steve grabbed his throw rope and hopped down the bank to stand in the slot above Willie's safety-valve eddy. It was the only time on the Tsangpo they set a rope.

Scott and Allan and Mikey cleaned it. Willie thought they made it look a lot easier than he remembered it being. So he launched again. "I made it with fuckin' 20 yards to spare. . . ." And then, safely in the eddy on the far side of the river, he had to watch the last three. But the rock blocked a view of the critical move. They didn't see Dustin get up on the peak of the rock and swoop down off the very top of the pillow with so much speed that he blasted across the far side of the river higher than anyone, hitting the shore yards above the Last Chance Eddy where everyone else pulled out. The vegan Clark Kent.

Willie said, "This is the fuckin' promised land as far as we're concerned. We made the crux."

The kayakers portaged a rapid, but the rock got too steep to traverse, and the only way to get back into the river was through a small tunnel or cave formed by massive rocks. The water surged into it and washed violently up onto a ledge. They had to set their boats on the wet rock and get in fast and seal the sprayskirts around the coamings before the next surge flooded the cockpits, then time their launches so they weren't crushed in the cave. Scott missed, and the surge shoved him to the roof of the cave and smashed him to the deck of his boat. They thought he was toast. But he held on to his paddle, and when the water dropped, he pushed himself through.

They slipped along the bank and got out and carried their boats up through a shoal of rocks that headed to bedrock. Scott got on the radio: "You know the biggest stepped drop? We're right below that. . . . It was fucking terrifying, to tell you the truth. . . . We're all okay. I'm going 10-7 here." Rock climbing carefully, they traversed the slab for a scout downstream. They were standing atop a 25-foot wall.

Using their throw ropes, they lowered the boats down to a ledge, then chimneyed down through a crack to a steep, stepped slide of rock, the only way back into the river. Fall straight off and the barreling current would plaster you into the berg of a rock close to shore. On the right was a deadly pocket; on the left, a big hole. You had to have enough speed when you hit the water to shoot beyond the rock, then tuck back right to miss the hole.

Scott stepped up. Willie gave me a play-by-play back in camp: "Scotty gives the seal launch a go—fucking beautiful little ricochet right into the river—no water loading on the deck—skims away from this— charges out midstream. . . ." The last step acted like the kicker of a ski jump, ricocheting him up and out, and he launched his kayak almost horizontal, hitting the water and planing like a skipping stone, taking the momentum into his paddle stroke and clearing the rock.

The rest followed. They fought on down the right side of the river, running, scouting, portaging. The power of the main current was ferocious, malign. They'd sally into it, no more than 15 seconds at a time, to get around an obstacle. Dustin mused later, "The exit of one put you at the start of another where you didn't want to be, so the whole puzzle didn't add up."

. . . .

Rob and I pushed across the ever-steepening slopes of jungle. We fought through thickets loaded with thorny blackberry and stinging nettles and then ran out of slope at the edge of a deep ravine. We sat down. There was a corner in the wet black rock falling into the gully, maybe a 40-foot downclimb to a shallower ramp. Probably the route, but a slip meant a fall of 150 feet.

Kusang and Passang and most of the porters caught up to us. They dropped their loads and looked over the edge. Then they took a piss. Everyone had sat down and started smoking when Jangbu the Everest Sherpa suddenly appeared over the lip of the cliff with a big smile and a long knife in his right hand. He had free-soloed up the rock. He smiled, his eyes sweeping upslope and fixing on a young pine. He climbed to it, dropped it fast with the knife, stripped it, leaving stobbed limbs for ladder rungs, and within 10 minutes he and Kusang had swung it down over the edge and propped it solidly in the rock corner leading to the ramp. Andrew climbed to us and set a rope for a handline, and the long file strung down into the bottom of the gash and up the other side like a line of army ants.

The radio coughed. Scott said they'd made it to camp. He said they'd paddled more than 65 percent of the whitewater. Dustin Lindgren was sitting beside me. "They *nailed* it!" he said. The Northeast Straits: Over a mile and a half, walled in, 200 to 250 feet a mile, 15,000 cfs, in kayaks, in the Himalayas, in winter. Damn.

. . . .

The ground crew descended out of the woods to a cove of beach carved out of vertical walls. It was the bed of a great flood eddy. Not sand, but river-smoothed rocks leveled with a mat of driftwood debris. Heavy water-seasoned logs with powdery, bleached skin lay against the banks. The Gorge was so narrow, the chalky cliffs across the green tailwater so tight over us, there was only a swath of sky above, going to cobalt. Hemlocks and pines from the opposite wall leaned into it. And higher still, we were ringed on all sides by snowy ridges. The twins stood together, peeling off their drysuits. Willie beamed.

"Big day. Good day. That's what we fucking live for, right there," he said.

After dark, the porters made a bonfire up against an elephant boulder on the beach. They gathered great chunks of driftwood and tossed them onto the fire. A group of the boys climbed atop the rock and sang with tenor voices, sweet and strong. The flames threw their shadows against the cliffs. Another group passed up a heavy butt log, and the boys lifted it over their heads and heaved it crashing onto the pyre. A dragon's breath of swirling sparks shot to the sky, whirling like flocks of birds and schools of fish, and for a moment they were a grove of bamboo overarching, like the ones painted by the Chinese masters, myriad narrow leaves sprayed on the wind. The sparks rose and spread, riding the heat column up to circulate among the cooler stars.

Allan sat apart with a mug of tea and pieces of the generator spread out on the stones. Yesterday, a porter had carried it upside down and soaked the sparkplug and carburetor in oil, and Al was making one more effort to get it going. Didn't look likely. We had a solar panel the size of a tea tray as backup; no more late-night calls to girlfriends. I'd used it last night to call my agent's office in New York. She wanted one report mid-expedition to add to the original book proposal so she could go to a publisher with a concrete story in progress and possibly close a deal. Charlie had the phone in his tent. I told him I needed it for five minutes and he asked why, as Charlie always did, and instead of saying "None of your business," I told him about needing to talk to my agent. Mistake. "So you can get your advance?"

"So I can maybe find a publisher," I said.

"Half a million, you think?"

"No, it won't be that much."

"Three hundred thousand?"

"I don't know, Charlie, maybe." He handed me the phone. Then he must have hustled off to Scott.

As I interviewed Steve at breakfast, Scott leveled a stare that I could only think of as malevolent. For the first time on the expedition, I had the hideous thought that if our course along the river went along cliff, I wouldn't hike it next to Scott. That is not to say that in the clutch, he wouldn't risk his own life to save mine. I'm sure he would. But I'd felt the force of the hostility.

. . . .

A warm, bright day, with a faint breeze stirring down the canyon. It smelled of fir trees and rock, of sagelike brush and the ozone of massed snow. The kayakers dispersed to claim their gear hanging to dry in the branches of trees and bushes. Drysuits and life vests and fleece hung like bright flags all around camp.

The Sherpas broke down the kitchen tent and repacked the food loads, and Passang, who is usually dapper and unruffled—he hikes in brown cuffed corduroy pants that never seem to get dirty, and his hair is always clean and neat—seemed upset. The set of his jaw was tense, his mouth tight. Dave told me quietly that back at the rest camp, after the big porter meeting, Passang had confronted two porters splitting a single load and had nearly gotten into a fistfight. Then this morning, the Sherpas discovered a burlap sack of rice that had been opened, robbed of half its contents, and sewn back shut. Much of the jerked yak meat was also missing, along with candy bars. I remembered nights when, at the edges of the dinner fire, clutches of porters watched us eat with impassive faces as we dug into the four or five big pots of sumptuous food the Sherpas set out.

Dave said he would let it go for now. We were so close to the last big push over the Senchen La. Diplomacy was key.

We climbed out of camp. Half an hour later, the porter train caught its breath in the sun on boulders 500 feet off the river. I sat on a ledge with Tuli and Tsawong and the policeman Ching Mi, and they laughed as they pointed for the third time at a group of goral goats on the opposite canyon wall. I couldn't make them out. I have good eyesight, but I couldn't see what was as obvious to these men as a stop sign would be to me. Tuli thought it was hysterical. He grasped my trekking pole and sighted down it like a gun. Holding it stationary with one hand, he put his other hand around my shoulders and tugged my head in line. I sighted down the pole: "Ah!" There they were. Tuli laughed and pounded my back until the dust flew. He gave me a cigarette.

The paddlers' voices came on the Talkabout, upset. They said that Johnnie and Scott's rescue knives had been stolen off their life vests, along with Johnnie's watch. On the radios, Scott and Dave agreed to keep it quiet. Tsawong clucked his tongue and said something to Ching Mi. Judging from the tone, it was something like "You're the cop—when are you going to rein in these sons of bitches?" Tuli's face showed nothing.

The paddlers ferried across the box canyon and portaged one drop and ran down the stepped corridor, through the exploding ledges, one, two, three, down the middle in big, gorgeous water with clean lines, reveling in the confidence they had earned. Dustin ran another insane rapid solo, in back of the others after they had walked it. He explained that he had been scouting and fallen behind and that if he took all the time to portage, he'd get farther back, so he ran. Also, he was tired of carrying his boat. Also, he thought, "Why didn't the others run this?" Just avoid a death sieve, slot a 90-degree turn above a 15-foot ramp, and melt the hole at the bottom with a back somersault to finish. Simple.

Willie said they were all bent over, studying a rapid on the sat map, saying, "Okay, it's this long, and . . ." when they looked up and saw the actual rapid tumbling out ahead. "Hey," he said, "we can go on visual cues now!" The gradient had eased off that much.

. . . .

Somebody knew about a meditation cave. It must have been Sherab. Many of the porters were so excited they dropped their loads and ran off into the trees. Ken and others from the ground team jogged ahead; I followed one of the porters. I had a tough time keeping up, and he looked back and waited politely, pointing out the cuts of knives, many years old, on old snags and downed logs. It was the curly-headed, fiery kid in the pink vest and mirror sunglasses, one of the angriest and loudest in the big meetings, and I was surprised that he waited for me. I thanked him when I caught up, but his face remained expressionless, and he just nodded and hurried on. Maybe he had seen my copy of the *Dhammapada*, too; he must have. And I thought by now most of the porters knew of my injury. Tuli understood it and would ask me with gestures how it was holding up. The rest had seen me limp at times and tie my boot painfully. Their pantomime nickname for me was One Who Writes All the Time, made with a short scribbling motion. Maybe the kid thought that if I was willing to make the pilgrimage and write it down, then I was worthy of this small decency. Maybe he was simply courteous, and his hostility at the meetings was a separate gearing, compartmentalized. Business is business, and this was something else.

At last we came to the edge of the high ground and the deeply shadowed cave. The porters were prostrating at its entrance. They touched their foreheads to a small depression and raised their pressed palms and went to the ground. I looked more closely. On the surface of the rock was a handprint, not carved but set in the grain like a kid's palm in the drying cement of a new sidewalk. They said it was Padmasambhava's. He had rested here in seclusion to meditate between battles with the demon gods. His presence was as real to the men as Sherab's. Just a depression in the rock and old white, block-printed prayer flags strung in the mouth of the cave. Back in the cold depths where no wind stirred, miraculously, were neat cones of tsampa left as offerings, the melted stains of yak butter candles, and stakes, taller than a man, driven into the earth and tied with longer flags. We were in one of the remotest places on Earth, and some of the flags didn't look more than a couple of years old. How could the tsampa remain in neat lines of finger-sifted pyramids? Didn't the wind ever howl through? Didn't small animals enter and eat it? Who had been here to make offerings and pray?

I found myself in tears. I wasn't sure why. I looked over at Ken, and he was overcome as well. In the hush of their prayers, we could hear the river, unseen, 1,000 feet below. Even muffled by distance, it shook and shirred the air and rose in a pulsing rhythm. It sounded like a giant breathing in sleep. Two of the porters glued small crystals to the palm of Padmasambhava's hand with buttered tsampa.

The back side of the cave sat on a point of the ridge with—good Lord—an eagle's view down the rest of our route through the Upper Gorge. Sherab sat on a prow of rock with his prayer beads. Directly below, deep in a fold of the forest-blanketed slopes, we could see the crease of the Churung Chu, the river that flowed from the massif between Namcha Barwa and towering Sanglung. The river we would cross this afternoon. Downstream was the drainage of Clear Creek, creasing up from the right bank into a wall of jagged rock and snow. Farther north, to the left of Clear Creek, straight downriver from where we sat, the eye traveled over a terrible-looking scarred face of rock and ice: the Senchen La.

Sherab touched me and held out his right hand, palm away. With a straightened left hand, he ran his fingertips left across his right palm and up into the notch between the thumb and forefinger. "Senchen La," he said. "Payi." Then he shook his head and waved his right hand in a quick dismissive gesture. Now he ran the fingertips up right, into the notch between pinkie and ring finger, and said "Luku." He nodded his head. I looked at him squatting next to me. His brushy black hair stood up in the sun. His face was as weathered and polished as teak on an old boat.

"No, Senchen La, Payi," I said, motioning up and left. The route we would take to get to the Lower Gorge.

He waved his hand again, shook his head. "Luku," he insisted, again tracing the route. And then he made a gesture that gave me the chills. "Senchen La," he said, angling the fingertips across his palm again, precisely along the line of his thumb; then at the top, he let them drop, wriggling them like falling men. He shook his head.

"Ahh," I said, not quite seeing it, and then looked again at the Senchen La. "Ahh," I said again.

"Luku," Sherab said decisively.

Charlie had gone ahead by himself. In a little while, he was on the radio, telling us he'd crossed the Churung Chu. He must have dropped down closer to the river, and now he was a bit lost. Every few minutes, with a note of increasing alarm, his voice crackled over the radios. "Charlie to David, do you copy?"

Dave, to his credit, was patient. He tried to describe the lay of the land as we made our way through the dense woods.

Then again: "Charlie to Dave, do you copy?"

"Yeah, Charlie, this is Dave."

"There's steep rock above me, and kind of a rough slope. . . ."

The kayakers could hear it all, and they began to call it Radio Tsangpo. Then, 20 minutes later: "Charlie to David."

"Go ahead."

"I've got trees all around me, and I can't move in any direction."

It took everybody a moment to digest. Then the kayakers laughed themselves to tears.

. . . .

Everybody called it Pine Camp. The trees were the beautiful weeping pines (*Pinus bhutanica*) and hemlocks, granddaddies six feet across that soared arrow-straight to the sky. Ward had remarked them with a botanist's awe. On a bluff more than 600 feet above the Tsangpo, they stood sentinel to a beautiful rapid of falling white that expended itself in a sliding pool of milt green troubled by upwellings and boils that stirred and overlapped and dissipated. Around the corner, the river entered the last broad bend before Clear Creek and the end of the line for a man in a boat. Ken and I came down through deep woods on a bed of fragrant red needles to the smoke of our fire ghosting up through the trees. Some of them were scarred with blazes where pilgrims had skinned off the resinous bark to start fires in the rain. The trees towered up into the twilight of their canopies. I took off my pack and lay against it and watched the smoke. In the round of my sight, the trees seemed to lean together and converge overhead, high limbs and needles against the evening blue. They stilled the mind like church.

After tomorrow, barring an accident, Scott and the expedition would have one goal: to get to the confluence and paddle as much of the Lower Gorge as they could down past Payi to the village of Luku—some 20 more river miles. Given how much effort the Upper Gorge had cost the team, there was a growing consensus that to split the expedition now and send a team to scout the Ten-Mile Gap—which gave every indication of being completely unrunnable—would be a mistake. The main objective now would be the confluence to Luku—which meant getting everybody safely over the Senchen La.

The kayakers climbed into camp, and there was some discussion about the porter situation. Tsawong had reported that more might leave tomorrow and trek all the way back to Pe, insisting on their return pay.

Scott squatted by the fire in the waning light and said that we would get over the pass, whatever it took. At the brink of triumph, of completing the Upper Gorge, everything else was becoming more uncertain.

Maybe Scott needed to blow off steam. Or maybe it was simply the rankling resentment over the book deal he could no longer contain. After dinner, in the windless dark, he tapped me on the shoulder where I was writing in a composition notebook by headlamp and said, "Peter, can I talk to you?"

"Yeah, sure."

I clipped the pen to mark the page and set the notebook on the mat of dried needles. Scott's tone was tense, and I braced myself. He walked around to the other side of one of the trees.

"How's it going?" he said.

"Fine."

"How's the hip?"

"No trouble. Thanks for asking."

"Some things have been said, bro."

"Yeah?" Not this again.

"You probably sense that things are getting stranger with the boys."

"I—"

"Nobody trusts you, dude."

Nobody trusts me? What did he mean? I'd been feeling like a solid part of the expedition after all the static at the beginning of the Gorge. "Nobody trusts you, and I'm sure you know they're withholding."

They are?

"You come in here after all our plans, set to write about controversy. And I hear you're about to get a $300,000 book deal. You haven't worked on this for years. You come in here, bro, at the last fucking minute. These guys don't even own a car. They have nothing, dude. They're broke most of the time. Mikey can't even afford a drysuit. And you're gonna get fucking rich. You should fucking think about that."

I took a deep breath. "Look," I said, and it came in a rush. "I don't

199

know what my advance is going to be. It could be $300,000, but I doubt it. I don't give a fuck. It's not about money. I never wrote because I cared about money. I care about these guys. Whatever I get, I share with *Outside* and my agent. Two years of work maybe, total. I'll be lucky if I'm making as much as my friend Sascha, who's a cop. Which is more than I've ever made writing. I don't give a fuck. I'm not here to exploit anybody. I believe in good karma. Whatever I make on the book, I'll give the paddlers 10 percent."

Silence. I heard Scott draw a breath. "That'd be cool," he said finally. "I'll tell the boys." Then he had to add: "Karma's one thing. Action's another." He was telling me I'd better not fucking go back on it. Jesus. Not a shred of grace.

. . . .

Jangbu was in fine form. The dawn was brisk and bright, pink tingeing the blue netted in the treetops. The smoke of a dozen fires floated up. Men warmed their hands at the flames. Kannuri chanted. Jangbu set out a pot of beef noodles, Enlarge chocolate hotcakes, and oatmeal. The boys raised their enamel cups to the Everest cook and cheered.

Willie unrolled the sat map and tossed a stone on each corner to hold it down. "Six rapids today. Then we're there! Amazing. Look—this rapid has flatwater on both sides! Stay to the side and you're golden."

Rob leaned over it. "They must've been shaking when they took that picture."

Dustin Knapp rubbed his fists into his lower back. "They have rapids on the Slave and the Ottawa like that."

Scott, a few feet away, dug in his pack and pulled out the Explorers Club flag entrusted to him by the venerable group. It was wrapped in plastic and labeled "117." A card that came with it stated that this very flag had been unfurled at both poles, in outer space, and at the deepest part of the ocean. It was a great honor, and today Scott would carry it in his boat.

We broke camp fast and climbed off the bluff down a small stream trickling through the remnants of a rockslide. The first rapid, the beautiful one, stepped down in three parts, through a constriction where the entire river rumbled through. The scouting was done with a swift efficiency. The paddlers' eyes had been calibrated and honed over the past two weeks. The eight-foot ledge that would have been questionable in the first days was speedily assessed: They could run it with angle and melt the hole at the bottom. The tight turn through boulders could be taken, no problem, with the right timing.

When they run, it is smooth and rhythmic. The groups of twos and threes, in a spaced line like a drill team, each man successively disappearing and torpedoing out of the first big hole, slicing left with precision through the next slot, regrouping in an eddy. They don't speak much to each other anymore; they just peel out one by one and go. When they all glide out into the glacial milk green of the final pool, they are in sync, like a bluegrass band where individuals riff and where what they all accomplish together surpasses what any one could ever do alone. The paddlers have moved beyond athleticism, discipline, risk, and sport and into something rare and fine.

It's fitting that on this last day on the water up here, when we climb over the ridge and come back down to the river, we hear cheers. It is sunny. The morning has warmed. The porters are all arrayed on the bank and yelling. Allan in his black-splotched H2 Zone is throwing a cartwheel against a breaking wave in the middle of the river. Is this the Tsangpo, really? Half a dozen kayakers in a big pool waiting their turn to play, like any benign rodeo spot not far from a road and a burger. The morning sunny and warming nicely. The river rolling down into gentle haystacks, with this one steep curler in the middle. The wave with nothing horrifying below, and perfect "eddy service"—the pool on the far side circling conveniently back upstream like a ski lift, so the paddlers can play again and again without getting swept. The audience, our surly porters of the day before, are now hooting and clapping like kids at a circus.

Willie peels out after Allan falls off, spins upstream just above the wave, and catches its face. He surfs, swooping back and forth, the curler breaking over his shoulder. Then, like the squirt boater he is, he leans back and throws in a powerful backsweep that sends his boat vertical on its stern. It bounces up and over the wave; he's holding his back-ender, one-two-three, as he careens downstream like the stem of a fishing bobber, an acrobatic breaching dolphin. The porters go berserk.

. . . .

At 3 P.M. on February 16, after two more miles of heavy water, the seven kayakers hit small eddies along the shore a few hundred meters below the outlet of Clear Creek and just above a tight left corner, hemmed by cliff that climbed 5,000 feet straight up into a world of Himalayan snow. They threw their paddles onto the pale boulders and celebrated the moment with high fives. The ground crew cheered. In 14 days, they had completed 44 miles of the Upper Tsangpo Gorge, paddling more than 90 percent of the whitewater and portaging only 23 times. Scott pulled the Explorers Club flag out of his boat and unfurled it. "The Upper Tsangpo Gorge is officially stamped," he said. As the group clambered up over the rocks to make camp on a narrow treed shelf above the river, Scott got on the sat phone and called his girl, Jen, and left a message for Outside Television producer Les Guthman. "Les," he said, "today we made history."

Nobody basked in the glory. Nothing was over. The ultimate goal was to get home alive, and that wouldn't be easy. We were at a dead end, surrounded by high rock walls and thousands of feet of near-vertical mountain face. The ground shook from the force of water. Just below and out of sight, it cascaded over Rainbow Falls and then, a few hundred yards later, the cataract of Hidden Falls. Between Hidden and the confluence with the Po Tsangpo was some 8 to 10 river miles, 5 of which—the Lost Five Miles—was so deeply incised, it had never been seen by a Westerner. Just upstream, the drainage of Clear Creek cut up into the flank of the mountain. The only way out was up.

Locals don't go near the high passes after mid-November. Down in the Lower Gorge, Bailey had waited until mid-May, when he figured enough snow had melted and the severe weather had passed, before taking on the Yonggyap La, and even then, storm and avalanche almost killed him. Now, with a total of 64 men filing in and converging on the cramped camp, there was no time to lose. We had to get up and over before anyone changed their mind, including the Spirits of Storm.

. . . .

The Sherpas discovered that more rice had been stolen. They showed Dave. Two 20-kilo sacks had now been opened, had half of their contents removed, and been stitched back up. Most of our jerky was also gone, and some five kilos of dried beef. They left us about a pound. "Which was considerate," Dave said wryly.

Tsawong brought a line of tense youngsters into the kitchen to apprise them of the situation. I could see Dave murmuring to himself, "Delicate, delicate. . . ."

The mood among the porters had shifted strongly again since the cheerful respite of the rodeo. Their unsmiling faces now spoke of fear. If we were worried about what we might encounter up in the snows, what must they be feeling with their low sneakers, thin sweaters, and army coats? And dwindling food supplies.

No time was wasted. Kayaks were dragged up into camp and emptied. Throw ropes were strung between birch trees and all the paddling gear thrown over them so that it could be dried and stowed. The boys got straight to work under the bare alder trees. They stripped their shoulder straps and hip belts off their packs and tried to figure out how to attach them to their boats. River knives were flipped open, duct tape was unrolled with a loud tear, and loops of prusik climbing cord were untied and set aside. Dustin was the first to come up with a workable system. He tied the tops of his shoulder straps to the back band of his kayak—the boat would be carried stern up—and hitched the bottoms through a prusik cord that ran through the broach loop—a plastic handle—on his bow. He hoisted it up to demonstrate and carried it comfortably, vertically, a very long backpack, through the double line of admiring comrades. What if he had to duck under a tree branch? "And when I need to go low," he said, anticipating the question and rocking the boat horizontally over his head so he disappeared inside the cockpit, "I can go low." His voice echoed inside the boat like a talking snail in its shell. The others nodded, impressed.

After messing with straps for half an hour, Willie said, "Fuck it. I'm carrying it. Johnnie, I'm carrying it just like always. Fucking gonna drag it, carry it, throw it around, every once in a while do this to stretch my arms." Willie had the boat on his head and shoulders, and he straightened his arms and lifted the kayak from inside the cockpit rim.

He dropped the boat back to Earth. The seat and thigh hooks were well-padded with adhesive foam. "I'm goin' Old School." He headed for the Sherpa fire to get a cup of tea.

Steve now had his boat strapped to his hips and back and was looking very pleased with himself. "You boys are in trouble," he announced. "I'm going to be setting quite the pace up the hill tomorrow."

"It's the annual How to Carry Your Boat Off!" Mike said, ungluing a strip of duct tape from his thumb.

Willie set his mug on the damp earth and stretched his hands. They were red and badly chapped from being constantly wet and cold. All the kayakers' hands were a mess. At the base of Willie's thumb and forefinger was a raw fissure. He had a pronounced callus pad there from years of holding a paddle, and the crease cut right into it. The tips of his thumbs, too, were nicked and chapped. "That's what keeps me awake right there. Just when I'm going to sleep they say, 'Neh-eh, we're right here.'" The thing about Willie was that he seemed amused by it.

Steve was satisfied with his rig and sat down beside us. I took advantage of the break to ask him if he'd finished school. He said he had studied biochemistry and genetics in South Africa and had six months to go. He was going to go earn some money and come back. That was five years ago. "I got caught up in kayaking," he said. "My interests now are video stuff, multimedia stuff, filming, photography, editing, and I'm learning Web design. I learn as I go. For my rafting video I'm editing, I designed the sleeve myself. It's a total one-man show." Steve's video is called *Slambezi* and is a collection of raft wipeouts on the giant water of the Zambezi. He said it makes audiences laugh out loud.

He made me think of my own disruptive encounter with paddling in college. I learned to paddle in March of my sophomore year, on a spring-break trip with the college canoe club down to the mountains of western North Carolina. Upon returning to New Hampshire, I canceled plans to attend spring semester. I convinced a good friend, also a beginning boater, to do the same, and we spent the rest of the New England runoff getting thrashed on the frigid local rivers and creeks. I did finish school, working as a river guide in the summers, and when I graduated, instead of pursuing a serious career as a writer as I'd intended, I spent the next eight years working on rivers as a guide and instructor, as these guys did, and paddling as much new water around the world as I could. Two long-term relationships hit the rocks because of it. My pickup was transport and home. I wouldn't have traded that life. A cautionary tale. I know more than a few doctors, lawyers, and engineers who just up and quit after experiencing the intoxication of a river.

THE GRAND PORTAGE

We got off promptly at 9:30 with all porters and clambered back up-stream 100 yards along the river rocks, the boys carrying their kayaks over their heads, and cut up left into the shallow rill of the creek. It was low in its bones after a cold night and burbling like flowing glass, true to its name, magnifying the smooth stones of the bed. Then Sherab pointed up to the left where the jungled slope climbed steeply out of the cut, and almost immediately we began to scramble. The Sherpas went ahead with their dirklike knives and hacked out the ancient trail. I climbed with Rob, which I had done often, as we share a pace. In touchy traverses above the cropping rock, we edged down huge old logs slick with moss and scarred with the old crosshatched knife cuts of previous travelers—how many decades had they lain as a bridge?

Tough going with a small pack. I wondered how the kayakers would fare and looked down behind me and blinked: There was a lime-yellow kayak, vertical, bobbing up the overgrown cliff. It was Steve, strapped in, hip and shoulder, stripped to an undershirt and breathing hard, feeling for a handhold, and climbing as fast as we did. People think kayakers don't use their legs; they do. Especially in the kind of dynamic rodeo-style paddling the boys employed. You constantly throw the deck of the boat to one side or another with your knees and thighs, flexing from hip to toe, and push with your feet against the braces in more than isometric pressure. While the paddling power comes directly from the torso, your legs are always working. World-class paddlers may have more available core strength than any other athletes, and it was showing now. Steve's expression was determined, set with focus, and he came on behind us as inexorable as a tank.

We climbed 1,500 feet and topped out on a knife ridge blanketed with a groundcover of blue-black berries and gnarled low rhododendrons. It fell off sharply into another deep drainage. The kayakers came along it in a ragged line like colorful shelled beasts, and we peaked at a prow of rock where a single prayer flag fluttered out of a cairn, frayed and worn to near transparency so that we looked through the sere cloth and written figures and saw the dark of the Upper Gorge winding back through the snowy mountains.

Steve unstrapped his boat and caught his breath. "If I'd known how sketchy that was going to be, I'd have run more rapids. I'd rather drown than tumble down and break my neck with a kayak on my back."

Willie joined him on the tight ledge. "I'm gonna fit shoulder straps tonight."

Allan dropped his boat and took a long drink from a water bag. As he swallowed, his eyes traveled upward, to the east, and they got bigger.

"The back of that peak, you're joking!" he said.

Everybody looked. Not far above us was snow, slope on slope at unappealing angles, etched with avalanches and broken by rock escarpments running northward, which was the Senchen La. The cliffs were nearly vertical, fluted and seamed, and they gleamed with ice. I swallowed too. Nobody had ever done a portage like this.

Ken cleared his throat. "It's foreshortened," he said. "There is some flat space up there."

Andrew craned his neck, scanning the terrain in a kind of reverie. "Look at that avalanche chute," he said. He didn't say it like "We better watch out"; he said it like he wished he had a pair of skis. He picked up his pack and set out to recon.

Scott stood next to a porter and raised his chin and pointed up at the route across the Senchen La. "Yeah?" he said. I think he was testing the waters. The porter made a sour face and shook his head.

We kept moving, around a knob of dense, stunted spruce and pines, and then we fell into an eerie hobbit forest of thick, gnarled trees and slick blowdown logs. Tatters of airy moss hung from the limbs and wafted in the breathy wind. I had never been anyplace like the Gorge. One moment we were trying to pick out a route in archetypal winter alpine; the next we were trying to keep our footing in a wet green, towering jungle. Everybody, especially the men with boats, went into their own zone of concentration, going at whatever pace they could manage, and the line stretched out over the next hours so that people could be alone with their feet and burning shoulders.

I ended up behind Willie and kept a respectful distance. He was a climbing monk, like the ones you see tiny in the old Sung landscapes, making their way up along billowing waterfalls. Except that instead of a staff, he had a kayak, his hands pressed on the rim of the coaming and his head in the cockpit, watching his feet. Willie negotiated dicey footing under low limbs, taking full squats and stepping wide, scraping the orange Gus under the branches. Immense leg strength. I offered to help him at a few spots, and he said, "No, thanks, I found my bliss," so in the easier places, I pulled a harmonica out of my pocket and, for the first time on the trip, played some blues. The repetitive chord progressions resolved like a lost train whistle in the shadowy green twilight.

> They call it Stormy Monday
> But Tuesday's just as bad.
> Wednesday's worse
> And Thursday's oh so sad. . . .

This felt like enchanted forest, a place where anything could happen. It would not have surprised me much if an elf had stepped from behind a mossy boulder and asked a riddle with pain of death or pleasure of paradise hanging on the answer. It occurred to me that the whole expedition was that riddle, in a way. Certainly the pain-of-death part. Figure out the puzzle of the Tsangpo and pass through unmolested. Make a wrong move and meet your maker. The Buddhist twist on the fable might be that the paradise was not a princess and a kingdom but simply this, the journey: gripping the rough root and hauling yourself onto the ledge and giving thanks for another breath. The blues was the same: the circling despair of simple living, clarified to sweetness.

I came on Willie pressing the boat back against a cropping rock and catching his breath. Sweat stung his eyes, and he looked whipped; he smiled and said, "Jeezum. That's sweet. Nice blues. That helps me out. Takes my mind off it."

We came to old log ladders propped against short cliffs, and cuts in roots for better footing, now scabbed over with moss. The trail, rarely used, was hundreds of years old. Steve took a bad spill and said later he was grateful he'd been alone. "A full-scale crash to rocks at the bottom," he said. "I just fucking lay there for three minutes. I didn't want to see anyone. Didn't want to hear any advice. I just wanted to be alone."

Finally we began to climb again, out of the Tolkien woods and into sparser trees, birch and spruce, and we skirted an overhanging ledge in a cut bank, and in the deep hollow were more prayer flags. A meditation cave.

Then we cleared the trees altogether and were kicking up a shallow slope of soft, dazzling snow into a basin squared off with high walls. Snow. On three sides were snow faces tracked with dozens of avalanche slides and cropping rock cliffs, and above it all, the sharp granite spires. The left escarpment was the back of the mountain we would need to climb, then traverse before dropping over to Payi. Snow and broken rock cliffs and gullies. Ahead was a faced wall a few thousand feet high and almost flat across the top like a broad saddle. Apparently that was the direct route over and down to Luku, farther down the Lower Gorge than we wanted to be. A few hundred yards above, cupped into the walls on the left, eastern side of the basin, were a pile of rocks humped out of the snow and a fringe of low brush, a natural camping spot. The avalanche run-outs swung around it, and if there was still brush showing, it was probably safe. We climbed to it and dropped our loads, and Willie and Dave and I sat on a boulder and watched the clouds tug their shadows across the Gorge and the flanks of Gyala Peri. Far, far down to the west-northwest, a patch of the river was visible in the bottom of a canyon so deep and twisting, it did not seem real. The river was white. Nor did it seem real that we could have come from there, that the orange kayak that now lay in the snow had glided and bucked across the winking shine of that patch.

"Holy shit."

"Yeah."

Just next to our rock was what looked like a 30-foot-wide bobsled run. It cut past and swept out of sight into the drainage below. There were bits of rock in the bed where the avalanche had carried away some cliff.

"Bloody fresh," said Dave.

"Ayup."

It gouged down 100 feet from where we would stamp out the snow and set up our tents. Another big run-out bulldozed off the face just beyond the campsite. Other recent slides scoured out of couloirs and gullies up and down the bowl. Mike trudged up the slope, dragging his kayak. He was wearing tropical swim trunks over long underwear and gaiters. His water bag was filled with dirty snow and slung over his shoulder. He drank the untreated melt. I guess, being the premiere paddler of northern India, he figured he'd already made friends with every parasite. Willie and Dave hit him with snowballs.

He slurped meltwater out of the bag. "Those overhanging tree branches were starting to get to me in the end—take a big step—*thunk*! Take another step—*thunk*!"

Mike reached down and packed his water bag with more snow. "You can get sick from snow, eh? This climber in Nepal told me giardia could precipitate out in snow."

Willie said, "You can get sick from being dehydrated. Another fun fact: You get dehydrated from eating snow. Like eating celery."

"Or Cheerios."

"Peanut butter on celery."

"Cottage cheese on celery."

Willie grinned. He said, "On the *Endurance*, with Shackleton, on Elephant Island, this one time they made a list of what everybody craved. Mostly it was sweets. They were so sick of meat."

Mike said, "I think the porters went faster today. They had a bit of competition."

One by one, the kayakers emerged from the trees below, entered a hail of snowballs, and collapsed on the rocks. Dustin Knapp said, "I was listening to Bob Marley the whole way—'More will have to suffer . . .'" and smiled his cryptic smile. That was his oblique way of saying that the portage was a bitch. Underneath his trim haircut, behind the amber-yellow wraparounds, Dustin's mind seemed to be vastly amused by just about everything.

Allan arrived and crashed over on top of the kayak on his back like an upturned turtle. "Kayaks where they shouldn't be, high up and away from the river!"

Willie pointed out some sick ski lines in the avalanche chutes all around us. Andrew elbowed his ski buddy Dustin Lindgren and said, a bit too seriously, I thought: "Duster, we should hike up that chute and boat ski it."

We were at 9,200 feet. We'd gained 2,000 feet off the river but had climbed much more, going in and out of the steep drainages. The top of the pass was something over 12,000 feet, all snow. We'd have to do it in one push in the morning.

. . . .

Charlie squatted next to me and asked how my hip was feeling, and I was surprised that I felt a strong repulsion, a resistance to answering even that simple a question.

"Good," I said.

"You know," he said, "the expedition could save money if you headed home as soon as we got to Payi. Give yourself a break, too." His voice had an edge. Anger I didn't even know I was carrying rose up in me like bile. I thought, "You fucking drama queen pain in the ass. You're nosy about everything, and everything I tell you, you repeat to Scott, hatching worry, fear, conspiracy."

"I don't think so," I answered.

"What are you gonna do, sit and wait for the kayakers to paddle to Luku and come back? You could hike out to Pelung, go to Lhasa, and fly home."

One of my Buddhist teachers would have said, "Charlie is your Buddha. He is here to teach you something." I looked at Charlie. He didn't look like a Buddha. He looked thin and drawn and worried.

I said, "I'm committed to the end of the trip. That's my assignment. Hal would be ripped if I came home without reporting the second half. I'm staying."

"Yeah, yeah. I was just thinking of the expense, how we can save money if some guys went out."

I stood up and went for the teakettle.

Dave said, "I'd even drink an American beer right now."

I said, "Milwaukee's Best."

"I wouldn't say no to anything."

Allan said, "Dave, give me a blow job?"

"This'll revolutionize kayaking," Dave said. "People will think nothing of walking 55 miles just to run a river."

Somebody said, "Hey, Dustin. How do you manage to look so clean-cut?"

Knapp swallowed a spoonful of couscous and smiled mildly, like Mona Lisa.

"Looks like he grew up on fast food, Nintendo."

Dustin Lindgren blurted, "I watch TV. Eat fast food. Drink a shit-load of beer. Fuck sluts." The statement hung in the thin, sere air; everybody looked at him and then laughed so hard they were spewing food.

Dustin's voice had a booming resonance, and his laugh was an eight-pound cannon. I looked up at the uneasy snow slopes all around us and thought it would be fitting if a Dustin chick story set off a slide.

. . . .

Rhythmic double cut and scrape of Andrew's ice axe, followed by the chunk of his heavy boots kicking out the footholds. Jangbu Sherpa right behind, swinging his own axe, deepening the steps up the steep couloir. Grunting chuffs of breath. Skitter and roll of loosed ice. Slowly, steadily, we made our way at daybreak up the narrow funnel of a gully edged with broken rock.

Surface slick as ice. I was just behind the Sherpas and kicked hard into each step, toeing the angle down for a better grip for the men behind wherever I could. I buried the haft of my ice axe deep and gripped it as I stepped up. The gully was too steep to climb unprotected, and we didn't have the gear or the time to protect 64 men. Most of the porters had whittled staffs. I saw the kayaks moving upward; it was dicey with an ice axe to hold on to, but the boys steadied their boats with their hands and had to step up into each hold and balance with nothing to grip. One slip, and you'd slide and crash out of sight, rag-dolled down the cut all the way to the bottom. And worse, one man falling could take out the whole train below him like a line of bowling pins.

We climbed up left onto a band of rock and then onto the snow shouldering the gully, and we were out of it and moving up. I was relieved. Then the sun hit. It sprayed down over the slope like blazoning trumpets and warmed our faces and lit the snow to a blinding dazzle. Within minutes the crust softened, and each kicked step went deeper and surer. I was right behind Andrew now, and it seemed like a gift, and then I heard him say, "We've got to haul ass. We've got to get off this," and I thought about the face above us, and the snow losing its stiffness, and all the avalanche run-outs we had seen.

Thankfully, the slope crested onto a little shoulder, we walked upright a few hundred yards up into the sparse relief of a grove of pine and fir trees, and we took a quick break to sip some water and catch our breath. We could see more of the great Upper Gorge now, but nobody gave it more than a quick glance: Above, we could see the first goal, the top of the white ridge, a shallow saddle going over. That's where we would begin our traverse left and north along the top of the rampart of the Senchen La. Nobody relaxed. Between here and there was a wide open face, steeper than anything we had done before, maybe 1,000 feet of climbing to the top. It started reasonably enough, steepening upward like the outrun of a ski jump into a flat, unrelieved wall of vertiginous exposure. The porters, who had a couple of pairs of sunglasses between them, squinted their eyes to slits.

We filed up onto the blinding expanse, up the short ramp, and then there were just the sounds of the axe again, less chip than dig in the softening wall. And the labored breathing, and the angle hardening until it was like climbing a ladder and Rob's boot heels were at the level of my eyes. The cut steps, though deeper, were slicker now, not the gritty bed of cut hardpack but greased with a microscopic layer of melt. Everything depending on the angle of a two-inch pocket. We were well over 50 degrees and unprotected. I heard Rob curse a couple of times as his boot slipped out, and I caught myself a few times.

I heard yelling. It started as a single cry, then a wave of shouts moving down the line.

Tsawong had slipped, scrabbled, and fallen. He was on his back, shooting down the line of climbers, gathering speed. "Flip!" came the cries. "Turn over! Flip! FLIP!" Somehow he did. At the last second, he rolled over and dug in his single ski pole and stopped himself above the precipice. He stayed in a little heap and cried. His left boot sole was starting to come apart, and he'd wrapped a piece of slick duct tape around the entire toe that morning, which wasn't a good idea at all. Instead of Vibram lugs, he now had a slippery skid plate.

Andrew swore. He scanned the face. Just above and off to the right was a crop of rock crowned by a few scraggly rhododendrons. "I'm setting a rope," he said simply, and began kicking steps, angling up to the rock and his only anchor. "You guys keep going," he said over his shoulder. He moved off to throw down a rope for a handline to help the rest, especially the kayakers, through this steepest section. I handed my ice axe up to Rob. He swapped me his trekking pole, which I was glad for. He'd done quite a bit of climbing in the Alps, and he began expertly cutting steps as we continued to move upward. The snow was softening. I kicked out his steps as hard as I could. Then he stopped. I was looking at the back of his boots.

He said, "Hey, Pete—you figure this is dangerous?"

I looked up. Running across the level of his chest was a compression fracture, about a foot wide. It jagged across the face as far as we could see in either direction. The surface of the snow was slushy, and I was sweating in the warmth of the sun.

I'd written a story once about a mountain rescue team who told me that sometimes they got a call on a missing snowmobiler and would climb to the site of an avalanche. There would be the great scar where the slab had broken away and slid, and just above it, in the snow above the fracture, a single sideways boot print. I asked what it was, and they said it was where the guy ran his machine straight up the slope and planted his foot to pivot and run back down, a move they do. Instead, he triggered a slide. The boot left a signature like a neat farewell.

"I don't know," I said to Rob, talking quickly, "but could you move up so that I can get above it?"

"Good idea."

Rob had a rope in his pack, and we climbed higher, and he said, "I better throw down another rope." This was the steepest section, and there was another little outcrop of rock and brush off to our right. "Carry on," he said, and handed me the axe.

I actually looked over my shoulder. Who, me? The guy who had repudiated the high mountains? I guessed so. I took the axe and swung it and kicked steps; it wasn't hard now in the mush, and the rest of the line came behind, and in a few hundred yards we stepped up onto loose broken rock and a scrub of berry groundcover and tiny junipers, the angle easing off, and I thought, "It's over," but it wasn't. Two excited porters scrambled up past me, heedless and fast, and one kicked loose a basketball-size slab.

"ROCK!" I yelled as it shot out of sight. I heard later that it glanced off Johnnie's forearm, cutting and bruising as he deflected it. Then it caromed and struck Ken's leg and went down between his feet. It nearly knocked both of them off the snow to oblivion.

At the top, the Sherpas and Dave and Dustin Knapp, who had taken a route all the way up the initial gully, were waiting for us. We filed into a hanging pocket just below a snow saddle that crested a few hundred feet above. An easy ramp of unbroken snow led up to it. That was the way to Luku. The Senchen La and the route to Payi lay across mostly rock cliffs beneath the top of the mountain, a long traverse northward before a swing east over the top. It looked icy and treacherous and riven by gullies.

Scott climbed over, unbuckled his yellow boat, and dropped it in the snow. He was flushed and grim. "That was fucked," he said. "That was so dodgy. That was not safe. Not in the least bit." He sat in down in the cockpit. "Fucking Tsawong fell twice—on his back, on his pack—he wouldn't turn over."

He must not have unpeeled the tape after the first spill. Man.

Steve shook his head and swung down his kayak. "That was the most unsafe thing I've ever done."

From Mr. Nerves of Steel, that packed some weight.

. . . .

We were now at 12,000 feet, 5,000 feet above the river. It was 2 P.M. The porters were mostly gathered on a pile of broken rock where the gusts had stripped off the snow. Bareheaded and windburned, they smoked in the sun. The eastern Himalayas spilled brightly away in a sea of snow in all directions, a tumult of winter mountains and thrusting rock. The porters huddled against the wind and squinted back the way we'd come. Tsawong told Dave that the porters were going over the top to Luku.

"Like hell," Dave said.

Luku is deep in the Lower Gorge. Deep enough. Only some 12 river miles downstream of Payi, but another hump of mountain spur separates them. Going to Luku first would set us back valuable days. It would take another tough trek and several more days to climb back up to Payi, where we wanted to begin the recon of the Lower Gorge. And Ken had said that in all his travels in the Tsangpo, the one stretch he and Ian Baker agreed they never wanted to do again was the high, steep pass between Luku and Payi. From the top, they had to slide and claw down a near-vertical creek bed. There would be a lot of snow up there, too.

Dave argued. The porters were vehement, obstinate. They told him they were not, no way, going over the Senchen La. They told him they were going to Luku first, period. No dicey traverse, just straight over the top. Sherab explained that the Senchen La was unsafe.

"No," Dave said. "Now look. We didn't get all the way up here to be told we're going to Luku." Dave is a tough customer. When Nepalese Maoist guerrillas recently showed up at his Kathmandu-based outfitting company, demanding tribute, he sat them down and told them how much he had already done for local schools and villages and that he wasn't going to give them a bloody penny. They gave him a cigarette, and he concluded with a lecture on the political realities of Nepal.

This time the porters just shook their heads: We go to Luku first, then upriver to Payi.

Dave demanded, then reasoned, then cajoled, and then finally decided that maybe the porters had a point.

Luku it was. We felt hijacked.

We picked up our loads and filed up the ramp and over the top. Before I fell in line, I looked again at the traverse of the Senchen La, at the rock faces and ice-filled gullies, and I thought, "Maybe they're right. With the equipment we have and the time of day in the middle of winter, it probably is too dangerous. We've been so lucky so far. The stars have lined up. Everybody is alive. Maybe this is our guardian spirit speaking."

And then we came over the top and looked down into the tropical green of the lower Tsangpo: a clearing of what must be a village and tiny terraces clinging to the edge of the inner canyon; the rampart of the Pome Range ranked high and snowy on the other side barricading the Lower Gorge; the silver river running beneath down into India. Cradled and remote and lovely, like a dream of sanctuary. Shangri-La. I thought, "There are still Bengal tigers down there." And India, to the south, the undulating jungles of Assam, a verdant vagueness floating in the distance. We took another step in the deep snow. It was possible—probable—that no man had ever been up here in this season. And then with the afternoon sun full on the west face, we fell into a clean snow gully and lost our feet and sledded into Shambala.

. . . .

It was wild. Andrew was out in front, and he jumped onto his butt and went for the long glissade. The gradient was perfect. Jangbu was behind him, his face lit like a kid's, and I was behind Jangbu, picking up speed and falling. I caught air and held on. At the bottom of the first slide, the three of us collided in a rolling tumble, a heap of snow, Jangbu laughing and laughing. I looked back up, and the whole line of porters was sliding now, yelling, and Mike was passing them all, one hand thrust in the cockpit of his kayak, the other stretched onto the snow as an outrigger, the boat plummeting at the edge of control. Down and down as the gully narrowed and steepened, hundreds of feet, and then it was too steep to sled and we edged carefully, and then it ended. Abruptly. In spring it would be a high waterfall; now it was cliff and ice.

We stepped gingerly onto steep rock on our left, and Andrew led us across a thin ledge a boot-width wide, with rhododendron brush hanging over it, above the dive of the ice fall. Edging feet, pushing through the branches with our heads, and grabbing the limbs for handholds and not looking down. God, how would the kayakers manage with the boats? We bridged across to a slab of rock steep and quilted in low-berried ground-cover and slick mud, and we descended carefully to a creek running with water. We drank. Then we crossed it and climbed straight up through bracken and bramble and dense rhododendron to a small shelf of jumbled sharp rock and mud and thick forest, and we made camp. Oh, man. The very last traverse had been the hairiest.

Willie climbed into the rocks beside me and Dave and threw down his boat. I'd never seen him like this. He was flushed and upset. "That's the sketchiest thing I've ever done with my kayak, hands-down," he said.

Mike pushed up out of the brush and dropped his boat. "Where the fuck are we? That was a mission, eh?" He tipped up his water bag and drank deeply. "Whew. We're up and over now, though, and into the other side." He looked at Willie. "Just trying to be positive."

Willie said, "If we were going where we wanted to go . . ."

Dave put an arm around his broad shoulders and squeezed. "No, it's fine," he said. "Wherever you go, there you are." He smiled at the bearded paddler. "Expectations are the key to disillusionment, Willie," he said. He should know. His hired porters had just told him to shove it.

We dispersed over the bench and pried up rocks and kicked out narrow places to sleep. Dustin Knapp said, "I was climbing steep snow, in little footholds, strapped into a perfect toboggan."

Dave said, "Luku's gonna have alcohol, boys. I know it's low enough that they'll ferment things."

Allan: "In the Himalayas in the middle of winter—with a kayak!" A chorus of Homer Simpson "D'oh's!"

. . . .

First dawn without room service; the Sherpas were sleeping in. The expedition was scattered in the sharp boulders and brush up and down the steep slope above the ravine, sleeping hard. Tucked in and crammed into any half-level space, curled around rocks, hammocked into pockets. Our first night in Pemako proper: the locus of the Hidden Place, the *beyul*, where one can attain in a single night the spiritual merit and enlightenment of a lifetime of devotion. For me, some harmony in the expedition would be nice. And a grease nipple installed in my left hip. The rift with the porters had gotten personal. Distrust and resentment had crept into the eyes and quickened greetings to cursory nods. How did this happen? Our attitude at the outset was surely tainted by an assumption that porters in the Tsangpo were cunning and untrustworthy, and the history of exploration bore it out. Our approach from the start was "Give 'em an inch and they'll take a mile," and all your beef jerky, too. By expecting scurrilous behavior from the porters, did we foster it?

Still, what happened on the pass was mutiny. In battle, the military's remedy was a bullet to the head. If there had been only 10 of them, we would have forced them across to the north. Instead, we were outnumbered two to one, and they forced the hand.

Dave said to Tsawong, "If you ever do this again, don't take any bloody headman, don't take anyone from Pe, and don't take them all from the same town. They had it saved up from the beginning. To be paid for hire and then dictate the terms of employment—that's not the way it works. It's like dealing with a labor union. We need Maggie Thatcher."

Tsawong blinked. He looked tattered. He had a large bandage on his left elbow that swelled out his jacket.

Scott sat by the fire and put on his flame-dried socks and running shoes. One sock was singed and split up the middle from being burned. "They control this expedition. They carry all our food," he said. He turned to Tsawong. "You talked to Mr. Liang, and he said we could go out of Pelung any day? Good."

Ken cleaned his glasses on a handkerchief. "Sherab says it's two days out from Tsachu to Pelung now." That's from the village at the confluence up the Po Tsangpo and out of the Gorge. The targets were shifting, people's sights already moving to the last push, anticipating the end. I knew I wanted to keep my own mind on the next step. Getting down the canyon we were in didn't look like any picnic.

"*Fuck.*" We all looked at Charlie. He snatched his running shoes out of the fire. "Damn."

Willie said, "I like mine poached."

Dave informed us that he'd done some sorting in the kitchen, and 15 kilos of meat had been stolen, nearly an entire porterload.

He said to Tsawong, hunched by the fire, "It's not just the meat.

It's the portering. We've paid 13 days of portering to carry the meat."

Tsawong nodded automatically. Poor guy. Frying pan and fire and duct tape on his boot. And worrying about his wife and the baby. He was a hinge on this trip, between us and them, and he needed some grease, too.

We broke to pack up. I went over to Tsawong and asked if he was okay. He tilted his head back and forth, whatever that meant, and looked like he was going to cry.

Down on the rocks near my bivy sack, Dustin Knapp looked down the ravine and brushed his teeth. I checked my watch and rolled up my bed. I heard the brushing stop. He spat. Three minutes almost exactly. I laughed. I loved the kid. Being true to form is one way of staving off the Great Uncertainty.

. . . .

Dustin didn't much like what came next. None of us did. Pemako was wetter than Kongbo. The track was greasy, and every step had to be considered. Place a foot on a smooth stick or root cocked downslope, and away you went. The exposed rock in the slides was oiled with a sheen of water. Within half an hour, we were scrambling up unstable and near-vertical cuts of eroded dirt, hanging from roots by one hand, reaching across to a jug handle on a chip of wet rock that might or might not stay beveled to the bank.

The kayakers were determined, grim, their jaws set in a way I hadn't seen even up on the pass. This was maybe more treacherous. Several times, I turned at the top of a cut bank to ask Mike or Willie if they wanted a hand with the boat, and they shook their heads and grunted and clung to holds and came over the top.

We crossed a 150-foot log that bridged a suicide gully, and it was slippery with wet moss. Nothing to do but step carefully across. And hump over the shoulder of the ridge on the other side. It was so beautiful.

Giant subtropical trees with new green leaves spread over the canopy. Banyan trees and giant figs. Lianas, thick as hawsers, plunged down. Epiphytes sprayed exuberantly from the crotches of limbs. There were flowers up there. Orchids, ivory and yellow. Rhododendrons flagged with brilliant scarlet blossoms. And weeping pines. Groves of them on the ridges. Trunks too thick to wrap your arms around, with long, pendant needles in soft brushes that quivered on the breeze. We stopped for a breather, and Dave handed me a sprig of pale cream orchid with orange leopard spots and a sweet fragrance like orange blossoms.

We edged our boots down another dirt slide and came at last to the rock bank of the creek and clambered down into it. It ran low in its stone bed, falling steeply, and we could walk along its angled slabs, dun-pink rocks embedded with nuggets and crystals, and now I felt I was dreaming again, the braids of it spilling to the next horizon, the edge of a little waterfall, boulders we could usually hop across, small cairns of stones made by someone to mark the best crossing places. Lacy waterfalls spilled in from the side over slides of rich green moss: a sheltered chasm overhung with jungle, descending and barely exposed to the winter sky.

We dropped into Pemako, and it was scary, worse for the kayakers than anything before, because the footing was so uncertain and they were so played out, and it was as beautiful as anything we'd seen. The creek was a passage, a bedrock canyon echoing with snowmelt, marked with cairns, stepped with waterfalls, with mossy rills and cascades spilling in from the sides, leading us down from the snows into the deeper green of a mythical country while the temperature warmed with every hour.

Andrew set ropes to rappel down the side of a short waterfall. I was hopping the creek with Mike and Willie, and once Willie had downclimbed the rock, Mike yelled that he was lowering the two kayaks on slings and sent them over the edge. The slack in a sling sent one boat plummeting into Willie's gut where he waited and knocked him down. He fell like a shot takin. Whoops.

"Sorry, mate!"

"The Grand Portage," Dave said. "The greatest portage in river-running history."

In a couple of hours, the track T-ed into a hunters' trail that ran high above a large glacial tributary of the Tsangpo, and through breaks in the forest we could see its jungle-draped gorge. It was the Yangden Tsangpo. We turned downstream and within minutes arrived at a big cave hollowed into the slope on the left of the trail and roofed with a jut of black rock. The trail itself formed a kind of lip, shadowed by tall hemlocks and weeping pines. It commanded a big view across the side valley to a sharp, pine-fringed ridge, and also to the left, northeast, down the tributary to where it ended at the deep incision of the Lower Tsangpo Gorge itself.

Shelter, water, a Cave with a View. A perfect camp—for a few people. We dropped our loads. And then we noticed the man and the boy. They were standing in the track, watching us quietly. The man, maybe 22 years old, carried a gun, an ancient Chinese .22, and both had long knives belted at their waists. They wore army fatigues. The elder had a shock of curly dark hair and carried a leather pack, out of which stuck the red-furred quarter of a goral. Two small dogs, shepherd mix, boiled around their feet, whining and quivering. The man, who wasn't much more than a boy himself, watched the guys with boats come around the corner with a flicker of curiosity in his still eyes. He watched them set the kayaks down in the trail. The boy stood half behind him.

To appreciate how it must have seemed to them, remember that no one, ever, ventured over the high passes in winter. That the last expedition to come through from the Upper Gorge was four years before. That Willie and Mike and Johnnie set what were obviously boats, bright orange and red, down in front of the cave, in the middle of a jungle at 7,000 feet. And that white people with beards and round, staring eyes are weird-looking under any circumstance. Then Mike made a gesture as if he were going to throw his kayak over the cliff, and that must have iced it.

I admired their composure. The composure of hunters. The dogs, hackles up, bursting with impressions of their own, wheeled, ran up to us, and reared back.

Ken spoke to the hunter. Somehow he confirmed that they were from Gogden, the first village down below, a few miles up the side stream from Luku. The man knew Sherab. Ken said he'd been to this cave before, when he came through in 1993.

The rest of our group began to file in. Steve chucked down his boat. "I'm totally bushed. The last few hours I've been cursing the descendants and the ancestors of all the porters."

Steve shook himself. "Let's get these boats out of the way." The four of them, Mike, Willie, Johnnie, and Steve, slung their kayaks together, carabinered them to a tree, and lowered them over the edge of the trail like fish on a stringer.

The back of the cave had a nearly level rock shelf, and the Sherpas started a fire in one corner of it. The porters dropped their loads in the cave, and when they attempted to linger, the Sherpas shooed them out loudly. The curly-headed kid in the pink sweater vest, Pemba, the 16-year-old who'd guided me to the meditation cave, refused to leave at first. He squatted by the fire, and the Sherpas brushed past him, irritated. The boy started yelling at them, then shot us all an angry look and left. Troublemaker.

Willie gathered up everyone's water bottles, jogged to the creek just down the trail, and filled them. Then he borrowed the crooked staff of one of the porters and began to rake the dirt floor of the cave into a semblance of smoothness. He excavated and raked and swept. He worked on it for half an hour. His energy was amazing. I think he was pissed and was channeling his anger.

"That's fucking nice, dude," Johnnie said.

We moved in our packs and staked out places to sleep under the overhang. Not enough room for all. The Sherpas would sleep back on the shelf, and Mike, with the selfless nonchalance he exhibited always, crammed his bag up on an uneven ledge. The porters dispersed up and down the slope in the trees, making a score of tiny camps wherever there was a pocket or hummock of rock that would hold them against the steepness. It was 5:30. On the eastern side of the great Senchen spur, the late sun had long departed, and the side valley was already washed in the first wave of night. Willie said, "Time to do dorm check." He wanted to catch some of the porters with our missing knives and meat, restore some order. And I surprised myself by wanting it, too. Fuck them. They were pushing us too far.

Willie took the staff, and we went up the trail and climbed the slope to the first fire on a ledge. A group of four porters looked astonished when we climbed over. "*Tashi delay*," Willie said. "How's it going?" They nodded, uncertain. A tense silence as we scanned their fire—nothing. A square can of tea on the flames, tsampa, butter. "Hey, have a good night." We dropped down to another fire, and this time the five porters looked vulnerable and poor—and startled. They had a little bit of tsampa, jars of tea. After all that climbing and descending, this was their meal. I thought of the relative feast the Sherpas were putting together up above, and I felt ashamed. We trotted over to one last fire, one older porter and three of the young hotshots, including Pemba, and they met our sudden appearance with silent wariness. But no purloined food, no stolen watch or knives in sight. We climbed back to the cave and announced it.

Scott said, "I want to have a meeting after dinner. I want everyone here."

We ate, looking over the last lingering light of the Yangden Tsangpo River Valley, and then Scott gathered everyone to the floor of the cave. "Day after tomorrow is a layover day to sort everything," he said. "Tomorrow will be a crux day for the porter situation."

He squatted in the dirt as if coiled to jump. He looked around the circle. "We're all really smoked with the porter situation. Fact is, we don't know who steals from us and who does harm. Granted there are a few items missing, but I just want to remind everybody, *look* where we're at and *look* what we're doing." He nodded. "Don't get so worked up about the porter situation. I was well clued in to how things work down here. I maybe should've been more open. All the little shoving, pushing, storming their camps—it's gotta stop."

Storming their camps. Is that what we did, Willie and I? I guessed so. I felt a twinge of shame.

Scott continued, "If people get involved with things they shouldn't, it just adds to hostility. It's something two people should be dealing with—me and David."

There was the reprimand. I didn't mind; he was right.

He looked at each of us. "We've all been through an epic three days, and it's been tough and it's been a grind and it's worn down the morale, but we've got to get through that. If you're unhappy with any decisions, come to me. I'm a pretty open-minded guy. Come talk with me about it. I'm here for everyone. Every single person on this trip is here for a reason, and we're here to experience it together."

Then came the logistics. "Tomorrow we're gonna break everything down to bare essentials, what you need for the next 18 days to survive."

Dave coughed and said, "Send nonessential gear out to Pelung. The kayakers will be doing the river section. There aren't many places to do bank support until Payi, and after that it's only till the take out that we can get some things down. We've got to go light." From the confluence down to Payi and then on to Luku, the trail would be way above, and inaccessible to, the river. The kayakers would have to self-support.

Charlie said, "Pretty much one pair of clothes, your bivy, and your sleeping bag."

Dave added, "I hear in Luku, too, there's some form of distilled alcohol."

Scott said, "The expedition will buy the first round."

"I'll buy the second," Dave said.

Andrew said, "Anyone wanna spark up a doobie?" He was joking, but only in that we didn't have any. The Lower Gorge, however, was supposed to be thick with weed.

And then somehow everybody started singing "Love Shack," and the nude Chinese playing cards came out, and we played Shithead until we couldn't keep our eyes open.

I could see now why Scott had had such fierce loyalty from his cadre of paddlers over the years. He was competent, no, masterful, in every respect, from his kayaking to river safety to filmmaking, from organizing an extremely complex expedition to leading it in the field. He delegated, trusted his lieutenants implicitly, and at the critical moment, he stepped in and led. My respect for Scott as a leader multiplied. Whatever issues he had with me and my story, that's exactly what they were. In the scheme of the expedition, they were minor. I think I'd misinterpreted his broodings. I think he was watching everything, often holding himself back, fighting the impulse to assert himself until he had to.

. . . .

A rote exhaustion took over. A steady, half-blind descent into more and more fervid jungle, of vines climbing serpentine up broad trees, lianas like the strings of marionettes dropping from the canopy, and orchids and epiphytic grasses bursting from mossy trunks. Mats of wild strawberries, violets, asters. The first strangler figs enmeshing their hosts in a cage of wooden snakes. We *felt* like marionettes, as if our own will, detached by fatigue, forced the legs and arms to move. For the kayakers, it was worse. Carrying the boats, they seemed like a weird parody of the Stations of the Cross.

Imagine, then, emerging in late afternoon into a field: a steeply sloping field blackened from the last burn and hazed with the tender green of new wheat and barley. Crossing it to a creek where hollowed logs sluice the water downhill to a small stone millhouse, following the worn trail down, and in the hut, the round stone grinding grains of millet from a big funneled bag—the turning of the stone vibrating the sack's stiffened mouth so that a grain at a time is shaken into the central hole. Into a pasture now, with black and white cows grazing, and tall prayer flags waving at the bottom, and a stand of banana trees and a house. A house. The implications ramify.

It was the house of the hunter we'd met at the cave: a high stone foundation walling the open stable—the animals lived underneath—walls of blackened thick planks, and a slat-shingled peaked roof, the shingles weighted with stones. I climbed a log stile with steps carved into it and dropped into a dirt yard where the revelry was already under way. Porters gathered around shallow baskets three feet across and filled with popcorn, and drank from ceramic bowls. Tuli raised his bowl, emptied a fistful of popcorn into my palms, hugged my shoulders, and motioned me inside. I stepped through the doorway, and it took a second for my eyes to adjust to the gloom. "Hey, Peter Sahib! Cheers, mate! Welcome to Gogden!" Dave, Andrew, Rob, Kannuri, Passang. Scott and Johnnie. They sat along a bench under a single unglazed window or shoulder to shoulder along the floor, against the wall. They held up ceramic bowls and toasted. A young woman with long, loose black hair appeared out of the corner. She handed me a bowl and sloshed out of a five-gallon plastic gasoline can something clear and—judging by the expressions on the expeditioners—potent. Kannuri beamed. He and Andrew slid over and indicated a seat between them.

"Petrol?"

"It's *rakshi*, mate, bloody top-shelf, too! And that's *chang*," Andrew said, pointing to a bowl of what looked like frothy piss. Chang tasted like beer, watery and bitter. Rakshi was pure, distilled millet alcohol and tasted like oblivion.

G O G D E N

The hut—walls, broad planked floor—was blackened by smoke. Soot-black, dusty bundles in odd shapes hung from the rafters: They were yak stomachs holding butter. A small fire burned in the open stone hearth, beside which gleamed the drum of a polished bronze prayer wheel. An old man, toothless, squatted and poked at the flames. A simple shelf above held a red battery with terminals that powered a radio and a single electric bulb. A lotus motif decorated the fireplace. Sacks of grain stood in the corner. A girl of about 10 in skirt and army cap, even more bejeweled than her mother, with bracelets jangling on both wrists, poured butter tea from a kettle. Another woman held an infant. These were Lopa, descendants of the Abors from the hills of Assam.

The girl and the woman and the hunter wouldn't let a bowl stand empty. They sloshed and poured, and no one would refuse. We'd get a modest bill the next day.

The radio played a tinny Chinese love song. The lama, crammed beside me, beamed beatifically and got affectionate. He kneaded my leg and shoulders and sloshed his rakshi into my bowl. I stepped outside to take a leak and saw Allan coming across the field slowly under his boat like a tattered revenant. Steve came over the fence, beat but clean-cut and looking relaxed as usual, then immediately squatted beside the porters, dumped some tea into a bowl of powdery tsampa, rolled the mush into a grapefruit-size ball, and devoured it.

The rest of the expedition was inside the next house. Andrew was here, too—how did he get here? He leaned forward and vomited on the plank floor, and an old woman stepped over and wordlessly swept it up with a twig broom.

I'm not sure how much time passed. The Chinese diva ululated.

I needed fresh air. I made my way out into the yard, which smelled of manure and turned earth and what I thought was cold snow. It occurred to me that I hadn't seen Rob and Dave for a long time. They'd been hitting it pretty hard. I climbed the lane and over the stile and found them in the dirt yard, sitting cross-legged around a basket of popcorn with Tuli, Ching Mi the policeman, and Sherab. Voices loud, emphatic. Angry. Tsawong interpreted. He looked like a zombie. Dave said, "All right. I'll pay you tonight. But only 14 of the 18 days. That 4 days is my insurance."

Tuli yelled. He wanted a written IOU for the rest.

Dave said, "Tell him, 'What's the difference? We're all moving together.' . . . All right, all right. Tonight at six. Fourteen days."

The meeting broke up. I sat with Rob and Dave, and they made toasts. The rakshi was working on everybody. Dave said, "You're bloody tough, mate. Never a peep. When I saw that pass, I thought, 'I hope his leg holds up.' Here's to Pete!" We drank—rakshi for them, tea for me.

"Shall we head down?" I said.

"Good fucking idea. Here's to heading down."

The lane was steep and had rocks eroded out of it like big steps, and it passed a hollow bamboo spout pouring water into a rill. Dave fell down laughing, and Rob fell, and Dave tried to piss on him, and he was laughing and laughing. It was cowboys coming to town. I led them to the second home, where the party raged and continued down the lane to a cluster of houses with a big view down the valley. One of them had been cleared as a lodge for the 45 porters. Chinese music and singing and shouts came loudly out of it. Behind it was a sloping pasture with a clump of banana trees, some flat boulders, and a few horned, dun-colored cows nosing over it. At the lower end of the field, the Sherpas had set up the kitchen tarp. A four-foot stone terrace edged the bottom of the pasture. I dropped my pack and stood at its edge. Just below it ran the broad, worn trail down the valley to Luku. A bamboo water spout stuck from its face, spilling into a creek that dropped off the steep hill.

Beside the pool, a group of little girls, a grown woman, and an ancient crone sat in a circle with a pile of tiny clay statues. They smiled broadly and tittered, and I squatted beside them. They passed around a brass mold like a bell, maybe three inches high. A feather lay in a bowl of yak butter. They dipped the feather and greased the mold, then packed it with slate-colored clay from the edge of the pool. They turned it upside down and dimpled the bottom and set in a single grain of barley as an offering; then they smoothed over it. They set the figurine neatly with the others.

"What for?" I asked, holding out my upturned palms.

The old woman pointed toward the pass and the mountains. She handed me the bell; the little girls laughed as I packed it, and one placed the single grain in my palm, and I set it inside the womb of the figure and smoothed it with my thumb and awkwardly tamped it out. It must have been late afternoon. I heard a commotion up above in camp and thanked them and climbed back up.

. . . .

Scott and Rob and Tsawong and Ching Mi and Tuli were up in the field holding a meeting. Knots of porters were gathered down the field. They kept surging uphill, trying to join the caucus, and Willie and Dustin Lindgren kept herding them back. I heard Scott's voice rising.

"You agreed! Eyes! You agreed! Eyes! Eyes!" Scott pointed his forked fingers at Tuli's eyes and then at his own. The old eye thing. "Nothing is for free in this world!" To Tsawong: "You translate—I pay! I pay all men. I fucking *pay*."

Villagers gathered along the hedgerows and spectated silently. A horse grazed under the bananas. The snow mountains of the Senchen spur reared beyond the stone houses. Ken and Allan and I sat together. "This period of time of extraordinary physical effort for 21 days wears on people," he said. "I'm sure the porters are under the same circumstances. I'm sure it contributed to the drinking. I think the bottom line is these guys are not porters. I think they were rounded up by cronies and friends in Pe." I looked at Ken. He consistently uttered perfect, well-shaped paragraphs. How did he do it?

"Where's Dave?" I asked Allan.

He smiled his gentle smile. "Last time I saw him, I was using him as a map stand."

Ken shook his head. "There just is not an established etiquette for porterage in the Gorge."

I'll say. What had happened was, Rob looked at his watch and left Dave in his cups at the second house, then came down to pay the porters at the promised hour of six o'clock. All the porters stumbled out of a large house at the edge of the field that had become the Gogden Saloon and gathered on the hillside. Rob found Dave's pack, took out the bricks of 100-yuan bills, and counted out 14 days' worth, 1,400 yuan apiece, $170 per porter, a king's ransom in Tibet. Tuli, drunk, counted it and exploded. He wanted the full 18 days. He shouted at Rob and lunged at Ching Mi the cop. The gathered porters began to shout. Finally, Scott and Rob and the head porters retreated up the hill to sit in council.

Their voices rose and died away. The porters milled restlessly and then broke uphill toward the negotiators. Willie and big Dustin Lindgren intercepted the younger, more agitated ones and pushed them downhill while talking to them and rubbing their shoulders. At dusk, nothing was resolved. The bright three-quarter moon floated in the sky over the snow mountains. Dustin announced: "Too many people have been having too good a time for too long. Forget about it till tomorrow." They broke, agreeing that payment would be made then.

We gathered at the kitchen tarp. The Sherpas made fresh nettle soup and dal. Scott sat on an overturned kayak, sweetly holding a village child in his lap and eating soup, brooding. Loud Chinese music drifted across the field from the big house, where the porters were hitting it again, partying with the local girls. Kids gathered around our tarp. They hummed the songs they'd heard 1,000 times—must have been China Top 40. Dave was still missing.

Allan said, "It's a blowout up there."

Mike said he had been checking with locals for knives to buy when another villager leaned in just as Mike was pulling a knife from its sheath, and he accidentally clocked him hard in the forehead with the bone handle. "He definitely went Hollywood on me. Andrew gave him a six-pack of antacid. Seemed to work."

Willie said that he'd walked to Luku this afternoon and looked down at the lower river. "I saw this wave."

Everybody turned toward him. A spoon tinked against a bowl.

"Dude, you could drive a Mack truck through it. The river takes kind of a bend to the left, and there's an eddy, boiling, with the current rushing by from this, like, *Hawaii Five*-O thing that curls *toward* the eddy. I've never seen anything like it."

A diagonal wave that angled *upstream*. The river that ran through Shangri-La would be different from any other river in the world. We forgot the porters.

"And the foam pile below it—there was nothing below. It looked like the most perfect foam pile. A perfect ball of whitewater."

Willie tipped his bowl and polished off the soup. "Now it won't be about rocks making the features. It'll be water colliding with water."

Somebody fetched Dave from above. We unlaced his boots and put him into his bag under the tarp. I kicked aside some cow pies and set up my tent under a roof of magnified stars and crawled into my own bag. Laughter and the music from Chinese radio came across the hill. I woke in the middle of the night and it was raining hard, and when I pushed my head out in the morning, there was new snow whitening the jungle a few hundred feet above camp. The mountains up the Yangden were blotted with storm. I thought that if we'd been on the pass just three days later, none of us would have made it.

. . . .

Most of us, glad for a rest day, drank our coffee slowly and played hours and hours of Shithead under the tarp. Local gals and hordes of children crammed in out of the rain. The young women were lovely, with long, loose or braided hair under their army caps and liquid dark eyes and high, scrubbed cheeks rouged by wind and sun. They all wore long skirts over rough pants and carried silver-sheathed belt knives adorned with shells and little bells, and up to 10 beaded necklaces—freshwater pearls and silver mandala medallions set with turquoise—and bone rings, and coral and crystals on leather cords. Bracelets, too. They jingled and tinked and clicked when they walked. One little girl, about four years old and with a shaved head like a nun's, carried a baby boy papoosed in a blanket on her back. The younger boys carried inner-tube slingshots in their back pockets, and the older ones had long knives in stamped metal sheaths. Boys and girls proudly showed me their knives, and I showed them my Leatherman multi-tool with little scissors, and we were all fascinated. A few, holding back laughter, reached out and brushed their fingers over the hair on my forearms.

At some point in the morning, Dave paid the porters the 14 days without a riot, and we could hear them making merry with their new earnings—laughter and singing and high female voices coming over the hill from the house across the pasture. Some of them showed up in camp with brand-new camo pants and fresh packs of Panda cigarettes. A matron with a basket on her arm sold us warm chapatti flatbread—she unwrapped the cloth, and the aroma struck the card players like a Pepé Le Pew cartoon. We devoured the chapattis with expedition jam. A boy sold sticks of sugarcane. Dustin Knapp showed up, fresh from a hike all the way to the river. The card game stopped.

He was still breathing hard. He was wet and carried only a water bottle and a small drybag, and his long undershirt was pushed up on his forearms. He'd found a trail descending to the cable crossing that strung to the other side of the Gorge.

"It's a whole different game," he announced, excited. "Fifty-foot-wide hole on one side of the river, 100-foot-wide hole on the other! And a highway going through." He turned to Willie and smiled his Mona Lisa smile. "That Mack truck–size feature you saw was more like a motorcycle." Someone passed him a chapatti. "The cable crossing—I tossed a rock. Five seconds, that's 312 feet, and the scour must've been 200 feet above my head." A 500-foot scour. It took a moment to register. A scour is what it sounds like, the visible strip of erosion on a riverbank above the surface of the water, washed away by high water and flood. Your local creek might have a scour a few feet high. Your local river, maybe 5, 10, an outrageous 20. But one as high as a 50-story building . . . the wall of water that caused that came out of some nightmare. This was nothing from a hobbit movie; this was *Independence Day* and *Deep Impact*.

We had all heard rumors of the flood. It was in June of 2000, just a year and a half before, and resulted from a landslide up on the Yigong, a tributary of the Po Tsangpo. It plugged the smaller river, creating a lake miles long. Then this natural dam broke, loosing an apocalyptic flash flood down the Yigong into the Po Tsangpo and the Lower Gorge. It had been big enough to destroy 20 large bridges and leave 50,000 people homeless in the Indian state of Arunachal Pradesh, 125 miles downstream. At least 30 people had died. The Indians accused the Chinese of causing it, of blowing the earthen dam and deliberately not warning them. We had heard all this, but nobody factored it into the expedition's plans. How bad could it have been?

Bad. From Dustin's description, it was one of the most dramatic hydrologic events in recent history.

Allan had dug out the zoomed-in pages of the satellite image, which, according to Space Imaging, was collected in May 2000, only a month before the flood.

"Was the rapid you saw all runnable?" Al asked.

"Oh, yeah. Boat scout."

"Was the water still green?" Scott said.

Dustin nodded. "Yeah, beautiful." Then he described the cable crossing strung between the cliffs: two cables so that whichever direction you went, you were sliding downhill. He said the cable from Luku to a hamlet across the Gorge called Gande was grounded with logs pounded vertically into a cave. Villagers used a simple rope harness that looped around the back and butt and hooked into a wheel. Nothing clipped in, no belay or safety, just a free-hanging zip line.

Dave came in under the tarp and caught us up on the porter situation. At first, he thought he'd pulled off a bit of a coup: The local chiefs said we had to hire all their boys. This was the old *ula* system asserting itself. Ken explained that villages were once required by the king or Dalai Lama to supply porters and provisions for official travelers. "This area may not have seen an expedition or travelers for many years. Probably over four years."

Dave said our porters were contracted through to Pelung, and the locals would have to deal with them, sort it out among themselves. We had heard the Pe porters and Gogden locals arguing with each other as we'd played cards earlier. The raised voices had stopped. Now the local chiefs had come back to Tsawong and demanded 3,000 yuan to let us pass through—$380.

Could they do that? Block our passage? Apparently so. They were following centuries of Lamaist precedent.

So now, in early afternoon, as the rain abated, we saw a bunch of our porters giving the haggling a rest and sauntering past on the smooth trail, going to Luku for more booze. They were singing, and they shouted *"Tashi delay!"* up at our camp, in what sounded like a mocking tone. It was the only Tibetan most of us knew.

Dave thought that as long as we were stalled out, he might as well get preparations and provisions ready for the final kayak assault from the confluence to Luku. Ground support would be minimal, and the kayakers would have to go self-supported, with heavily loaded boats, just the way Walker-McEwan did on their attempt from Pe in 1998. They would have to plan on six days to run the 20 river miles. Dave said he would send one or two people with their hiking shoes and clothes for the hike back.

He and Passang Sherpa started in on reassessing and re-sorting porter loads. It would help in all future negotiations to know how many porters we'd actually need for the last section. Dave didn't look even the least hungover. He made a scale by taking a length of stout bamboo and tying a piece of purple seven-millimeter climbing rope in the middle of it. On either tip, he tied a short line with a carabiner on the end. One liter of water equals 1 kilo. The porters would carry 18 kilos of expedition gear. He took a liter water bottle and poured it 18 times into a water can and clipped it from one side of the crosspiece and balanced the loads against it. In less than an hour, he got our provisions down to nine loads of food. There were two big bundles of prayer flags we'd planned to leave at Rainbow Falls. Someone suggested we leave one bundle here to lighten the loads. "Nah, I don't think so," Dave said. "I don't feel very good about this place. I threw up everywhere." He winked.

The locals were fascinated. Knots of freckled girls, their hair braided and shiny, stood shyly off to the side. Young men asked for medicine and were given the standard palliatives—ibuprofen or antacid. Kids crowded in. Willie scraped a line in the straw and dirt under the long tarp, leveled his eyes at the children, and boomed, "I'm defender of the line!" That was all the provocation they needed. The kids instantly understood the new game. They jumped across it and back and pushed each other. Willie shook his head, uncoiled a climbing rope, and nodded to Andrew. They stretched the rope across the line. This incited hysterical laughter. Within five minutes, there were 10 kids hauling one end in a tug of war with Giant Willie. He released it and they collapsed into a gleeful pile. Two little boys jumped out of it and immediately tackled one of the quiet young women watching at the edges. She seemed to be wearing her Sunday best, and I thought she would react angrily. Instead she rolled with the boys on the wet grass and tickled them and laughed until I thought she'd pee. Willie waded into the scrum as instinctively as a bird dog jumps into a marsh.

While Willie upended eight little kids on a boat like a seesaw, tumbling them into a tangle of squeals, another man approached Tsawong to ask for medicine. Scott looked up from his cards, exasperated. "You know what," he barked to Tsawong, "tell them no more medicine. We're out." He turned back to Mike. "It's gonna be war tomorrow. Tsawong says Mr. Liang will pay for it. If he doesn't, I'm gonna take it out of his wages."

Dustin Knapp asked, "Why is Mr. Liang gonna pay for it?"

"Exactly," Scott said. "He wants to call Mr. Liang and ask him. He just wants Mr. Liang to pull the plug, just say 'Okay, come out.' That's it. Don't let Tsawong use the sat phone."

Scott called everyone together. "I've been thinking about things. We don't want to get locked in with 80- to 160-foot holes to dodge and no way to scout. I'm not into that. All it takes is one bad section. Because as you all probably know, from Payi to Luku there's no way out of the river, we're without ground support, and we'll have loaded boats. So I think we need to take a good look at it and come to a group decision."

Dustin Knapp said, "What I saw was really easy to run and really hard to scout."

Scott suggested the team take a good look. "By just going confluence to Payi," he says, "we'll save six days." As opposed to going on down to Luku.

"I'd also like to send a team to Rainbow and Hidden falls," he said. "To peek around. For the expedition and for the film."

Everybody digested it. It was a new objective, pretty ambitious and brash. A Hidden Falls party would have to come over the Senchen La from Payi—not the hairy, long south-north traverse we saw and avoided but straight over the top and back down to the river.

Dave worked over his leg like a preening monkey. "I don't understand all these ticks," he murmured. "I asked to be a *chick* magnet."

. . . .

The waxing moon waded into a tide of stars. Scott came back from up the hill, where he'd just called his girl. "The Kings are still number one," he announced, "and the Lakers lost three in a row. As of an hour ago, *Aerated* was duplicated. In Montreal, get this—an American won a speed skating event!" Laughter.

Remote expeditions in the third millennium.

Talk of other, more somber news. Two nights ago, up in the cave camp, Dave had called his wife, Louise, and she told him that 134 Nepalese were killed by Maoist guerrillas in the countryside.

"Supposedly, the King of Luku and the King of Gogden were involved in that meeting today with Tsawong about the payoff," Scott said.

Dave said, "The standard practice here is, you drop your porters at the next village and move up with the next set."

"Yeah, they have guns here. We have knives," Scott said acidly.

"We have Sherpas!" Allan said.

At 9:30 the next morning, the negotiations with the Gogden headmen were already under way. Most of the boys were eating pancakes, sitting near the tarp on the piles of packed bags. A little ways off in the field, Dave and Tsawong and Scott and a knot of locals were getting into it. A young man in suit pants and camo jacket was arguing loudly, on the edge of fighting. An old man in a frayed and stained black suit and army sneakers, with a belted knife in an old wooden sheath, was shooed away by a few of our boys. It turned out he was a headman, too, and his loss of face ignited angry recriminations.

Dustin Lindgren made a comment about the loud one, how he should shut it, and his brother yelled across the slope, across the piles of gear, "Don't fucking say anything! No stealing comments, no nothing!"

"I was just—"

"Not a fucking word!" Scott snapped.

Dustin turned and muttered under his breath, "Fuck you."

Dustin wasn't having a good day, and it had barely started. Apparently, he had just shown his knife to the Gogden headman and explained that there'd been stealing, and the headman thought Dustin was accusing *him*, which wasn't the best PR.

I thought of a Hell's Angel funeral I once went to where the chaplain, in leathers and beard, had said, "Every day I thank *God* I haven't stole today, or cheated or lied or murdered—and then I get out of *bed*."

I got a cup of coffee and watched the spectators come. They strung all along the lower edge of the field, on top of the stone wall. Gogden-Luku has 76 souls, and they must've all been there, every one. Efforts to stop them from drifting down into the pasture, to the very edge of the negotiations, were fruitless. A clutch of young girls in burnt-red vests watched from the limbs of a flowering fruit tree. With their turquoise jewelry, they looked like exotic birds. Boys occupied another tree. More locals huddled beneath the copse of banana trees on the low terrace.

I noticed that Ken and Andrew and Johnnie weren't eating anything. They looked drawn and shaky and had the guarded immobility of the nauseated. The three of them had eaten food yesterday at a local's house and were sick all night long with vomiting and diarrhea. Dave was also up with the all-night shits.

Just shy of noon, Dave, Rob, Scott, and Tsawong sat cross-legged off in a cove at the eastern edge of the field with a kettle of tea and Tuli, Ching Mi, Sherab, and another head porter from Pe. Dave began by talking about the *ula* system, how the Gogden locals were insisting we hire their people instead. "If we keep you on, you men from Pe, this will keep happening. Here, Luku, Payi, all the way along. Fighting our whole way . . ." Dave was angling to fire these guys, handing them the pink slip as gently as he could. He needn't have bothered: None of them seemed too upset. They seemed, in fact, delighted. Tuli kept nodding sympathetically, smiling, sipping his tea as if he could feel Dave's pain. When he saw me, he grinned and patted the ground beside him, but I shook my head, and Scott shot me a murderous look.

Dave said, "We thank you from our hearts. These kayakers have made history. You will remember, you will tell your grandchildren, of the expedition when the kayakers came down the Tsangpo. And you have been a part of it. We thank you. We're sure we will see you on the trail in the future."

The porters raised their teacups in toast. Then I did the math, and it occurred to me why they were so pleased at getting canned. If they worked the extra nine days we had promised, out to the road at Pelung, they'd only get two days' return pay to take the bus home. About the same pay, but one version with all work and one with none. Dave was giving them the no-work option.

"Peter. Peter, please leave. I'm asking you, please." I looked up. It was Scott. His lips were compressed, and his head was trembling. I looked at him and didn't move. This was what I was here for. Our expedition was somehow hanging in the balance of these talks, and I had an assignment. Scott said, "Peter, *please*! I'm asking you!" Jesus. He was going to blow his lid. He wasn't going to let the wrangling continue while I was there.

I got up, walked five feet away, turned my back, and stayed there. I could still hear the discussion. It felt like another power play to me. My presence wasn't affecting the discussions, unless Scott was going to make another bad-faith deal. A few minutes later, they broke to get more tea. I walked over to Scott.

"Scott, can I talk to you a sec?"

"No, *please*," he shot back. "Sorry, I'm in the middle of negotiations."

They talked a few more minutes, Dave wrapped it up, or thought he did, and they shook hands all around and broke. Scott walked by me, heading up the hill.

"Peter, you want to talk a sec?"

All right. I remembered his strong speech up in the cave, when he said he wanted us to come to him with any grievance.

I said, "I need some cooperation. That was a power play. I wasn't interfering at all. You don't want me to write about controversy, and it'd be hard to find any. But this is drama, this stuff is important—"

He cut me off. "Peter, it's a matter of trust. I asked the whole village to stay back. You have never been a part of these negotiations."

What did that have to do with it? "I'm the *press*," I said. "The press sits in on meetings between the president and Putin. I need some *cooperation*. This is the story—"

"You don't have a *story*?" he shouted. The whole camp could hear. You're making a deal out of this? Are you saying you don't have a *story*?"

"No. I'm saying—"

"Fuck your story!" he yelled. He looked like he wanted to take a swing. Instead, he threw his half-full teacup down the hill and stomped away.

I looked down the hill, and the whole expedition was silent, watching, all the porters, the villagers. I walked down to my pack.

Charlie said, "That probably wasn't the best time."

"It's a distraction for him," Willie said.

Andrew said, "We know you didn't mean any harm."

"You tell a story with details," I said.

"Anyway, maybe it wasn't the best time," Charlie repeated.

"Yeah, maybe not," I said.

. . . .

I saw Tuli walking back toward the porter house. He gave me a cigarette. I asked him, motioning, "Are you going to Pe?"

"Pelung," he said. He motioned that he'd be carrying my pack, I think. I was a bit confused. He put his hand on my chest, nodded, and smiled. "Okay," I said, and walked back to our camp.

Scott walked back up to the rest of us. "Just so you all know," he said tensely, "there's a good possibility we won't be leaving here today." Then he retreated back down the hill.

I dug a little bottle of liquid soap and a clean pair of socks out of my pack and headed down the trail toward Luku, past the tall prayer flags to a creek that cascaded down the lush hillside. I turned up the creek for privacy, following a stony path, then came to a small, clear pool below a stone mill house and stripped and bathed. The shock of the ice water raised goose bumps, and I did a quick pushup in the stream and washed my hair and dunked again, then clambered gingerly up the pebbly bank on tender feet and air-dried in the sun. I looked up and saw a group of young girls, the ones in the burnt-red vests who had been in the peach tree, peering down from the brush above the mill hut, their faces lit with mischief. I laughed and hastily pulled on my polypro long underwear.

When I returned, a large meeting was taking place on the open hillside. There were 30 of the porters from Pe and Scott, Dave, and Rob at the center, with Tsawong. Ken was there, too. Willie and Mike had returned, dazzled by the river and perplexed at the ongoing scene.

I walked up. "They want 20 days' return," Dave said.

Things had certainly progressed. I scanned the standing porters. They pressed into the circle of negotiators and looked fierce.

"They want as much pay going out as they got going in, without carrying anything," Dustin Lindgren said. "Mr. Liang witnessed the contract in Pe—it's just absolute idiocy on their part."

"Let's walk away for a while," Dave said.

Tsawong announced a break. A loud murmur of protest swept through the porters. The younger ones started to yell. They jostled together in a press toward Tsawong, and they looked like they wanted to tear him limb from limb. Where were the older ones, the elders? We backed down the hill to the tarp. This didn't look good at all. The sun, balanced on the ridge above the village, went over. It dwindled for a moment, hanging on the high snow, and was gone, throwing the field into sudden cold shadow. Extra jackets came out.

Dave said to Tsawong, "Tell them that you're calling the Chinese authorities for advice and we'll wait."

Allan said, "The cop says he's useless in this. It's out of his control."

We were at the edge of the big tarp. Instinctively, we began to pull in the outer bags of gear, circling the wagons.

Dustin Lindgren said, "The punks are taking over. The leaders are useless."

Tsawong approached. "I just talked to my wife, who talked to Mr. Liang, and he will bring the money to Pelung."

Dave pulled someone's pack down onto the pile of gear. "The chances of them going to Pelung to collect money are near zero when we have money to pay other porters." He blew out his cheeks. "Can we have the porter leaders again?" he called, and walked back up into the fray.

The younger porters, the curly-headed kid in the pink vest and a dozen others, were arguing with Ching Mi. They turned on Dave and Tsawong and Scott, talking over each other. They said they wanted their money now. Ching Mi tried to reason, and they shouldered him aside.

The rest of the porters were just back of them, all around us, like a tide backing up a breaking wave. Their elders, even the pugnacious Tuli, had been pushed to the back of the crowd. A bunch of the hotheads had their hands on the hafts of their long knives.

Forty-two days or nothing. The demanded paydays kept growing. *Now!*

I did the math fast. What they seemed to want now was over the top: 18 days on the trail plus 10 days' return pay—the deal made at Pemakochung. Plus the promised days out to Pelung, say 9 more, full pay, even though they wouldn't be working, plus 5 more return days for that phantom leg—42. Dave kept trying to reason, prodding Tsawong, and Tsawong would start to speak, and they'd shout him down.

We'll kill you all. . . .

"Now look, we're willing . . ."

Pay now. NOW. We'll take everything. . . .

The crowd was backing Dave and Tsawong and Scott and the rest down the grassy hill toward the tarps. I looked into the crowd, and Willie was in the middle of it all, praying. He was standing in the middle of the two groups in his fleece skullcap and beard, hands to his lips in prayer like an obsessed mendicant. His lips moved as his eyes went from porter to porter.

Ken said to Tsawong, "You need to call on the sat phone. You need to let Mr. Liang know the seriousness of this particular incident right now. It has to be made forcefully. Our safety is on the line. And it could turn violent. It'll be an international incident if there's an attack in this Gorge. That's the last thing China wants."

Steve said, "CNN, everybody will cover it."

Dave raised his voice. "I want to speak to the porter leaders."

"*Mare! No!*" The young bucks pushed forward.

Charlie, frightened, said, "These guys are ready to make the decision for us. Pillage our shit and take our money."

"They've already threatened that," Steve said.

Scott said quickly, "We have seven grand for a helicopter ride out of here."

Andrew said, "Is it big enough for all of us?"

Tsawong, a few feet away, called for Scott. He said he had Chinese Peter on the sat phone, Mr. Liang's lieutenant.

Scott grabbed the phone, and the hotheads backed off a few feet. They seemed to understand that suddenly there was a line to the outside world and all that represented—probably government, the Chinese army maybe. Scott yelled into the phone: "We're in Luku. The porters are threatening our lives. Threatening to kill us, and they're stealing all of our money—stealing all of our money and threatening to kill us. They have us surrounded right now. Seventeen days. Yah. Seventeen days. They want us to pay them 42 days for 17 days of walking. That means we don't have enough money to leave Luku."

He handed the phone up to Tsawong. Tsawong spoke in Chinese, emphatic, rapid.

Scott said, "Are you telling him they're threatening to kill us? *Tsawong!*"

Scott grabbed the phone. The satellite bars, the black bars showing satellite reception, disappeared. The phone was dead. It would be another few minutes before another satellite swept over and we could call again. Everybody looked at the phone. It seemed to have an iconic power. No one moved.

Scott looked around at the porters. "Bad news for you guys," he hissed. He forked his fingers and pointed them at his eyes. "You all are fucking liars!" He couldn't help himself.

The porters leaped up, shouting—

The bars on the phone reappeared, and Scott hit redial. The porters drew up short, like horses yanked taut on a lead.

Scott yelled, "Peter. Peter. They're demanding all the money pretty much. Yah, it's out of control."

The phone went dead again.

The next two minutes were maybe the longest of the whole expedition. The crowd pressed forward. Willie was praying. Some of the porters had their hands on their knives again.

Reception. Two, three, four bars. A satellite—

Scott into the phone again: "They're threatening us with knives! You tell him something needs to happen!"

Tsawong talked on the phone. The cop talked.

Scott looked up at Mike. "You like what you saw down there, Mikey?"

He was talking about the Tsangpo.

Mike said, "It's pretty intimidating. But everything I saw was beautiful."

"It's the most beautiful river I've ever seen," Willie said.

Tsawong talked fast to the cop and porters, his long hands, holding a cigarette between two fingers, gesturing emphatically. The whole crowd riled, shouted, even the older porters in back; Pemba, the hotshot in the pink vest, spat, yelling—and then Tsawong just went off on him, shouting back. The crowd surged. They backed us up to the tarp. Dave and Tsawong were side-by-side. Dave looked scared for the first time. Tsawong whipped out his porter book and looked straight at the pink-vest kid and ran his fingers down the list of names. The import was clear: *We know you; we know your name. We will report you to the Chinese authorities.*

At the same time, Dave stuck out his arms and made a sign for handcuffs—

That was it. Eruption. Pemba lunged for Tsawong, swinging. Just behind him, the group of hotheads attacked, spitting, yelling, punching. The whole crowd exploded forward.

Dustin Lindgren was a practiced bouncer. He waded in. Willie was in the middle, too. They wedged and yelled and pulled and separated. So did Ching Mi. And Tuli, the old fighter, was yelling and grabbing the punks away.

Ching Mi the cop now stepped up. He waved the porters away, and they backed off a bit. Everybody breathed.

Dave said, "I don't really see any other solution than to pay the 40 days. Unless we want to stand up to them, and I don't think that's a good idea."

Tsawong interjected. He was shaking. "They say they want all the trip's money."

Scott took the phone and called.

"Peter," he said. "They just attacked us, bro. Not very well. . . . They just attacked us. They're threatening to kill us if we don't give them the money. Peter, are you there? Are you there? All of our lives are at stake right now. I wonder if there's a possibility of a military helicopter or other ideas. . . ." Scott cupped the phone, looked around.

Charlie said, "What'd he say about the helicopter?"

"There are no helicopters in Tibet." He cupped the phone again. "Peter, we're at a point here where we have to give all of our money— okay. Where's the cop? Ching Mi!"

That was it. Tsawong told him and the porter leaders that they should come here at 8:15 to get the money. Tsawong stood between us and the porters and rubbed his face. He was crying. The porters said, "Okay. Okay." And then the final jab: "*Tashi delay!*"

Dave slapped his head: "Ow. Fuck."

Scott said, "We just got robbed."

"At knifepoint," Mike said.

Half an hour later, by the light of headlamps, Dave pulled out his pack and counted out the bricks of yuan bills.

Ken and Andrew comforted Tsawong. I started up for the pile of gear to find my pack. A three-quarter moon hung directly above us, and a bright planet down to the east of it, maybe Venus. Scott saw me and called across the camp. "Hey, Peter, did you get your story?"

I stopped in midstride. I wasn't sure if he was genuinely making up for losing it earlier or if he was angry.

"Yeah," I said warily.

"I really appreciated that, this afternoon," he shot back with obvious sarcasm.

I didn't take the bait. When I came back down to the tarp, Allan sat next to me on one of the kayaks and said gently, "Pete, did you get a lot of notes?"

"Yeah," I said. I smiled at him. "Thanks."

. . . .

I passed 100 prayer flags strung on a wire over the creek with the morning sun shining through them and thought how adventurers, the truest and the finest, were the least encumbered people I'd ever known, had the least to protect. The rest of us acquire not just material things but also education, careers, advancement, everything entailing politics and caution. We acquire lovers, spouses, children, homes. We repeat the moves that have succeeded before, and eventually, security triumphs over risk. The seven paddlers didn't own anything. Most of them didn't even have a car. Most of the time, they had no steady girl to go back to. They collected nothing but stories. Maybe freedom really is nothing left to lose. You had it once in childhood, when it was okay to climb a tree, to paint a crazy picture and wipe out on your bike, to get hurt. The spirit of risk gradually takes its leave. It follows the wild cries of joy and pain down the wind, through the hedgerow, growing ever fainter. What was that sound? A dog barking far off? That was our life calling to us, the one that was vigorous and undefended and curious.

THE LOWER GORGE

The expedition was on the move again. Thirty-seven new porters, one from each family in Gogden-Luku, were hefting loads and tying them up with tumplines. There were women now, jingling in their long dresses and jewelry, and kids, whole families, each with a length of hemp rope and a hook. They shouldered the loads, the kayaks, too, and went over the wall and down the sunny, smooth trail to Luku. We followed.

These were happy porters, and for good reason. Dave was giving them all a flat rate—500 yuan for the 2½ days to Payi, period, no fussing with return pay. The sooner they got it done, the sooner they collected.

We descended to the village and turned north onto a good trail that would take us upstream. At a stout house hard against the trail, some of the old porters were continuing their party, and a few of us turned into the dirt yard. The blackened planks of the house's walls were scratched and chalked with prayers. Small pumpkins lined the stone foundation walls, and big baskets of black roasted potatoes and corn and chile peppers were passed around by the hosts. Everybody was in a fine mood now, sharing cigarettes with us as if nothing had happened in Gogden. Hanging from the eaves was the carcass of a cat.

What was this? It was tawny, the color of dry wheatgrass, and the size of a yearling mountain lion. Its eyes were sewn shut, crudely X-ed over, which gave it the look of a cartoon character that has just been clocked, and it was stuffed with straw, light to pick up. When I asked the old man in mime where he had gotten it, he said he'd shot it up there, waving vaguely toward the mountains.

We moved on. Mike and I hiked together, up the good trail that climbed steeply into a dry forest of pines. After an hour, it leveled for a bit, and we stumbled on a rock stupa at the edge of the canyon; for the first time, I looked down into the Lower Gorge and saw the river far below. The cut of this canyon was, if anything, more severe than the Upper Gorge's—narrower and more vertically sided. It marched undiminished into a haze of ranked mountains, and I could see the great scour of rock from the flood. Lush jungle poured over the rims. The river was green, milkier now, more jade than turquoise, and flat, maybe 50 yards wide. At the corner, it broke into a flurry of white, a river-wide feature whose scale we couldn't imagine. It was big, this lower river.

Mike said, "On a river of this volume, not only is there gradient downstream but from the sides as well, which makes it quite hard to get to the edges." In other words, current piling against and deflecting off the walls humps water all down the sides, so a kayaker in the middle of the current has to fight his way uphill to get to an eddy along the shore. The danger of getting swept out of control downstream was multiplied. Mike took out his camera and took some careful shots—"For future expeditions. Maybe the only chance we get to visually document this part of the Gorge. . . ."

We found the main trail and soon came on Tuli and another porter sitting beside their light personal loads, smoking. Tuli grinned and motioned me to sit beside him and have a smoke, but I waved and hiked on. He blinked, perplexed, as I passed. It perplexed me, too. I guess he thought the whole scene in Gogden was just business.

We were heading toward Go La Pass, a high, snow-laden knife ridge that divides the villages of Luku and Payi. Namcha Barwa sent it zigzagging northwest like the tentacle of a great octopus, and it ended only when it plunged into the Tsangpo. As far as we knew, the top of the pass we were now climbing was nearly as high as the pass to Luku, and the back side looked just as steep.

The fern woods ended abruptly at the edge of a deep side canyon and a creek that cut down toward the big river. The canyon was in deep, cold shadow. Across it, the wooded wall of the ridge we would have to climb tomorrow reared straight up, 3,000 feet more. The top was obscured in frayed cloud. Mike and I sat on the canted stump of a fallen tree, talking about nothing in particular, and learned that we had both worked for a man up a tiny "crick" in the kudzu hills of western North Carolina, Silver Creek, in a paddle maker's shop where a gentle giant named Homer King made exquisite custom paddles out of local ash and basswood and cherry. That's how big the kayaking world is.

Willie climbed up out of the shadows with his paddle and a big smile. He dropped onto the stump and leveled his paddle across the trail. "Toll gate. We're gonna charge the old porters 100 yuan to get through."

"What were you praying for yesterday, Will, in the middle of the brawl?"

"I was praying *Please let this work itself out. Please let this work itself out.* . . . I got some good eye contact with a lot of people. I was taking the Martin Luther King approach."

That night, we camped near another collapsed hunter's hut in deep, damp woods. Jangbu, evidently assessing the still-ragged fatigue of the group and having seen the ridge we'd have to climb tomorrow, broke out two cans of sweetened condensed milk. One went straight into the fire, where it cooked into a cylinder of gooey caramel. We devoured it by the spoonful. The other went into steaming cups of the last instant coffee. Then he cooked up a five-pot meal that included dim sum pastries stuffed with a nameless meat.

Scott, in another turn of mood, was talkative. He spoke of plans for the coming year, kayak video expeditions. "The boys want to go to Russia," he said. "Sumatra, Swaziland, Mexico, the coast of B.C., and a ski film to Argentina are all on the agenda."

Then he talked about his mother. At age 56, she had attended a special federal agent school, and now she works with the feds as a special auditor investigating corruption in education funding in the state of California. She leads a squad that will show up unannounced at a suspect institution and tell everyone inside to freeze at their desks while they seal the building and corral files and evidence. She carries a gun.

. . . .

February 24, Day 22—can it be? Some of our former porters crapped one after another in the middle of the trail, a sign of scorn. We went straight up the far slope, on a ridge back of forest, thick, wet, and spongy. From this verdant spine straight down, sliding, skiing in mud, swinging around small trees like light poles, down into another creek bottom, then straight up the other side, following another ravine into spruce forest, this time up wet slabs of rock that would be waterfalls in another month. A girl from Gogden carried a kayak, in her burnt-red jacket and ticking necklaces. A young boy carried another. Up between craggy formations of rock that looked like poured and frozen lava and might be, up into the snow and wind above 10,000 feet, into a ripping fog of cloud and a forest of stunted and wind-bludgeoned spruce all rimed in ice, the gusts blowing the frozen snow out of the limbs. Near the top, in wind-packed snow, I turned around and looked down into a miasma of boiling cloud blindingly sunlit as if from within, and saw the shifting shapes of great mountains. The dark peaks swam in it and the wind froze my face; the clouds tore and ramps of light bore downward, and I saw the shape of the Tsangpo Gorge like a river of deeper shadow flowing into India, the depth of it like out of a dream. The Tsangpo would hold something back, not in stinginess but in the generosity of mystery.

On the other side, the snow was knee deep, then thigh deep, then waist deep where it washed into the contours of the falling slopes. I stopped to put on my gaiters, and Scott passed on the trail in front of me, head down, carrying his paddle. I said a hearty "Hey!" He turned and glared at me and put his head back down and kept walking.

Just over the top, under tall hemlocks, was a sturdy hunter's lean-to on a bench of shallower slope, and the porters piled into it and made a couple of fires and warmed themselves. They took turns sledding the kayaks down the easy hill before it dropped off sheer.

Sometimes the only way through precipitous country on foot is to follow a creek bed. The falling water carves a rock trail down a mountainside where the footing is otherwise too loose and overgrown. That's what we did now. We came out of the high snow into black timber that barely clung to the canted world and dropped into a creek that fell through wet, dark forest with an abandon that threatened to go airborne at any moment. The problem with following a creek bed is that it's full of water, and where it's not, the rock is often wet and smooth and you hop at your peril. But the stream was low and left exposed slab. Johnnie and I hopped down together. He said, "I knew that everything Willie and Chuck and I had learned, everything we've thought about and experienced, would be tested on this trip. I knew it would be scary as shit and test everything I knew. It did. There were a lot of times out there where I was pretty scared." He stopped on a small outcrop of rock and took a deep breath.

"But it all went so smoothly, it was almost like the stars were lined up. I'm skeptical. I think, 'It's going so smoothly—what am I missing here?' But I knew, I had a feeling that it was meant to work out—which didn't jibe with my skepticism.

"Willie and I have this feeling that all our lives led up to this trip. And it's almost like it wasn't my choosing—not my choosing, but like the decisions I've made all brought me inevitably to this point."

We pulled up on a mossy rock shelf between two small, coursing waterfalls and camped almost in the stream. The porters knew the place. On the underside of the shelf, below the second cascade, was a large cave where they squeezed in.

I took my books into the bivy sack with me. It had two short poles that made a tented hood for my head and gave just enough room to prop on one elbow and read. I opened the Ziploc and pulled out the little stack. The paper covers were stained with tea and mud and were curling. The book on top of the three in my hand was Hemingway's collected stories, the one with the canoe in rapids in big woods on the cover. I looked at it, and a lifetime of associations rose out of the picture. Hemingway had been my hero when I was boy. His clean images of wild country transported me out of the streets of Brooklyn, where I grew up.

It rained on and off all night. The pattering and drumming against the hood of the bivy rose and subsided against the sifting gush of the little waterfall and the burble of the water eddying into the pool a few feet away. I crawled out to pee in the middle of the night, and there was the cascade angling down, sluicing white against the black rock, and the outline of the lone spruce at the top of the cliff, and behind it, swimming in mist, the gibbous moon. It was as it had been since the landscape painters of Ming and Qing had dipped their brushes and washed black ink against cream parchment and, through sheer love and consummate craft, transmuted the motion and sound and luminosity of a mountain night onto a scroll. That, in the end, is what we were here for: to give ourselves. None of the petty human scrabbling—the "Dusty Earth," as the Chinese mountain poets liked to say—mattered in the end. We would finish our expedition, gods willing, all alive. Scott would make a movie; I would write a book. The moon would fill and empty itself. Snow would blow onto a high ridge and drift into the pines and melt, and a nameless creek would spill into the fog and the night.

. . . .

Down and down into the shifting fog and the intermittent rain. Somewhere the rain stopped, the chill mist transformed into a warm steaminess, and I looked around and we were surrounded by great, broad-leafed trees, some with buttress roots, trees wrapped in the mossy, wrist-thick ropes of strangling vines, wild bananas with exuberant fronds, a midlevel canopy, epiphytic red flowers, and a fecund smell of matted leaves turning to earth. Bird cry pierced the subtropical jungle. Then we broke out of the forest into a wide, slashed field. There was a hut at the far end, tiny beneath its backdrop of dark woods that climbed the ridge straight into the scouring clouds. And at the bottom of the field, graced with a few tall trees completely covered in pink flowers, maybe peach, was the inner lip of the Gorge.

The paddlers almost ran to the overlook. This section, between Payi and Luku, was on the original master plan. The kayakers stood sentinel on a fallen log and looked straight downstream. The river bored through thousands of feet of sheer cliff. Jungle poured over the rims. Waterfalls streamed in from both sides, cascading in 1,000-foot seams to the river. The solid gray, horizontal band of the bedrock scour was easily 300 feet wide. The Tsangpo moved too fast to hold its opalescent green for long. Just below us, it broke into an exploding river-wide drop. Humongous wave trains erupted into two more rapids below that. Jesus. On the steep slope above the inner box canyon on the opposite site, river-left, was a mile-wide landslide. We were looking straight down at the "Landslide Rapid" that had so concerned the paddlers on the sat maps in Auburn.

Willie pulled at his beard and summed up the collective feeling: "Max on."

It was the first view of the Lower Gorge they could positively correlate with the satellite images they had memorized. It did not look runnable.

The rocky bank that was their margin of safety in the Upper Gorge had mostly vanished, destroyed by a cataclysmic flood. Even from here, they could see that the water volume was considerably bigger than what they had run. It was not as steep, but the easing gradient was canceled out by other factors. The drops looked like ledge falls, and they tended to be river-wide. The doubled current galloped between smooth rock walls. No take-out spot in sight.

What may have been the greatest disappointment was that the whitewater, the actual moves, might be doable. The first of the three big rapids was a river-wide terror that just might be walkable—there were some rocks along the shore. The next two looked runnable. Big, dangerous, but within the pale. The mood shifted a bit. A breath of excitement swept the group. They traded off using the binocs.

"Looks like a run down center, then drop left behind the rocks," said Dustin Knapp. "Or all down the center."

They strung across the field and dropped into woods, down into the cut of a forested creek that looked like some artist's view of paradise. The creek was spanned by a little wooden footbridge. It spilled in a series of little waterfalls. In the big pool below the bridge, two lumbering dzo with tremendous horns, one with a ring in its nose, waded knee deep in the cold water and swung their heads up to look at us. We clambered up the cut rock on the other side of the bridge and emerged into a climbing field of tall grass. We crested the rise in patches of scattered sun, and suddenly we could see what lay ahead for this expedition.

The first few wooden houses and fields of Azadem, a hamlet of a few dwellings just this side of Payi, strung down beneath the steep forest on our left. A smooth trail descended through these terraced fields. Ahead and to our right was the Gorge. We were looking up into it and could see a straightaway a few miles long before it turned. Behind it to the north, a ring of stunning mountains cupped the apex of the Great Bend. Some of us nearly jogged down the trail. Rough plank house on the left with animal hides hanging from the porch like stiff shields—more Buddhist hunters. Another hut surrounded by shredded prayer flags and crazy carved weathervanes spinning on tall poles. Dogs barking and someone singing. In the cusp of the bend, we looked down on two things. One was so lovely I stopped and just took it in.

Below us, beneath some small, steeply stepping, rich green fields, is a cluster of wooden houses among garden patches of yellow flowers. A few dzo graze, and a peach tree blooms brilliant pink beside a stack of raw lumber. Just past the houses, toward the lip of the canyon and a sort of overlook at the corner—a prow of ground—is a tight grove of swaying bamboo 30 feet high and a cluster of white prayer flags just as tall. We can see up the stretch around the bend now. The relentlessly deep-walled chasm is laced with tributary waterfalls and layered with descending spurs, two of which must hide the Po Tsangpo; straight up the Gorge, behind everything, is the towering perfect pyramid of snowy Ka Chiri.

The second thing: Right at the corner is a thundering waterfall, river-wide, left wall to right wall, maybe 40 yards across and 40 feet high. Above it, upriver, are five more drops—not as high, but also river-wide and just as terminal—and more sheer cliff before the river bends out of sight into what the kayakers call the S-Turn.

What it looks like is an ending.

. . . .

Johnnie was speechless. He snapped a few photos and trotted on into Greater Payi. I sat on the trail and took out my camera. Soon Scott and Ken came up the trail.

What are the stages of grief? Denial, anger, bargaining, etc. Scott looked as if all of them were paying him a visit at once. He stared at the Gorge, his eyes traveling up the slides and rapids. The Tsangpo sent up the roar of storm surf, only more continuous. Scott slumped against the dirt bank. "That's probably all she wrote."

Ringi, the youngest Sherpa, passed on the trail with a few porters—girl porters; he'd been pouring on the charm all day—and Scott asked him for a cigarette. He lit up. "You guys can maybe run above the confluence."

"No take-out."

"Hmm."

We made camp on the beaten open ground of the overlook at the corner, beside the tall bamboo and the flags. I walked down between the little houses. A pretty girl looked up from the wood-fenced garden of yellow flowers and smiled. "*Tashi delay*," she said shyly. An old man with long, loose gray hair and missing teeth sat on the steps of a porch, holding a baby; he smiled and waved. Three tiny boys with shaved heads hung off to the side and watched the procession, looking a bit scared. A few pigs rooted in the weeds. In the last hut, partly fallen in and abandoned, the Sherpas were already setting up a kitchen and directing the loads of provisions. Scott wandered in. Dave walked over to him, said something in his ear, and put his arm around him. He squeezed and smiled. Scott went to the big tent duffel bag and sat on it alone as the camp went up around him.

We paid off our porters from Gogden peaceably, without a hitch. Meanwhile, the plan for a side expedition to Hidden Falls was firming up. Dave, Ken, Andrew, and Tsawong were meeting with some local hunters, working out the route—over the Senchen La in reverse. So far, only three nonlocal expeditions in history had made it to the falls: Ken and Ian Baker in November 1998, the Chinese a few weeks later, and a woman from Texas who paid an immense sum in 2000 to be guided in by a Kathmandu-based outfitter. Nobody had ever done it in the middle of winter.

In the waning hours of the afternoon, the Hidden Falls crew finalized their roster: Dave, Ken, Dustin Lindgren, Andrew, Kusang, Passang, and three local hunters, including the village chief and a man built like a linebacker: Bullock, who had guided Ken and his group in 1993.

An early breakfast, and then the Hidden Falls crew shook hands all around, posed for pictures, picked up their packs in the beaten dirt outside the shack, and climbed out of the tiny hamlet. Sherab decided to go along at the last minute, which made the team even stronger. They strung out in a single line through the houses and past the peach tree and switchbacked up into the field, and just as they did, the sun broke through and washed the slope in warm light. We cheered. They waved and then lost themselves in the woods. The ceiling lifted, and we could see clouds tearing along the slopes above and new snow on the peaks. The Gogden porters took off, too, back up over the steep creek and the snowy pass, and I was surprised to see them pulling seven cows and a little black piglet on a twine string; they'd bought them here with their wages. The piglet ran from one side of the trail to the other and screamed.

The whole Gorge was in motion today. Fog surged beneath the inner rim and flowed up into the jungles. High clouds massed and broke up and scudded northward, and the long light again sprayed down. Light rain fell in gusts. I sat against the wall of the shack and caught up my journal. A pretty woman in an army cap sold us hard-boiled eggs and squatted down next to me and wouldn't leave until I'd bought some clear crystals. Sometime about midday, I realized I was starving. Last night, a local had sold us some dried salt pork, and the Sherpas had simply stuck it in the fire and flamed it until it dripped, then handed it around. How delicious. I'd lost about 20 pounds since the start of the trip and craved fat. Tsawong ate a piece now over the fire that still burned in the shack.

"Hey, Tsawong," I said. "Can we get more of that?"

"You want pop?" he said.

"No, *pork*."

"Yes, yes. We get pop."

I followed him out. We went to the house next door, to the pig man. Bristly hides tanned on his porch. He led us in—smoke-blackened plank walls, butter stomachs hanging from the rafters, an open hearth—and I gave him a few yuan and he went straight to an entire back of pig hanging on the wall. He took out his long knife and cut off a strip. He flipped it onto the table, skin down, and made crosscuts through soft white lard laced with pink meat, down to the rind. Then he added a few sticks to his fire and flamed it briefly and handed it to me and Tsawong, and I devoured it. Gluttony. A deadly sin.

At four o'clock, Willie and Mike came back into camp, exhausted from scouting the Lower Gorge. Willie consumed a fruit roll. He said, "The rapids are huge. What it boils down to is: Do we want to do this thing and climb out 1,500 feet where it's fucking sweet, or go farther and portage a bunch and take out where it's a bear?"

"How was the S-Turn?" Charlie asked.

"Fucking beefcake. The take-out above it is fucking solid gold. We haven't seen the straightaway in the S-Turn yet. We definitely have more scouting to do."

The plan was shaping up: They'd have a good look at the stretch above the S-Turn and see what they could run between the confluence and the reasonable take-out on the north, upstream side of the bend. That left them only five or six river miles of the Lower Gorge to run.

Sitting in the Sherpa Hotel after dinner, we watched big old Babu, Tsawong's boss, come in out of the wind. He lifted his nose exactly like a bear searching out a meal, and then went straight for the fire. One step, two steps—CRACK! He went straight through a broken floorboard, up to his hip. He blinked, frowned, then climbed out, dusted himself off, and continued toward the Dutch oven full of Jangbu's cake.

Willie nodded with approval. "He went down like a sack of taters. But he was good about it. He looks like the only one who's gained weight on the trip." He really did. I'm sure part of it was that he didn't stress out about anything. I'd never seen Babu once look anything but obliging and content, even up to his crotch in floor joists.

Willie talked about his brother Chuck. He died in sight of his brothers in the Black Canyon on a Friday. Their mother, Julie, got the call in Moscow, Vermont, while she was helping her neighbors prepare for their daughter's Saturday wedding. The old clapboard houses sat below a field and lined the single county road that ran along the Little River. The river was across the road and ran past the town ball field. "They were having a party for their daughter's wedding," Julie Kern told me later. "We had one of the coolers of wine. I think it was maybe six, seven o'clock, late in the afternoon. It was just getting dark here. We were out on the porch. A thunderstorm was beginning, and the herons were flying out of the Little River and nesting in the ball field. Willie called. He described a helicopter. I think it brought the kayaks out.

"He said, 'There's a thunderstorm coming and the birds, the eagles, are flying, and I said, 'There's a thunderstorm here, and the herons are flying.'" Mother and son held the receivers to their ears. The herons' wings, beating slowly out of the trees along the Little, were the slate color of rain. In both places, the sky rumbled and cracked.

. . . .

Pop. That's what Tsawong called it. I called it Satan. The singed little piece of half raw lard grew in the night in my gut into a Stephen King dog. I beat it back and bolted the door. It flattened itself to the width of an abattoir stench and oozed under and reconstituted itself, bigger, meaner than before. It smelled awful, it smelled like—*pop.* I bolted out of the tent and slid into the bamboo and was racked with a convulsion that emptied me from both ends. I breathed. Crawled back into the tent and here it came again. We did the same battle half a dozen more times. Me and *pop.* In the morning, trembling, I packed the tent and walked toward the Sherpa Hotel. The breakfast fire was already lit, and the smell of Jangbu's frying wafted out and gagged me again. I told Charlie I was starting out and left the bag by the door and fled. If I was going to make it to the next camp, at Tsachu, I'd need a head start.

I'm sure the Gorge was lovely in the lifting fog. I walked half a mile and detoured off the trail and wrestled the dog, who won again, and I just wanted to curl up in the brush and pass out. Not an option. I passed some houses. Some more prayer flags. Children ran to a fence. I dropped into some woods and confronted a pole fence, maybe chest high, and just stood there, head hanging, leaning over the trekking poles. The fence and I had a conversation. I glanced up at it. "I'm gonna figure out a way."

Ha.

"In a little while . . ."

Ha.

That's when Mike and Johnnie came around the corner. Mike said, "You don't look so good."

"Guts."

He took off his small pack and rummaged for pills. "Here. Take one of these." I don't know what it was, but in a few minutes I felt a little better. The trail steepened and we walked over another pass, this time in woods, on good trail, no snow. At the top, there was a tangle of small prayer flags, scores of them, tied into the trees. The girl from the flower patch passed, carrying a kayak. Her little son, maybe six years old, carried her baby in a sling.

The trail we were on dropped straight down, broke out of the trees onto a steep scree slope, and landed beside the Tsangpo on a broad beach of fine sand scattered with smooth cobbles and boulders. The big river. It chugged and heaved in a train of rolling haystacks, maybe 20 knots, with tremendous volume. Steve said he figured 25,000 cfs at least. At the lower end of the beach was a rough cliff. More cliff across the river, and above it woods. We'd walked for nine hours, most of it a blur for me.

Before I turned in, I saw a kite over the river. It flew on the wind from one side of the Tsangpo to the other, 100 feet off the water. Then another. I squinted in the dusk. It wasn't a kite; it was a cable crossing, a zip line like Willie's, and the porters were flying across the river. The bridge had been torn away in the flood, and now there was the cable. The kids flew headfirst, belly up, legs bent in a sailing tuck, probably harnessed to the wheel just at their sternums. In that light, you couldn't see the wire, so they looked like human birds. Must be two cables, as Dustin had seen in Luku, which zipped downward each way, because they came back just as fast. They were doing it for fun. Boys and girls. Back and forth.

Kannuri came with a plate of food, couscous and beans.

"Thanks, Kannuri. You're the man."

He put his hands flat together and was gone.

. . . .

From Tsachu up the Po Tsangpo to the Chengdu-Lhasa Highway was 18 miles, a two-day walk at most on good trail through a steep canyon. Two cable crossings and a couple of swinging bridges near the top. A cold beer and a yak steak were two days away.

We packed up and brought the loads zagging up the cliff to a platform of rock. The cable was half-inch steel simply looped around a boulder for anchor and clamped with two cable clamps. It passed over a forked stick for tension. Andrew, the mountaineer and cliff-dangled Canadian Highway stabilizer, said later he couldn't even look at the tensioners and anchors, they were so rickety. "They saddled a dead horse," he said with a kind of awe—meaning the clamps were on backward, which made them much weaker. The cable was 100 feet off the river and maybe 200 yards to a boulder platform on the other side. The river rushed and surged below. Willie, who had designed rope courses and zip lines in high school, smiled philosophically at the complete lack of safety.

Each porter carried a three-inch metal wheel with crudely welded hooks winging off it on either side. They slung the wheel over the cable, wrapped a frayed, quadrupled piece of rope around their waists, and snagged the hooks; some looped a single strand of cord around the backs of their necks for support. Then, grinning like any kid at Six Flags, they kicked loose and zinged headfirst down and across the river. Multiple bags and baskets were slung the same way, and three boats glided across together like a bunch of weird bananas. The flower girl was trussed up with her little son and infant, three bags, and a teenage boy from Payi, who was added to pull the load hand over hand for the last sagging 20 feet. The cable hummed, the forked stick shook, and locals on the other side hauled the loads onto a rock ledge. The Sherpas and some of our guys had fancy climbing harnesses, but Willie grinned and said, "I'm going native." The porters grabbed him and slung him to the cable with a very worn rope. I went the same way and learned quickly why you needed to bend your knees to your ears: At first, I let my legs hang, which levered my neck dangerously close to the humming cable and burned a greasy line in the collar of my shirt. Also, it felt like I was tilting out of the loose slings. With knees up, you sailed fast and smooth. It was a rush. At the other side, Willie said, "Man, they trussed me up like a Christmas chicken."

"You guys must have been poor growing up," I said.

"Turkey," he corrected himself.

The whole process took a couple of hours. Then we climbed 2,000 feet up to Tsachu. It was on a kind of peninsula of ridge that ran out between the bending canyon of the Po Tsangpo on one side and the Gorge of the Tsangpo on the other. From our camp, high on a boulder-strewn green field, we could look down at the Po Tsangpo and up its flood-ravaged Gorge. The air smelled of blossoms and tilled earth and rushed with the sound of the two rivers. We could hear chopping and distant singing. Also the ringing of a hammer on a stone chisel. Out along our ridge, the little houses and flags were dwarfed by a magnitude of landscape.

The paddlers didn't waste any time. It was warm and sunny, and they dropped their gear and jogged out to the edge of the ridge on the Tsangpo side to study the river with binoculars. It curved gracefully around Abu Lashu, which was another sacred peak, and then headed for Payi. It didn't look promising. There was the bedrock scour, little or no bank, and below the apex a big river-wide drop with no clear portage. Another big drop thrashed white below that, also river-wide. With nearly twice the water volume they'd had in the Upper Gorge, it looked like an invitation to disaster.

. . . .

In the middle of the afternoon, they gathered on the high, stony field of our camp and held a meeting. Scott sat on the thin grass, shirtless and pale. He looked around. "As far as I'm concerned," he said, "we're all wearing gold medals right now. As far as anyone else coming in here, no one's gonna paddle to Payi. I'm probably gonna end the film at the cable. You come to the cable, it's a natural end point. Going by the confluence, getting a few more rapids in. If we hiked up here another day"—he gestured with a stick back at the canyon of the Po Tsangpo—"we could run that and get a whole bunch of rapids in. My biggest concern was like—is somebody gonna come in here and fucking plug this thing? I'm pretty much 100 percent convinced that no one's gonna do that anytime soon."

Steve got up and walked away. He sat against a rock 10 feet off and looked out over the big river. His silence was another point of view: Give this Lower Gorge a college try.

"Okay," Scott said. "Do we have consensus?" He squinted into the sun over his shoulder. "Steve! Come over here."

Steve poked at the ground with his own stick. He craned his neck around.

"We're gonna take a little vote," Willie said. "What are you thinking?"

Steve said, "I think that if I wanted to paddle down to Luku, it wouldn't make a difference."

"How about down to that gully?" Johnnie asked.

"That would be my vote," Steve said.

Scott was irritated. "Why are you sitting over there?"

"I'm sleeping." It was half curt, half joking.

"You're a fucking cunt over there," Scott said, also half joking.

"Okay," Willie said. "All in favor of going to Luku?"

No hands.

Scott said, "Okay, all in favor of going to Payi?"

Steve got up and walked over. He squatted. "I think we could paddle around here"—he gestured at the apex—"and scout from the river. And if we get into something bad, get out."

"We're talking about going around the apex and paddling back up," Scott said.

"If we got around that apex there," Steve insisted, "and we looked downstream . . ."

"You can't see downstream," Dustin Knapp said.

"I'm for going up the Po Tsangpo," Allan said. "Checking out our attainment option today and either taking out just after the bend or stopping at the cable."

Scott nodded. "What we do is get to the wire, take all of our shit out of our boats, put it on the beach, paddle down around the corner, and attain back up with empty boats."

"That means a lot of whitewater," Allan said.

"And another first descent," Willie said. He meant the lower few miles of the Po Tsangpo.

Scott pried up a piece of turf with his stick. He made his decision. They would do some new, challenging whitewater on the lower Po Tsangpo, camp at the mystical confluence—there was reputed to be a hot spring and a sacred prayer site there—and then a dramatic paddle around the foot of Abu Lashu and the apex of the Great Bend. From there, right at the northernmost point of the Tsangpo, they would take out and not mess with trying to attain anything or scout the big rapid below. They'd meet a group of local porters and hike straight back up here to camp. Scott nodded once. It was like a gavel coming down. The rest of the group seemed relieved.

Steve got up and looked out, up the Po Tsangpo canyon.

"One cool thing," Scott said, "is to camp at the confluence. It's a fucking powerful place. It's got a beach, some shelves. That'd be sweet for us. All in favor, raise your left hand!"

Hands shot up; then everybody laughed as they switched hands.

. . . .

In the small hours of the morning, new snow lay in the trees on the hill behind us. Out ahead, all across the southern sweep of sky, from west to east, the mountains were bathed in radiant pink. Gyala Peri, breast of the goddess, shone like a crystal mountain. A nearly full moon, bright, whiter than the rose snows, floated in the soft blue, setting over her western flank. The last stars paled. I hustled from the tarps to the tents and woke everybody up. It was the first of March, 2002. It was the loveliest sunrise any of us had ever seen.

The paddlers packed light after breakfast, hired eight porters, and

walked down out of the village, down off the western side of our ridge. The rest of us had a quiet day. Kannuri took out a bundle of prayer flags and made a small fire at the chorten just below our camp, sprinkled juniper into the fire and chanted, then climbed a tree and tied the flags in with a tangle of others. He led me around to the back side of the rock and showed me a cave that held the face of Padmasambhava in the stone of the ceiling. Kannuri put his hands together and prostrated and said the saint had lived here, too.

Locals gathered in our camp. They said that when the flood roared down the Po Tsangpo in the summer of 2000, they thought the world was ending, and they gathered in the middle of the night up in our field, the highest point in the village, and the ground shook for 12 hours. For days after that, landslides fell from the slopes above the river.

An old man named Chom Pe looked over our big sat map and, squinting his clouded eyes, pointed out right away the Senchen La and Payi. He said he'd been to Hidden Falls in 1998 with the Chinese and that there was no good trail over the pass for our falls party. They would be on rough game trails and would encounter much snow. He said that the falls were sacred, that they were a gate to another world.

Somewhere nearby, the steady hammer rang on stone.

The villagers told us that something unutterably sad was about to unfold in Tsachu and Payi and Luku and all the other hamlets around the Great Bend: They were to be depopulated by the Chinese-controlled government. The residents would be relocated to new towns such as Bayi and farmland outside the Gorge. No one was sure why. There were rumors of a national park—or a huge hydroelectric project.

No one will live here anymore? we asked. They shook their heads. They didn't want to leave. The farmland was poor up on the plateau. But the government said they would get new houses with electricity; their kids would go to school.

. . . .

It didn't take the boys long to drop down to the Po Tsangpo. Then they launched onto 10,000 cfs of steep, technical, bronco-busting mayhem. They loved it. In the third rapid, Mike tried to clip a giant hole, got nailed at the edge, flipped, and was sucked upside down by a wide backwash. He threw in a giant stroke *upside down* that broke the momentum, Eskimo rolled in a flash, and back-paddled away from the gnashing hydraulic. Willie went over the top of what looked to be a wave; it was a pourover backed by a mean hole, and he fell right into it. It grabbed him like a bear trap and he began to cartwheel. Johnnie, speeding down just behind him, taking the same line, went right over the top of his brother and skated clean. Willie was tiring fast and thinking that in another second he would have to pull his skirt and swim, when the hole miraculously released him. They all worked downstream.

In the late afternoon, the river emptied into the flood of the main Tsangpo and they paddled into the confluence. It was in deep shadow. There was a cove of sand beach across the Tsangpo, backed by cliff. They ferried hard and pulled their kayaks onto the sand. Steve made them all a fine dinner of mixed pasta and green tea, and they sat at a crackling driftwood fire, toasted their accomplishment, and raised their cups to the Tsangpo.

The next morning, they launched one last time.

The side of the canyon was naked, smooth rock wall, bared by the flood and twisted and layered with the grains of ancient strata. They paddled through monster water for the apex. What had looked like a Class III wave train from shore was a Class V juggernaut. Eddies along the bank boiled up and domed and rejected them. They had to fight to stay out of the middle. At last, they strung out in a line, and their boats spun and skated on the swift flatwater. Abu Lashu, the sacred pyramid mountain, clothed in jungle and streamers of cloud, presided at the bend, and they drifted around the curve of her base. Then they stroked for an eddy and a sloping slab of granite along the left bank. One by one, the boats, red and yellow, glided like birds in flight over the green jade of the river, veered up into the pool, and hit the shore.

TAKE-OUT

That night, the Hidden Falls crew called in on the phone. They were ju-
bilant. They had climbed into deep and hard-blowing snow and camped
beside the marshy lake called Tso Dem near the top of the Senchen La.
The next morning, it snowed heavily and they struggled up through it
and over the top. They worked their way down the plunging wall of the
Gorge, through woods and down onto the exposed, nearly sheer slopes
of rock and dirt slide and rhododendron brush, and hit a perch directly
above Hidden Falls. The cataract, 112 feet high, shook the ground.

Sherab knelt and worked his beads and prayed. He had never been
there. Beneath the falls, in the rock of the left wall, they could see
through the spray the keyhole cave that was said to be the portal to the
magic realms. Andrew the mountain man rappelled to a tiny perch right
at the lip of the falls. Then he scrambled solo and unprotected along the
cliffs upstream to the lip of Rainbow Falls, where certainly no man has
ever stood, and raised his arms to them all.

On the sat phone, they said they were now back in Payi and would
join us in two days.

Scott got a chest infection and hacked and coughed. One night, he
pulled me aside again and began yelling. I couldn't understand why.
Something about the book, what's fair, 10 years of work. He screamed,
"What did you do for this expedition? What? Nothing! You didn't pack
food, you didn't spend years planning—*nothing!*" I guess he was out of his
mind that it was over.

I called everyone over at dinner and told the kayakers that they were my heroes. I said if I did get a book, I'd give them 10 percent, so nobody should feel exploited. Somebody said, "Well-said." "Spot-on." "Decent." I looked at Scott, who stared into the fire.

The next day, I walked up behind camp and discovered the source of the hammering: a man and his wife and their young daughter were chiseling the back of a big boulder. It said, *Om mane padme hum*, "Hail to the jewel in the lotus." They wore scarves around their faces against the rock dust, and the mother and the girl took turns holding the chisel. All day long they worked; they wanted to leave this behind when they abandoned their homes.

At night, waves of cranes flew over, and their disembodied cries fell out of the dark. The paddlers hiked up and ran six more miles of the Po Tsangpo. The Hidden Falls crew rejoined us. On March 6, with the paddlers all back and jazzed, we packed up and hired some porters from the village. We dropped off the high ridge, down into the flood-ripped chasm, and hiked out.

The box canyon of the Po Tsangpo had been devastated. The old trail struggled through the debris. It climbed high onto cliff, crossed steep slides, and dropped to the river. It meandered among the boulders washed into the bends like pebbles, and over sandbars where wooded banks had been. It climbed over landslides 80 feet high that had dammed the river again and then burst. Great trees had been tossed into the fringing forest 300 feet up. In the new green of these woods, babblers and warblers hopped and sang. Spring was coming.

We walked toward Pelung and the road, strung out in a long line, each in his own thoughts. The kayakers carried their paddles like Samurai with their long spears. The Kern brothers were quiet, probably thinking about Chuck. Scott walked with his head down. He'd coughed through the past few nights. I crutched on the trekking poles, the doctor's palliatives used up, favoring my flaring left hip. Scott passed me, and I said

"Congratulations," and he looked up out of a trance and said, "Sure. Thanks." I watched him hike across a boulder field, bent, thin, carrying his weapon.

Steve hopped over the steep scree and didn't even look tired. He wanted to paddle some hairball firsts in California, surf some sick waves in Uganda, and try to win the Freestyle World Championships.

The Lower Gorge would remain untested. Dorje Pagmo allowed a way through for the worthy, but she would not yield herself up entire. There was more for someone in the future to dare.

On the second morning, we came to a long suspended footbridge strung with colored prayer flags. The bridge swayed in a strong wind, and the flags snapped stiff and loud. Pelung was just a little farther. Willie stopped. He didn't want it to end. He said he wanted to cross the bridge and keep going. Just keep going into more canyon, forever.

In a couple of months, the villagers below would begin leaving. The Great Bend had been designated a National Park and a National Treasure of China. The government told everyone in the Great Bend to evacuate. The Lopa farmers would no longer carry their barley to the water-turned mills and grind it into tsampa. The peaches would ripen on the trees and fall beside the empty houses. The Monpa hunters would no longer haunt the high trails, replenishing prayer flags as they went. Next fall, there would be only the cries of cranes flying over, and the wind, and the unceasing sound of the great river. The wind would whip the white flags and take their inked prayers, little by little, into the Gorge until they were washed clean.

BIBLIOGRAPHY

Charles Allen, *Mountain in Tibet: The Search for Mount Kailash and the Sources of the Great Rivers of India*. Sterling Publishing Company. London: Futura Publications, 1982. Kailash is the sacred mountain that inspired Scott Lindgren.

F. M. Bailey, *No Passport to Tibet*. London: The Travel Book Club, 1957. The classic British explorer's memoir. (Out of print but available through rare and used bookstores. It's worth the search.)

Todd Balf, *The Last River: The Tragic Race for Shangri-La*. California: Three Rivers Press, 2001. A superbly told reconstruction of Wickliffe Walker's tragic 1998 kayak expedition down the Tsangpo.

The Dhammapada: The Sayings of the Buddha. Translated by Thomas Byrom. New York: Shambala Pocket Classics, 1976. Wisdom and consolation, straight from the source.

Michael McRae, *The Siege of Shangri-La: The Quest for Tibet's Sacred Hidden Paradise*. New York: Broadway Books, 2002. McRae tells the history of exploration in the Tsangpo Gorge, beginning with Francis Kingdon Ward's journey in the 1920s and ending with the Gillenwater brothers, who helped discover Hidden Falls.

Karl Ernest Meyer and Shareen Blair Brysac, *Tournament of Shadows: The Great Game and the Race for Empire in Central Asia*. Washington,

D.C.: Counterpoint Press, 1999. A well-told story of empire—British, Russian, and American—and the wonderful characters who participated in a power game for control of the most remote terrain on Earth.

Susan L. Taft, *The River Chasers: A History of American Whitewater Paddling*. Mukilteo, Washington: AlpenBooks, 2001. The most complete history of extreme kayaking and canoeing.

Robert Thurman and Tad Wise, *Circling the Sacred Mountain: A Spiritual Adventure Through the Himalayas*. Reprint. New York: Bantam Books, 2000. Wise, a skeptical journalist, follows the Buddhist Thurman to Mount Kailash and becomes a convert to eastern spiritualism.

Wickliffe W. Walker, *Courting the Diamond Sow: A Whitewater Expedition on Tibet's Forbidden River*. Washington, D.C.: National Geographic Society, 2000. Walker's personal account of the expedition that led to the death of Doug Gordon, one of the world's great (and great-hearted) kayakers.

Derek Waller, *Pundits: British Exploration of Tibet and Central Asia*. Lexington, Kentucky: University Press of Kentucky, 1990. A well-researched account of the spies trained by the British to map forbidden terrain. (Out of print but available through rare and used bookstores.)

Francis Kingdon Ward, *Frank Kingdon Ward's Riddle of the Tsangpo Gorges*. Edited by Kenneth Cox. Second. Suffolk, United Kingdom: Antique Collector's Club, 2005. The botanist Ward's description of the Tsangpo's Upper and Lower Gorges proved to be precisely accurate three-quarters of a century later.

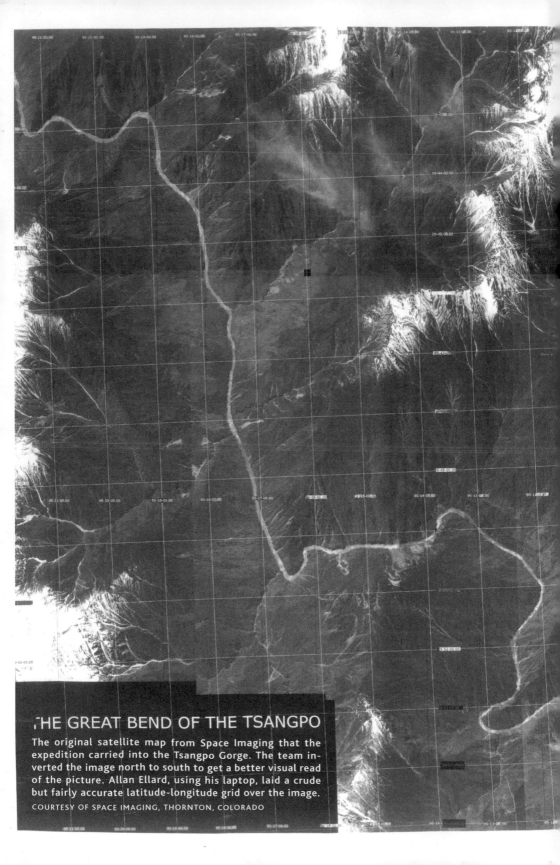

THE GREAT BEND OF THE TSANGPO

The original satellite map from Space Imaging that the expedition carried into the Tsangpo Gorge. The team inverted the image north to south to get a better visual read of the picture. Allan Ellard, using his laptop, laid a crude but fairly accurate latitude-longitude grid over the image.

COURTESY OF SPACE IMAGING, THORNTON, COLORADO